From West Limerick, Tom Nestor now lives in Ennis, Co. Clare. A regular columnist with the *Limerick Leader* for many years, he has had numerous short stories published, was a prizewinner in the Ian St James Competition in 1993 and has written plays for RTE and BBC radio. He is currently working on a novel.

THE KEEPER OF
ABSALOM'S ISLAND

For Tom Nestor, childhood was a soaring adventure across a rural landscape. With no place for him on the land or affinity with its toils, he resolves to escape. With his pack of dogs he strides off into the carefree world of a curious boy in a magical time. Set in the countryside around Rathkeale in County Limerick, not twenty miles from the poverty-stricken lanes and ashes of Limerick city, this memoir is peopled with such characters as the mad aristocratic Absalom Creagh, and Miss James and Miss Abigail who taught through the medium of religion and terror.

Books by Tom Nestor
Published by The House of Ulverscroft:

THE BLUE POOL

TOM NESTOR

THE KEEPER
OF
ABSALOM'S ISLAND

Complete and Unabridged

ULVERSCROFT
Leicester

First published in Great Britain in 1999 by
The Collins Press
Cork

First Large Print Edition
published 2003
by arrangement with
The Collins Press
Cork

British Library CIP Data

Nestor, Tom, *1936* –
The keeper of Absalom's Island.—Large print ed.—
Ulverscroft large print series: non-fiction
1. Nestor, Tom, *1936* – —Childhood and youth
2. Large type books 3. Ireland—Social life and
customs—20th century
I. Title
941.7′0822′092

ISBN 1–8439–5100–2

Published by
F. A. Thorpe (Publishing)
Anstey, Leicestershire

Set by Words & Graphics Ltd.
Anstey, Leicestershire
Printed and bound in Great Britain by
T. J. International Ltd., Padstow, Cornwall

This book is printed on acid-free paper

For my wife May
and
for my brother John
who did not live to see this book

In the sun that is young once only,
Time let me play and be
Golden in the mercy of his means,
And green and golden I was huntsman
and herdsman, the calves
Sang to my horn, the foxes on the hills
barked clear and cold,
And the sabbath rang slowly
In the pebbles of the holy streams.

Fern Hill, Dylan Thomas

1

I was let down on a sunbeam. One morning, in the spring of 1936, the light lasered a hole in the pewter sky above Harold's Wood and the sunbeam floated in the kitchen window. I was borne in the column of dust particles that slanted through our kitchen like a block of perspex. None of the other ten children came that way, so my father said, and my mother gave a quizzical nod to his rare flight of imagination. The others had been found on the doorstep or under heads of cabbage in the haggard.

In those early days I had the kitchen to myself for long periods. My father was at work in the fields; the older children were away at school or called to arms to hay field or turnip drill. The younger ones were too infantile to matter. My mother had a myriad of tasks in the farmyard and I was alone. So I waited for the sunbeam, which I knew would come when the light broke through. It linked me, like an alien spaceship, to that strange world in the sky where, my father said, all things begin.

'Beyond here be dragons.' So wrote the

ancient cartographers on the margins of their maps to signal the limit of their knowledge. My secure territory was marked by the boundary of the back door. I could look out the kitchen windows and watch the landscape and all the creatures that traversed it. But I would not venture beyond the back door for out there was the country of the dragons.

My parents had warned about that. It seeped into my brain and locked me within. The warning was a strategy. I would be a nuisance around the yard, stumbling my fretful way in the dragon shadows. My mother had enough to concentrate on without having to worry about her floundering child. So I watched the swirling dust in the sunbeam column and kept an ear and an eye on the sleeping infants, one in the cradle beside the fire and another in the room below where my parents slept.

I tended the fire and shooed the hens and ducks away with the most blood-curdling cry I could muster. The back door was always open so the hens would try to invade my territory. There was an old Rhode Island Red that seemed to be the chief scout and the instigator of all mischief. She would come crabwise across the cobbles of the yard, head outstretched like a searching antenna, eyes glinting with a fervour of curiosity, a talon

2

raised in mid-decision. Whenever I lapsed and missed the cues, she would be in the middle of the flagstones with a retinue of her disciples filling the doorway. It seemed to me then that the only reason she came was to shit on the floor. Any hint of excitement and she would leave her calling card and her comrades followed suit.

No matter how I tried to scrub away the calling cards, the smell lingered on. My mother would wrinkle her nose the moment she stepped inside and wonder what class of a fool I was. I hated that. She had appointed me the custodian of her kitchen and I had failed. My mother was goddess of my universe; the fountain of love and warrior queen. She could read into my soul and exorcise the things that bothered and frightened me. So when I failed her, my dignity collapsed and I felt removed from her citadel.

When she was out, I shivered in trepidation. The rear door was always open while the light held. Beyond it I could see the dragons and they all looked gargantuan compared to the shapes and the sizes in my kitchen habitat. The Rhode Island hen and the gander were huge to me, the cows that looked in the door and the horses that passed that way were creatures of such size that my

3

comprehension could not grasp their enormity. When there was activity around the yard, as there was at milking time, I would retreat to the shadows in the hallway near the entrance to the parlour. I was comforted by the truncated view of the giants that moved in the yard, because the part had to be less dangerous than the whole.

Fear enclosed me like a wall sometimes. The dragons, like the hens, would come over the threshold and have me for their breakfast, as Johnny Murphy, the hired hand, once told me. There were other times, especially around mid-morning and in that lull hour between the afternoon tea and the milking, when it seemed that the world slowed down and the giants went into siesta. My mother still hotfooted it around the farmyard with my eldest sisters. They were like spokes from the hub of her energy, darting this way and that as she called out the task and the beat.

In those quieter times, I would clamber up the cliff face of the window ledge and look out on the landscape. West was where most of our fields were. Each had a name, sometimes a collective name like Waterfield, distant and redolent of a language and a people far beyond our perimeter, echoes of Anglo-Irish wealth. The fields nearest the house had been in our family for generations and were named for familiarity and the nearness of intimacy: the Grove Garden, Hayes', the Nursery, the Ferny Field. Two great beech trees at one end and a grove of pine at the other marked the range of Waterfield. We had acquired that portion in the recent past; it had once been part of Absalom Creagh's demesne. The purchase was partly funded by selling a smaller farm near where my mother's family lived. They had met when my father was putting cattle into a roadside paddock. He called out some banal preliminary to conversation when a young woman cycled past and she stopped to decipher the accent and vent her curiosity. Such are the fickle links of chance and fate on which hang the destiny of generations. From such an innocuous start, she fell in love, gave ten children to the world and acquired an infinity of work and toil.

It seemed from the east window that we lived in the hollow of a saucer-shaped country. On a clear day, especially from the square air vent at the top of the hay barn, you could see all that flat space gently sloping towards the Shannon, which glistened far-away like one of the silver ribbons my sisters wore in their hair. Then the land sloped upwards to gentle hazy hills far out on the rim. Mannix's Folly, a great house now in ruins, dominated the skyline to the west. I feared that too for it stood there as a reminder of God's terrible power.

According to the lore, this man Mannix harboured a dream that he would raise a great house on a rocky hillock, which would be the focus of his power and a declaration of his wealth. He was not a God-fearing man so he ordered his workmen to raise the roof on a Sunday. When they did, a great wind blew and plucked off the roof like thistledown and spiralled it into the nearby fields. In a fit of rage and humiliated before his superstitious tenantry, he ordered them to work again on the following Sunday. The storm hit every Sunday thereafter until finally he bowed before the greater power. The house was never finished. It stands there today: four walls of red brick on a hillock surveying the hollow of the saucer. I fully believed that story then though the more plausible reason was sometimes offered by my mother. Mannix simply ran out of money.

The ruins of the great Creagh house stood ivied and crumbling as a backdrop to Paddy Danaher's cottage. He was reclusive and eccentric, sane and perfectly normal one minute and as mad as a hatter the next. I would experience the gamut later in life of Danaher's moods and be at once scared and drawn by the complexity of his nature. I knew him then for his occasional visits to my father. He always came late at night and especially on wild raging nights. The hair would be plastered to his head in separated hanks; raindrops were like crystal pearls in the foliage of his eyebrows, and his mad eyes blazed forth the demons that tormented and amused him.

Paddy Danaher was the living representation of all the portents that had been dreamed up to frighten us. He was the driver of the headless coach or the devil himself who sometimes took the form of the black dog that went abroad late at night when all good people should be in their beds. That dog crossed the road at the Four Piers and woe betide the luckless human whose eyes beheld its passage. But sometimes Danaher would sit in the hob seat and talk of simple mundane things with the measured words of the innocent and untroubled. And you wondered then if you had dreamed the madness of last time.

Absalom Creagh, the landlord, had been mad too. So we said, but perhaps we confused the condition with the eccentricity of ennui which had afflicted the landlord class. It was he who had brought the spur from the stream that marked one boundary to his estate. He brought it almost a mile, carving a canal through limestone strata and the networks of hazel and whitethorn roots. The stream was fed into an artificial pond surrounding an earthen mound on which a lone ash tree grew. We called it Absalom's Island. Creagh stocked the pond with fish and he would sit by its verge on his shooting stick, casting a fly, in the heel of a summer's evening. When the lure failed or boredom took hold of him, he would reach for the shotgun and wait to pepper the rise, if rise there ever was.

That was well before my time, but its last link was brought in when I was still the kitchen custodian. At the time we had a labouring man called Gerry McKenna. It must have been a good year, because we did not always have the money to afford such a luxury. He had been herding in Waterfield and while searching for an errant animal in the island of the pond, he found a fish in a mud hole. It was the topic of wonder all through the breakfast and in the days that followed. I know now it was a bream for the colouring and shape stuck in my mind. Old mad Absalom had been dead for a hundred years or more and yet, here in the kitchen, on a raw morning in February, was a tentacle of his oddity, seeking us out. Perhaps they were fellow travellers, Absalom Creagh and Paddy Danaher, for eccentricity is like imagination, like religion — a device to cope with the limitations and fears of one's environment. I suspect that Danaher's was founded on loneliness and drudgery, Absalom's on the boredom of opulence.

We shared the front yard with the Barrett family. It was a replica of ours: thatched roof, stone walls roughly plastered, small porch over the front door, all looking squat and utterly stolid as if any embellishment was a sin against the creed of the practical. We were dominated by the practical; sometimes it went to extremes and you would see outhouses better appointed and more comfortable than living quarters. When electrical power came into our community in the early 1950s, I worked for a few weeks as a clerk on the central site. The practical ones came to the fore, some refused the service, others opted for the minimum — a single light fitting fixed to the rafter in the cow-byre. The old paraffin lamp was good enough for the dwelling house.

We had come from the same stock, the Barretts and us. Originally the founding brothers had arrived from the shores of the Shannon to avail of a land resettlement scheme. They had first been granted a much bigger spread of land, but they feared they would not be able to manage or finance it and so settled for the smaller one in Kilquane. My father would regret that he ever told this story of our ancestral arrival. When they grew older and ambitious, my brothers felt hemmed in by the size of our holding, and chafed him about his ancestors' lack of foresight.

The Barrett house was as yet outside my range, but from the vantage point of the windowsill I watched the comings and goings of its occupants and fitted their features in my mind: Mary Ellen, her husband Jimmy and sister Madge. They looked friendly and pleasant but the rare appearance of the old mother filled me with anxiety. She was dressed all in black, a long flowing skirt that almost trailed the ground, and an equally black bonnet that was tied at the throat and allowed her features to peep out one moment and disappear again behind the dark shell, as if she were a gigantic snail. Her face was the colour of old parchment, her chin jutted forth in constant pulsing movement like she had a plug of chewing gum in her mouth. No matter how I wished it otherwise, she would stop and look directly at the window and send me scuttling into the shadows before the parlour door.

Jimmy Barrett came and went more than

the others. He was driven by a great fever for work and it drove him forth in all weathers. It seemed always he had a cigarette butt between his fingers and walked bent towards the ground as if down there was the very inspiration for his existence. Jimmy was an inordinately shy man who was seldom found in the places where people congregated. On Sundays he ducked into the sacristy as soon as the priest was on the altar, and was heading down the fields before the congregation came out from the chapel. He had been in Chicago during the heyday of the gangster mobs. Once, several years later, as I hunted rabbits in his fields, I came across him under a crabapple tree, taking his afternoon tea break. He shared it with me and then suddenly, perhaps in response to some desultory remark of mine, he began to talk about Chicago. He had been on a street nearby when John Dillinger was shot and had seen people press forward to collect macabre souvenirs of the gangster's blood. On that evening in high summer, the words and stories poured forth unhindered. I often tried to recreate that moment, seeking him out in the solitary places, but it never happened again.

Between both our houses there were long periods of deep friendship and shorter spells of intense coolness. No matter how silly the disagreement or how senseless the event that generated it, the families stood four-square behind each other, like feuding families in the Appalachian mountains. But then, the argument would cease as suddenly as it had begun: the shared concern for a lost animal would cure it or some expression of conciliation from either side that thawed the frosty climate.

I would never leave the kitchen or even contemplate venturing outside its four walls, except to tiptoe to the open door of my parent's bedroom when the baby stirred. The parlour, just off the kitchen, was beyond the limits of my security and I would not venture there. It was our only courtesy to ostentation and we kept it at a distance, turning it into a shrine, as if usage or familiarity would erode its character. I disliked the parlour. There was something about it that was redolent of death and long past associations. In its musty odour it held the ambience of a mausoleum. There was a portrait of a Franciscan, clad in full regalia, dominating one wall. His expression of severity was awesome, his eyes followed me around the room in constant admonishment. He knew the innards of my soul and written in his eyes was the count of every transgression enacted or contemplated.

The most striking feature of the parlour was an over-mantel above a lovely iron firegrate. The sepia wedding photographs of aunts and uncles, the work of the Egleston studio in Limerick, dominated the collection of mementoes on the over-mantel. On the sideboard another kind of collection was arrayed: Toby jugs and miniature vases with folksy English village scenes like the pictures in *The Wind in the Willows*, a pewter toast-holder, silver sugar tongs, a pair of matching rose bowls. The standard lamp, with adjustable pitch and reach, stood in the centre of the room. It was always examined and commented on by the distinguished and rare visitors who were offered the privilege of the parlour. My father smiled indulgently at the compliments for in that moment he was patron of the artistic imagination, a Renaissance man.

I was drawn to the Egleston portraits and when there was someone to accompany me, I would take them down and study them. The flowering of beautiful youth lit up the features, especially the women on my mother's side who were strikingly handsome. In later years I would be struck by the horrible transition that father time had inflicted on them, all that bright shining beauty in its pristine promise washed away by the ravages of age and toil. My father and mother had never sat for the Egleston studio; they had no wedding portrait on the mantelpiece. I was glad even then and still am.

★ ★ ★

Johnny Murphy slept in the loft room. He was one of the last of the migrant workers, rootless, alone and sickly. My father put him up and was rewarded by a work performance that was wildly at variance with his wishes. Like many of his ilk and time, my father was master of the routine; he was utterly confused by the unpredictable. His sleep would be disrupted at the crack of dawn as Murphy prepared to set off on his madcap day. The loft was never intended as an attic room; at best it was a limbo place where things could be stowed in case they might be needed again. There was no stairway leading up to it, so when Murphy was retiring for the night, which he did with absolute certainty as soon as the evening meal was over, he would fetch the ladder from the gable end and pull it after him through the loft doorway. Great as the racket was then it was magnified a hundred fold in the silence of the dawn. Murphy never came forth again and we youngsters would make fantastic conjecture as to what he did all evening and all night, alone in his loft.

He had arrived with a portmanteau in hand and a bundle tied on the end of his walking staff. We wondered what the portmanteau and bundle contained, but his habits and his use of the ladder made a Fort Knox of his secrets. The noise that woke my father was the sound of the loft door being dragged open, for it had but one hinge, and then the clatter as the ladder was poked through and settled in place.

My father was a long way back in the queue when the early rising habits were granted. If he had his way, it would be mid-morning before he surfaced. Murphy made his leaden-footed way into the blackness of the new day and went about chores that were in total discord with my father's priorities. If it were a day for the hayfield, Murphy would set about laying a hedge. If we were stacking corn sheaves, he would be mending tackling in the outhouse. When he was called to task, he sulked for days; he smote the implements as if they were the personification of his enemy, breaking shafts and blades and leathers to signify his manic mood.

I quaked before him. I feared the dark intensity that lurked in his eyes, the fierce kestrel's glare that was fixed on my face whenever I lifted my eyes to his. My mother told me he was harmless, but I knew better. He was forever telling me that he would have me for breakfast. But worse: he would suddenly dart towards me, claw in the direction of my crotch and cackle in glee when he showed me the top of my willie, yanked out and imprisoned between his index and middle fingers. I knew it was a trick, but there was something about that leer that always made me slink away and check. He took ill one day as suddenly as his moods and behaviour. I remember him coming down the ladder dressed in his Sunday suit and carrying the portmanteau and the staff with the bundle tied near the crook. He never returned. He was buried in a pauper's grave somewhere near the city of Limerick. It dispelled forever the notion that there was wealth of some kind in the portmanteau and gold sovereigns in the rag bundle.

★   ★   ★

The day wore on. Fears and trepidation ebbed and flowed. The child in the cradle woke and howled and the fire went dangerously low while I was occupied by the rocking. Outside the world moved by in the gargantuan steps of the dragons, the wind picked up and the smoke billowed about the kitchen. My mother poked her head inside the door and called out a rapid-fire checklist of questions, never waiting for answers. Would she ever appreciate how onerous my responsibilities were or realise any of the problems that beset me? Shit on the stone floor, the fire burned down, old Paddy Danaher, festooned with rabbit traps, slinking by the orchard wall. All these things on a good day.

There were worse days when the sky darkened, God's thunder raged overhead, lightning ripped the sky over Harold's Wood and my mother stayed in the shelter of the outhouse. There were times when Murphy, with blackened face and fire in his eyes, came in dragging the ladder and barricaded himself in his room, too consumed by his rage to notice me.

Over the great beech trees in Waterfield the sun dipped and the shadows came across the land. Cows lowed in the fields and the dogs barked. My heart soared. I heaped peat on the fire and blew it into flame. I lowered the kettle on the iron hook and waited for its song. These were the harbingers of ease, of coming safety. It was like hearing my father cough when I woke suddenly in the dead of night, knowing that we were both safe in our own place. Soon they would all come in from farmyard and fields. The night would spread a warm glow and banish the world beyond the back door. The kitchen would be a babble of noise and talk. My father would sit on his throne — that armchair that stood in the corner near the fire and on which no one else would dare sit in, even when he was absent. My mother would hold court in her rustic Camelot. I would languish in the cocoon of it all, washed, fed and cosseted by the eldest sister Mary, winked at by my father as if we shared some great conspiracy or a great intimacy. It was the safest place in all creation, and the noises, the ragings or the deathly silence of the world outside only emphasised the pleasure and the warmth.

2

My father stretched his long legs to the fire and sighed his weariness. From now until the fire died down and the crickets sang their dead of night chorus, he was lord and master. The opening play that demonstrated his supreme presence was the shedding of the boots. He merely had to nod his state of readiness and it was all hands to his bidding. If someone did not immediately respond, my mother would bark a sharp command to the person nearest the legs.

It puzzled me why I was always the nearest one, until I understood the strategic movement of the others away from the fire the moment my father came through the back door. It was no easy task because his boots were laced with leather thongs; the knots were as tough as sinew and slippery as eels. He clucked clucked like a brooding hen and pursed his lips in annoyance while I fumbled with them.

The kitchen had been transformed. It breathed life and sound from every direction. When we sat round the table to take our evening meal, the sound grew by several levels. The stream of voices eddied and swirled, rose in strident bursts when someone provoked an argument, tapered into cadence when order was restored. Around the vocals was the percussion section of other noises: cutlery and delph, tea slurped from saucers for that was the habit of the time, scratching chair legs and creaking table.

Early in the meal there was a period of intense concentration. The best way of safeguarding one's portion was to wolf it down. A moment's distraction from the plate and a piece of bacon or sausage had disappeared. 'Look at the butterfly on the wall,' my brother John would whisper, and I was a sucker every time. He was a few years older but cuter by ten. I turned to look and the prime morsel I was saving was plucked away.

'He stole me sausage, Ma.'

'I did not. No such thing.'

'He did so, Ma, did.'

'He ate it himself. I saw him.'

'Did anyone see him swipe my sausage?'

Then would come the silence of conspiracy. It was accepted practice and my siblings would all conspire in the cover-up. To confess any knowledge of the crime would pave the way for a new regulation and no one wanted that, even my father. I had once seen him drop a slice of bread, bid his daughter Kathleen to pick it up, and while she did, he had snatched her piece of bacon.

'He did so, Ma. I saw him.'

'He's telling lies, Ma. I didn't touch his ould sausage.'

'Michael.' My mother appealed to the man on the throne. It was a tactic and he, like me, was a sucker too. My mother was a very strong-willed woman; it was she, not my father, who was King Arthur round that table. But tactically it was politic every now and then to make deference to my father's nominal status. She delegated to him those matters too trivial for her to be bothered with, like keeping order. He rose to the bait and said in a tone of limp conviction, 'Not another word out of ye, or ye'll all leave the table.'

My father sought no prominence within the home. He was satisfied with the apparent deference and would make soft murmurs of acknowledgement when it was shown to him. He had little of the will and self-motivation of my mother, and it suited him perfectly to delegate to her all the authority that she needed to fulfil her aspirations as the family driving force. However, every now and then — perhaps it was tactic from him too — he would quibble a little about the erosion of his

21

power, and how he wasn't being consulted any more. So she threw him sops and they were usually like nettles. 'Another word from you, Tom,' my father said, 'an' you'll be off to bed.'

It was enough and, though I had heard it a hundred times, it had an immediate effect. Being banished early in the night was the greatest punishment of all. I had suffered trial upon trial, trepidation heaped on trepidation, to arrive at this period of security. It made me seethe within, to conjure up visions of revenge, for I was shattered by the inequity of it all. When they would find my dead body in the wilds of Waterfield, they would remember this moment and their grief would afflict them forever. So I held my peace, and the first stirrings of an unequal world began to take shape in my thoughts. If I had been the perpetrator, I would have been forced to return the sausage. I was fifth in a family that would grow to ten children, the lowest one in rank of those gathered round the table.

The evening meal was not over until he signalled it so by pulling his chair slightly backwards. He exploited that to the full, though really it was just another sop to the pretender on the throne. When it was time by her agenda, my mother would rise, bidding the rest of us to follow, and she led a charge of work flurry around my father's seated figure.

He sat there, worrying a crust of bread between his clacking jaws. The table would be removed to its normal place under the window looking west, the floor swept around him, all the delph washed and stored and he would still be in situ, jaws munching and eyes cast desultorily on a roof spar as if nothing was amiss. He would affect surprise when told by my mother to move himself, as if all that activity had gone on around him, unnoticed.

There was a very distinct division of labour about the washing up, which prevailed for all things associated with the kitchen. Washing up, sweeping, tending the infants, readying clothes, stoking and minding the fire were all female duties. So ingrained was that culture that I was frequently insulted by being called 'a minder of infants' and 'a guardian of the fire.' Not only did I hate the allusion to a gender inferiority, but the smirk on my father's face was enough to make me mentally head out for Waterfield and die in desolation. Only years later, when eight-tenths of the family had pitched their tents in far flung locations, and the remaining fraction had die-hard convictions, did I see my father take a dishcloth in his hands. Even then, if someone's shadow passed by the western window, the approach of most callers, he would dump the dishcloth and head for his throne like a scalded cat.

As soon as the washing up was complete, the table was brought back to the centre of the room. Electric power was still years away and so was our knowledge of the technology. We had a fixed paraffin lamp above the mirror on the east wall. It was our secondary light: it lit the mirror and cast shadows. It would serve as a poor substitute when the main light failed. That was the hanging lamp, suspended on a pulley from a roof spar and let down over the centre of the table. It had a bottle green glass oil well that splayed wonderful patterns of refracted light when the lamp swayed in the draught. Those broken shapes decorated the curvature of walls and angles, glided around corners and etched on the loft door, a craftsmanship in light that a turner would have gaped at in wonder.

★ ★ ★

My mother had come from a background of books and education. She was convent-schooled and devoured everything of the printed word that came her way. She read literature and trash, from Jane Austen to a silly true love magazine called *Red Star*. There was a press by the western gable that was overloaded with books; it was so full that when the door was opened, all its innards tumbled out. My mother had read everything in the press and perhaps that was why its shelves were never attended to. The hours after the evening meal were her exclusive time. Darkness had set upon our world and the creatures that dominated our lives were at rest: cows were in the byre, calves in the outhouse, the pony in its stable, fowl in their cramped quarters fashioned in the angle where two walls met. All except the fowl were bedded down for the night.

There was an eccentric division of labour also about the fowl. Breeding, feeding, exploiting, were my mother's sole domain and my father kept those things very deliberately at arm's length. He hated fowl and the management of them, but my mother had foisted upon him the responsibility for their safety. It was a kind of inverse flattery; founded on the notion that no one else but he could be trusted with that duty yet. He had always to be reminded about it. Late at night, when he was savouring the company of the crickets, and the hatches of his world were battened down for the night, she would call from the bed in a delicate balance of command and request, 'Did you lock the fowl house door, Michael?'

He would groan and mutter. I think he waited deliberately for the eleventh hour, hoping that she would forget and be culpable, for in his excused omission the fox might raid and sweep the house of every blasted hen, duck and goose. But she was too sharp for that. As he would say himself, 'you'd have to be up very early to best that woman.'

My mother read in the circle of light. The light played in her hair, tinting it with aquamarine. I would see her in mid-morning tend the lamp and know that the care which she lavished on it was intended for her reading time. She was good at it. No one could trim the wick like her or buff the globe with newspaper until it lost every streak. Sometimes in those minutes of sheer luxury, as her lips moved with the pleasure of her reading, the flame would flare in the globe. It happened when someone opened the front door, or a gust of wind struck the back door with the force of a squall. At best, it left a blackened sooty globe that would take long care and attention before it was clear again. At worst, the flame reared past the rim of the globe, the man on the throne voiced out his fear for the thatch, but it was lost in the shattering glass and the onrush of awful darkness that swallowed all in its terrible maw.

We brought an uneasy sense of respect to my mother's exclusive period. It never lasted more than fifteen minutes. By then the school books had been arrayed, the assembly sat in silence round the table, eyes feverish with brimming questions, bodies tensed like greyhounds at a starting trap. Some strange collective sense of moment decided when the reading time was up and the clamour arose with an ascending buzz.

My mother had been well versed in her convent school. She knew arithmetic, geography, English composition and reams of history. It was just as well that she had that prolific knowledge because her progeny were already showing serious leanings towards specialisation. One was good at arithmetic and another 'handy enough' at composition, but rarely, if ever, was anyone good with the twain.

'Give us a sentence, Ma. Start me off.'

'If I multiply inches by inches, will I get square inches?'

'What are the nine counties in the province of Ulster?'

'Give us an example of a possessive pronoun, Ma.'

'Ma. Will you listen to me?'

She threw answers and suggestions and words and phrases that primed the well of submerged knowledge and dimly-remembered learning. But it didn't work for the one who had an essay to compose. Sentences were drops of blood; blank copybook pages arid deserts.

'Give us a start, Ma.'

My mother sighed deeply and dragged her eyes from the book. She joined the tips of her fingers, contemplated the triangular shape she had created and leaned it against the bridge of her nose.

'Every year in October, when the harvest is finished, there are races in the town of Listowel, in the County of Kerry.'

The she closed the book and looked for a long envious moment at the pretender to the throne. He was smoking his Gold Flake, his first cigarette; he never smoked during the day. Such was the welter of work on the land that he would never allow something as frivolous as a cigarette to distract him. It was a neat piece of conniving; he sometimes let it slip that he had no craving during the day. But it evoked my mother's sympathy and that sympathy was cast in edicts of stone. If my father ran out of cigarettes, no matter the lateness of the hour or the foulness of the weather, we were duty bound to go and fetch him a packet. The nearest shop was a mile away across the fields. My mother would explain that duty in collective 'we' terms but in reality it was always the singular 'you' because that duty affected me only. It filled me with despair. He would wait until the last cigarette was in his mouth before he would say; 'I'm out of cigarettes.'

It had the clap of doom about it. Outside the blackness was over the land, the wind was creaking in the eaves and a stray curlew calling in melancholy desolation back towards Waterfield.

'You go, Tom,' my mother said, 'there's money in the rosebowl.'

Why was it that her command always fell on me? Why was it that every eye swivelled on me the moment my father made his announcement? Wasn't it obvious? In the opinion of the queen and the pretender, I was the most expedient. I had no place in the scheme of things, no talent for husbandry or domestic skill to make me important.

And so I went, skulking out into the night like a whipped cur. I was scared to go into the unlit parlour for the money, let alone face the devils of the night. I would be set upon by bulls, by black dogs and crying curlews. I was terrified as I stumbled through the fields in the utter blackness.

I will never understand why my father behaved as he did, for he must have known from the previous night that his supply had run down. I would have gladly gone in the light, even in the gathering dusk. But for a word of praise — because he never thanked me when I returned — I would have gone through a legion of savages.

'What's after the town of Listowel, Ma?'

My father blew smoke rings at the ceiling, luxuriating in his comfort. He was ensconced in the allegiance of his family, wrapped in the convention of its adulation.

When I grew older and began to understand human characteristics, it struck me how paradoxical my parents' behaviour was. She was a female Arthur; he was a male queen bee — a strange exhibition of role reversal. I know now that it wasn't really that way at all. They were playing at roles. It suited my father fine that all the hard decisions were taken away from him and all he had to do was rubber stamp them. As the queen bee, he was lavished with attention, waited on and enthroned. Because my mother had the intelligence for strategy, it suited her to lay schemes. I think now that they both understood each other perfectly. Ultimately it was their achievement that mattered, not the manner of its accomplishment.

'Give us another sentence, Ma.'

'Ma, will you check this long division for me?'

We were a step advanced from the quill, light years away from fountain pens. A chrome holder fastened a writing nib at the end of a stick. 'Far away from fountain pens ye were reared,' my father would tell us. In my mind, writing nibs and cigarettes are inextricably linked. Nibs were forever breaking: they slipped off the holder and were trampled on, they fell out of satchels and makeshift copybook bindings. Gold Flake and Osmiroid, cigarette brands and nib-makers, were the bane of my life. The moment a nib broke, I was forced again into the night to buy a new one. I was soldier ant, passenger pigeon, pack mule. I went compelled, without compassion or sympathy, into the heart-thumping fastness of the night.

Maggie Barrett had a huckster's shop under the outcrop of rock beside the school. She was a spinster, moody and often abrasive. She got up, with bad grace, from the chair beside the range and wondered aloud what kind of parent would let a child out on such a night. I wondered the same but never voiced it even to my inner person who was forever protesting about my treatment. It would be flying in the face of God to think such things.

I could be struck dead, or turned into a pillar of stone. Osmiroid was the brand name on the nib face; it became etched in my mind as a symbol for all downtrodden persons, all those who were appointed to be lackeys, and drawers of water. I never recovered from that state. I was an Osmiroid until the day I went into the brave new world of my first job.

'Give us another sentence, Ma.'

'When we got out of the railway station the streets were black with people There were tinkers with piebald ponies, a three-card trick man and a trick of the loop.'

My father read the local newspaper out loud. His voice was the drone of sing-song poetry being learned by rote, or the chief ports of Britain being loudly committed to memory. The paper was days, even weeks, old; it would be read paragraph by paragraph, line by halting line. My father read of murders and court cases and the price of cattle and corn. He read of the ravages of the Second World War and halted before names that were an obstacle course of strange shapes and sounds.

'What do you make of that name there, Kitty?' My mother's name was Catherine but he always called her Kitty.

Place names fell off her lips with the ease

of a seasoned traveller: Monte Cassino and Montevideo, El Alamein, Prague, the Ukraine. The war was thousands of miles away — an altercation in another planet. It had no relevance to our time and place, to cattle, corn and seasons or race days in Listowel. After a while my father did not read about the war any more because he attempted Versailles himself and made a hash of it. He was constantly reminded of it by what he called smart university professors of children who could not do their own long division when it was put up to them. 'If you're so bloody clever, why are you stuck for a sentence?'

I had nodded off before the youngster at the races had bought a bag of periwinkles. I never felt sleep coming on. One moment I was listening to strange names from continental Europe or imagining the music of the wind that shakes the barley — a poem by Katherine Tynan in my brother's schoolbook. It found a place in my soul the first time I heard it.

There's music in my heart all day;
I hear it late and early.
It comes from fields far far away;
the wind that shakes the barley.

I would try to keep sleep at bay after my mother had put me to bed. I was alone in the room, watching the ray of light coming in from the kitchen, framed by the partially closed door. It was my lifeline to the safety of the kitchen. Lessons were finished, voices drained into murmurs. The front door opened and then banged shut as the eldest trio ran across the front yard to Barrett's house. In Barrett's they would play card games, and drink brimming mugs of heated milk and sugared bread, called goody, at which they would turn up their noses at home.

Silence settled over the kitchen. Sometimes, depending on the angle of the door, I could see my mother at the table. I would see her head drop forward, her book fall on the floor and hear the rustle of the newspaper as my father peered around its side, checking if she were snoozing or fast asleep. Suddenly her head would snap upwards, she would resume reading, but it was always like a remission; she would drop off again and again. My father used say that the books and the characters ran through her dreams and she would call them out and have the characters talk in dialogue: Baroness Orczy and the Scarlet Pimpernel. E. Phillips Oppenheimer, Annie M. P. Smithson.

My mother had no ear for music, but she sang her way through her farmyard chores, in a tuneless monotone. She mined snatches of poetry and doggerel from her memory bank and set them to that universal tune. They seek him here; they seek him there. Those French they seek him everywhere. Is he in heaven, or is he in hell, that damned elusive Pimpernel?

She made tea and laid a cup on the arm of my father's throne. Then she made arrangements for the morning. There was a chipped and dented old alarm clock on the board above the fireplace. She would wind it; move it forward ten minutes and put it face down on the bedside table because it would stop if it were placed erect. When she awoke in the morning she reset it to the correct time. The wanderers from Barrett's returned, stripped before the fire and headed off, clutching bundles of clothing, to the inner reaches of the rooms beyond the parlour, which to me were out on the margins of the known world.

My father would sit before the fire alone, reaching frequently for the packet of Gold Flake and more than compensated for his abstinence during the day. The cigarettes were an accompaniment to his vigil. I wondered what he used think about, what dreams he dreamed, what wonderful landfalls he made alone in his kitchen. I think he loved that time. I could hear the sighs of comfort, the protesting creaks from the armchair as he formed a recline off its back legs. He was no longer pretender to the throne; he was alone and the power in his kingdom.

The wind rattled in the eaves, the rain hissed soft sibilance on the embers. Far away in Waterfield a vixen cried and one of the sheepdogs in the barn growled its vigilance. The crickets emerged from the ashes and their secret valleys of crevices. My father told me that he had the gift of communicating with the crickets. A fairy had come one night and taught him; she had made him promise, under pain of dreadful retribution, that he would never share the knowledge with another human being. So he could not tell me. But perhaps, he added, one day the fairy might come to me.

The vixen cried again from the covert in Waterfield. The dog answered. My mother heard them both.

'Don't forget to close the fowl house door, Michael.'

3

My ignorance exasperated me. I would look at book pages and try to figure out what the pictures were implying or what the words were saying. When he was out in the fields or occupied at night with his lessons, I would sneak my eldest brother's English reader from his bundle of schoolbooks. There was a picture of an Indian chieftain adorning the centre page; he looked out to a landscape of mountain and lake and he seemed to be uttering words of great import. I could sense that because his hands were outstretched and his eyes had a look of severe intensity. I could hazard no guess at all at what the caption underneath the picture said.

I played at going to school for one whole year. I made myself a makeshift canvas bag, stole a pen from my sister Mary and salvaged a collection of used copybooks that had been discarded in a heap at the bottom of the haggard. When the house awakened, I rose with the school-goers and brought my bundle to the kitchen table. They laughed at me, indulgently at first, and then with glances and headshakes of the kind reserved for Paddy

Danaher. John told me that I was an idiot. No person, sane in his head, would volunteer to go to school.

John was a rebel who fought the school at every turn. He would find a pretext to go out into the schoolyard; and when our creamery cart passed by, he would be down the stone steps and hidden behind the milk tankards in a twinkling. McKenna, who drove the cart, must have been in collusion with him. Why else would the grey pony slow and crop the margin as they came past the high wall of the school? Once home, having run the gauntlet successfully, John was allowed to stay, as if his daring deserved reward. He was certain it would be; he would jump off the cart with a whoop of delight, throw the book bundle on the horsehair couch and head for the fields.

I suppose it was that devotion to land and husbandry that influenced my parents; John, the second eldest son, was the natural inheritor of their joint vocations. I tried his ruse once, a year or two later. But McKenna whipped the grey pony when I tried to mount the cart. I struggled up, and when I arrived home, I was taken by the lobe of the ear, frog-marched by my mother up the Hill field and thrust in the direction of the school.

There was a piece of folklore about the siting of the school. It was perched on top of a craggy hill though there was flat land all around. The landlord, averse to an educated peasantry, reluctantly granted the most awkward site. The builders carved out a platform from the outcrop, built a high stone wall, a flight of stone steps and set a limestone plaque over the door. It looked out over all the land, the ribbon of the Shannon, Mannix's redbrick ruin, the Norman keep-tower at Lisnacullia, the spire of the church in Rathkeale.

In the summer of 1943, I started school. My makeshift bundle was under my arm; I had hunks of buttered bread wrapped in brown paper and a Nash's lemonade bottle filled with milk. The class I joined was the smallest in the school's history: four girls and me. The opportunity of that wasn't lost on my father and it went into his armoury of conversation and ridicule. It was logical, he supposed, that it should work out like that: the minder of hens and the guardian of the fire had found a natural place in the company of girls. In time, what was a singular blow to my pursuit of masculine status, would become a benefit.

That class was lavished with attention. We raced through the curriculum and when I went away to college after eight years in that grey stone building, I was well ahead. What most of my college classmates were first encountering, I had been apprenticed to and mastered a couple of years before. But I had paid a price for that apprenticeship.

I was seven when the new teacher, Miss James, arrived. I never knew exactly where she came from, though there were overtones of County Kerry in her accent. Up to then I had been enfolded in the warmth of Miss Early. She was round and fat and a teacher born. She infected us with the bounty and the magic of her skill. Then she went away, to marry a farmer from the hill country beyond Carrickerry and they sent us an opposite to replace her.

Miss James was cast in granite. I seldom saw her smile. Her world was dominated by religion, black and humourless. Everything had a religious connection; education was merely a device to overlay its strictures and principles. We were taught through doctrine. There was only one way to bless oneself, one way to genuflect, one way to display sanctity and the observance of devotion. I recall Miss James in the front pew at church, her features set in rigid concentration, lips moving like pistons, eyes unwavering on the tabernacle. When school was over, she spent long hours in that same front pew. She frightened me because I could never see over that wall of blackness and she prompted my first misgivings about aspects of religion. Where I had come from, God was kind and warm; Miss James was in rigid disagreement with my legacy.

I was found to be the carrier of obscenity, an offspring of Satan. It happened when I was nearing my eighth birthday. We were around Miss James' desk, wrestling with the complexity of the seven times table. Seven times one is seven; seven times two are fourteen. Voices climbed and fell in cadence, droned away into whispers, gathered volume. There was nothing in our class-work that could not be converted to Roman Catholic reference. So it was that day. Seven times tables reminded Miss James of the child saint, Maria Goretti, who gave her life rather than be forced to sin against holy purity. I made a backward movement with my hand and she instantly concluded that I was groping under Hannie's skirt, one of my classmates.

She went berserk: her granite features reddened in anger, shreds of saliva sprayed from the corners of her mouth. She had seen the devil; he had the guise of a seven year-old. He had possessed my body and occupied my mind and I was a willing receptacle. It was madness. There wasn't a single sexual notion in my head. I believed that children were found under cabbage heads, now and then one was let down in a sunbeam.

Miss James beat me about the legs. It was summer and I was barefoot. Then she put me standing on the bench and invited the other pupils to mock me. A little girl named Birdie whispered something in sympathy, and she was made join me.

I never recovered. In Miss James' mind I was evil. She would look at me with simmering eyes, laden with hostility. I was beaten at every opportunity; the weals rose red and fiery on the calves of my legs and burned like stigmata on my palms. The intensity of her anger befuddled me. Perhaps I really was evil and it was apparent only to the adult wordly eyes of God's chosen. But then the injustice of the punishment took hold of me and cried out for redress.

I took my case to the court of our kitchen. My father clucked clucked in sympathy and some anger, but he did not find in my favour. I must, he said have done something wrong. He was in the grip of the establishment: church and school were inextricably bound and he offered them his total allegiance.

My mother opted for a pragmatic judgement. I could not be guilty of the crime but, given the forces ranged against us, my second state would be worse than the first if she protested. Once an outraged man had taken issue with the teacher in the senior room and she had simply invoked the higher authority. The parish priest called to the man's house, berated him, threatened to talk about it from the altar and advised him to leave education to those who were qualified to administer it. That man's son was ignored forever after.

I remember nothing of my time in that small classroom except Miss James and the effect she had on me. She haunted my sleep, leering over the side of my bed, face creased in anger, stick raised in punishment. I quaked at every glance she gave me, baulked at every question, though I knew the answer. I wet the floor because I was afraid to ask her permission to go outside. She willed me the seeds of a stammer that affected me then and later in times of tension and distress.

When I was nine, I left her classroom and my heart soared. She went away a few years after that. It was said that she had entered a convent and had gone to preach the good news to pagan souls in Africa. She had talked incessantly about black babies and how it was our duty to pray that Catholic missionaries would have reached and converted them before the Protestants and Anglicans arrived.

Miss James was the flag carrier for the small army in the official church who turned the simple message of love and charity into a complex dictatorship of rules, hellfire damnation and the promise of eternal doom. It was all so oppressive: the constant message of fire and brimstone, the virtue and the dignity of poverty, the evils of the flesh. I was terrified of church and priests and the power they represented.

The day I crossed the threshold of the small room to the senior, where third to sixth class were taught, Miss James disappeared from my world. I was filled with happiness. It should not have been so because word emphatically had it, that compared to Miss Abigail, the teacher in the senior classroom, Miss James was benign. I willed myself to ignore that opinion. I had met Miss Abigail once with my mother when we had gone into Thornton's shop in Rathkeale. She had smiled at me, patted me on the head and bought me an ice cream. It was another inexplicable example of the contradictions that were besetting my life. She had sometimes smiled at me too, as I passed through her classroom. I was ribbed cruelly about it because no one willingly offered a shred of fellowship towards this living terror. No one ever remembered Miss James taking so strong a dislike to anyone as she had towards me; there must have been something strange and odd about me to deserve that. But courting the favours of the virago, Miss Abigail, really set the seal on my oddity. I never did go courting her favour. I was too fearful of the tradition to do anything like that. But in truth, I suffered less and was treated better than most of my contemporaries in the four years under her tutelage.

Abigail was an extraordinary woman. She must have been in her mid forties then. Her face was masculine, with dramatically cragged features. She had a tongue like a rasp and could construct in a twinkling the cruellest pastoral analogies that sunk like barbs and banished self-esteem. We were as thick as double ditches, she said; we had the finesse and the manners of rutting puck goats; we were as mindless as day-old chickens, as smelly and unwashed as a wallowing sow in a mud hole.

Miss Abigail had ethics that shrieked of hypocrisy and she practised them as if they were written in stone and delivered personally by Moses. It was common knowledge that she had borne a child out of wedlock. When the same fate befell one of her pupils, she railed about the sin of impurity and forbade us to talk or associate with the hapless victim, because victims they were in the morality of that time. She had a sense of social status that was extremely opposed to the equality tenets of her profession. Her people were farmers; those who held land she esteemed in direct ratio to the size of their holdings. At the bottom of the pile came the labourers and people who lived in cottages. She made exception in their case only to the few who qualified on the grounds of exceptional intelligence.

I was fortunate that I came somewhere midway in her range of qualifying criteria. So too did my classmates, Moira and Birdie. Bridget came a few steps higher. Hannie hardly touched the bottom rung of the ladder, but she accepted everything that was thrown at her with the tolerance of the born stoic. School was a limbo only — a transient, compulsory prison cell whose walls would collapse the day Hannie came of age. Then, it was as certain as night follows day that she would be on the mail boat to Britain, awash, like thousands of others, in the tide of mass emigration.

I spent four good years in the senior room and I look back on them with a mixture of pleasure and pain for everyone fell foul of Miss Abigail at some stage. I had little problem with the normal business of school. I liked learning, discovering, the delight of abstraction. I could work out mathematics and do composition without hardship. Miss Abigail used me as a roving substitute when the inspector called, demoting me for the day to a lower class or promoting me to a higher as she judged the need.

I got on the dark side of Abigail for extra curricular activities, like mitching school to follow the foxhunt or causing trouble in the playground. Once my cousin Con Enright and I were sent as family delegates to attend the Holy Hour devotions on Sunday afternoon. Holy Hour was never in favour; it was dull, interminably long, and it interfered with a prime period of our freedom. But the priest demanded respect for it and ruled that one at least from every house should attend. In keeping with my fortune to be delegated the unpalatable tasks, I was nominated.

It was a lovely day in late October. The hazelnuts were ripe and abundant in the hedges of McAuliffe's field. We never went to the Holy Hour nor gave it a second thought. At break time the next day she called us separately to her desk. Why had we not attended the Holy Hour? Con had had a pain in his stomach and I had had to take a cow to the bull. We were beaten with a broken chair rung and put kneeling in opposite corners until we told the truth. We were kept there for three days, including break times. Miss James shared lunch with Miss Abigail and I heard her say, as I was intended to, that it was no surprise that I was developing into a liar and a heretic. Miss Abigail said that I was a treacherous slimy weasel.

Bridget was waiting for me when I came down the steps to go home. She was full of distaste for Miss Abigail and sympathy for my plight. Her concern uplifted me until I discovered that she was the one who had ratted on us. She had seen us from the gallery of the church.

I was uneasy about being cast in the role of favourite because, however infrequently it occurred, it set me at odds with my schoolmates. I hated it when she read out some of my written work or praised me to the inspector or priest. She would give me books to read, like abridged versions of *Treasure Island* and *The Deerslayer*. She would announce to the whole room that I had talent and that she would look for my name in the roll of future greatness. It would all be retracted when some escapade went wrong.

Miss Abigail didn't know it, but that was when she brightened my days the most. It was a great time for devilment. We had no form of amusement other than what we created ourselves. Our world was ordered and predictable; it bowed to the dictates of religion and the conventions of mature behaviour. A few of us, in the dead of night, took a ladder to the drills that Owney Casey had formed in his haggard. He was renowned for drills that were as straight as lines from a draughtsman's board and for ridiculing all those who hadn't his eye or inclination. We levelled the drills with a ladder, reducing them to a field of red earth. We listened for the reaction from neighbours, and did the same when he repaired the damage because the response was favourable. Listening for the reaction was essential; there was no point to devilment unless one could see or hear how it had been received.

I told my father about it walking home from mass and he sat in the ditch with the laughter. That same evening he lectured me severely about hurtful pranks and the suffering they caused unsuspecting people. A few days later, Con's father did the same, though he had earlier seen the funny side of it too. So we kept our counsel and forswore each other to secrecy when we locked the puck goat in the schoolroom for a whole weekend.

We were coming home from the hurling in Dunne's field when the idea took root. Most farmers ran a puck goat with the dairy herd in the belief that the stench kept cows and heifers from aborting their unborn calves. At the best of times, puck goats stank. The animal with Liston's cows was at the height of the rut. It was shooting jets of urine, aiming the stream into its mouth and along its flanks. The goat had wallowed in the urine pool; its coat was matted with dried dung, and the smell reeked to high heaven.

Miss Abigail kept a spare key under a geranium pot on the windowsill. The whole parish knew that, so it could be any one of a hundred people who had put the goat inside the school. We released the goat on Sunday night; had it been recognised as Liston's animal it might have cast suspicion on us. I was hot on the heels of Miss Abigail on Monday morning when she opened the school door. The stench burst out like a nauseating wave: earthy-cloying musk loaded with ammonia, stale urine and excrement. It rose from the wooden floor, reeked from the desks, fell from the ceiling. Along the corridor, between the desks and in that square area where Miss Abigail held court, were mounds of goat droppings.

Pupils ran up and down in pandemonium looking for a place to breathe. Miss James had a face as red as a beetroot and a handkerchief daintily pressed to her nostrils. I enjoyed that moment and its memory thereafter as she tried, with a look of abject disgust, to remove the droppings from the soles of her shoes. Abigail went wild when she recovered her wits. She lined us against the wall and marched up and down like a sergeant major, flaying the desk tops with the chair rung. No one knew a thing about it. We were sent home.

But I had a suspicion that Miss Abigail suspected. The word was that she had gone to the parish priest with her complaint and demanded that he come and grill every pupil. It was said that he had refused, prevailing upon her not to make a laughing stock of them both. For a few days after, my classmate Bridget was sniffing about looking for morsels of information. But I knew Bridget by then; the confidential whispering of admiration was but a lubricant for the unwary.

Miss Abigail sent a message by my nephew, fifteen years later, that I should call to the school to see her when I was next home on holiday. I was welcomed with great sincerity, introduced to her pupils and she told them that I had once been the star of the show. She pulled an old copybook from the press and read out one of my essays. I was paid the supreme accolade: the pupils were sent home early in my honour. We talked for an hour after they had gone. She told me that the pleasure of teaching had gone out of her life: the pupils had descended to a most witless level. She could hardly say boo to them now, and there was an appalling indiscipline. She walked me down the stone steps and at the bottom asked, ever so innocently, if I had put the puck goat into the school. I still hadn't the courage to admit it.

I languished for most of my final years in the school, from eleven to thirteen. I tried to compete with John Joe. He was very bright, one up on me in every department: he could write faster, in bold confident copperplate, and never misspelled. He had a wonderful dexterity of mind and he blithely weaved a facile passage through the most difficult mental arithmetic tests. It was all so easy for him: history, geography, English and Irish. When I first came across the creed of the gunfighter — that no matter how good you are, there is always someone faster and better — I saw John Joe as my personal nemesis. I stopped trying and for the rest of my life, every which way I turned, there was always a John Joe.

Perhaps I settled too easily for mediocrity. I was, in the vernacular of my place and time, like a middling good greyhound: always expected to do well but invariably occupying one of the minor placings. John Joe went on to become a teacher and ultimately to become the principal in that same school.

I worked hard at becoming accepted. Miss Abigail's relationship with me hung round me like a millstone. Every complimentary word, every essay read out for priest and visiting dignitary, was another stave in the fence that separated me from acceptance. I spent most of my time dreaming up pranks and devilment and sharing them round like favours to curry goodwill. I was invariably found out and chastised but it was sometimes tinged with unspoken amusement.

I knew then that work on the land held no attraction for me. I escaped it in every way I could. It became a battle between my father and I. It would erupt in angry words and accusations of ingratitude. I would comply guiltily for a while until the prison of routine and the hankering for freedom would make me escape again. I don't think he ever understood that. It was all very simple to him, as most things were that affected his beloved land and his credo about it. I was betraying the credo.

'What class of son did we raise, at all, Kitty?'

4

They flit across the landscape of my mind, inhabit my dreams, the kids who populated my childhood. I see them walk down the Long Road, from Rathreigh and the road to Ardagh, from Creeves and from Kilbrathern, from the Pike and Sluggarah Cross. They come from a place called Riddlestown, with its great house in the grove of beech. And Benson's Cross and Cooltomin and Ardlaman.

I could once reel off those place-names as if they were a five times table. I could put names on the faces that inhabited them. They are mostly made of cobwebs now; a face here, a memory there, shreds of dialogue, all brittle and flimsy. Trying to remember them now is like groping for a memoryhold in the darkness of time. But some still stand out like standing stones in a flat plain, moulded indestructibly by the impact of yesterday, standing erect through the march of years.

Youth was predominant then in the demography of our parish. It was as if emigration had missed out a generation and the vitality of youth that followed was a glorious experiment, stumbled on by accident. I think of Coolcappa now as Brigadoon, a place that came out of the mist, showed itself in a brief flaring exultation and, as quickly, spent its youth and disappeared again behind the veil of mist and myth. I always search for it; I see misformed shapes and hear echoes as if someone has found the pathway through the veil. And sometimes for brief moments, at funerals, wakes, weddings, I think I have found the doorway to Brigadoon. But it will never appear; it is all a collective Humpty Dumpty that cannot be put together. The parts are in London and Sydney, in Boston and New York, the living and the dead.

So I have built this mental Brigadoon in my head. A private place in a lush valley, a land of ever youth, kids from the Long Road and the road to Creeves, happy as endless summer. I allow none of them the slightest trappings of adulthood because then they will escape and sadden those who are left behind. I make constant visits to that personal Brigadoon, on sleepless nights, in dark moods. It keeps the flame alive.

★　★　★

I hitched my wagon to Ally Rafter. I did so because he hated Miss Abigail and I thought it would be expedient to be associated with that camp. Ally had learned that there were ways of alleviating the terrors of the learning system and he pursued them with a resolve that fooled even her. He knew he was going to inherit his father's farm, and he could work that inheritance with the minimum of learning. It was enough to read and write, to understand the basics in arithmetic. Anything else was superfluous.

Ally deliberately cultivated the image of the dunce. That alone, however, wouldn't save him from the dark side of Miss Abigail. So he had to find a way to counteract that. He became the factotum, the dogsbody for all chores that were unrelated to classwork. Ally served mass, so he had an hour off every morning. He fetched the pail of water from the well in McAuliffe's field, he tended Miss Abigail's beloved geraniums, cleaned and polished her bicycle, supervised the fire, drew peat from the outhouse. When he needed assistance as he frequently did, he chose from a favoured few.

I watched and envied him. He mooched around the room, finding a geranium plant with withered leaves and tending to it with the care of immense devotion. Ally brought allegiance to an art form. Miss Abigail had great regard for that allegiance and misread it for respect. I tried hard to follow his act; but he was the one who played Hamlet, leaving the minor parts in his wake.

It took two to fetch the bucket of fresh spring water and an hour to make the journey to McAuliffe's well. The County Council had erected a pump beside Dunne's field; it was hidden from the school by the bend of the road and was just minutes away. The pump broke down soon after it was erected and I believe it was Ally who wrecked it. But he never told Abigail that it had been repaired and, though the neighbours drew water from it daily, she lived in ignorance of its working state.

I loved that trip to McAuliffe's well. It was freedom and I remember the way my heart fluttered when I got the beck from Ally. That pathway through the fields was a pilgrimage route to a sanctified shrine. The freedom was one thing; listening to Ally's stream of invective built on the pleasure. He had listened well to Miss Abigail's barbs and insults. He flung them back at her on the road to McAuliffe's well; he took her analogies, amplified their lewdness and ejected them like verbal javelins every step of the way. It was the only conversation. It started the moment we set foot on the last step of the school and Ally hardly drew breath until we had returned. If I interrupted, he would jab me in the ribs and bid me to stop.

We had almost returned to the school's stone wall one day when Paddy Maumb came by on the hay-float. He asked for a drink and Ally gave him the bucket. He quaffed long and then emptied the rest of the water on to the dusty road. I watched in amazement, hearing it hiss as it evaporated. No one, pupil or adult, crossed Miss Abigail. Then Maumb got off the float, put the bucket against the wheel, drove his horse forward and flattened the bucket. He collapsed against the horse's flanks with laughter.

Ally had a very short fuse and I was expecting him to react, but he was there on the other side, bent over, clutching his stomach. Tears came out his eyes with the fun of it, his head lolled from side to side.

'There,' said Maumb, handing me the ruined bucket. 'Take that back to Abigail, the rotten bitch. Tell her it was me, Paddy Maumb, that made shite of her bucket.'

I stared at him dumbfounded. There was no mistaking his intensity of hatred.

But Ally seized the day. 'Will you be here again when we are coming back from the well?'

We beat out the bucket and went again to the well. It took us two hours in all to return to the school. Maumb was waiting for us each time; twice more he spilled the water and flattened the bucket. Ally went crestfallen to Miss Abigail's desk. He was the picture of broken dignity, fluttering his sad spaniel eyes, catching his breath as if he was having trouble keeping his tears in check. He repeated verbatim what Maumb had said, with sob-like pauses. Miss Abigail apologised for the *amadán*, who, as a former pupil, hadn't the wit, the intelligence or the manners of a bullock with two heads. And who now, in his thirties, was even more stupid. She forbade us to talk or consort with him.

We promptly did the opposite. We couldn't wait to express our appreciation. Maumb was already a folk hero: he kept goal for the Rathkeale hurling team and, according to local tradition, could stop hayseed. I went with Con to the Bog field in Rathkeale every time he played there. We stood at one side of the goal, almost under the shadow of our hero. His sister, Mena, stood at the other post, a bicycle pump in her hand. Every time a fracas developed in the goalmouth, she was in the thick of it, making noises like a samurai warrior and wielding the pump as if it were a katana. 'Come inside that square again', I heard her say once, to a corner forward with crooked legs, who had flattened Paddy in the back of the net, 'do it again, you horny oul' ram, and you won't have to worry no more about the machinery between your bandy legs'.

As usual, I got on the wrong side of Ally. His mouth always hung open and Abigail remarked that he should be careful if he ever found himself in Limerick city lest a bus might park in his gob. I laughed in spite of myself when all the others in the class had the prudence to suppress it. At lunchtime he marched straight up to me in the playground and laid me low with a looping uppercut. I was never in favour again. But I had a driving thirst for vengeance, which like the pranks, nearly always boomeranged on me.

Con Enright and I sneaked into the school one night in November. We were first cousins, born within months of each other, partners in escapade and devilment. We hammered nail holes in the bottom of the water bucket, removed some of the earth from the geranium pots and replaced it again when we had doused the roots with paraffin. Ally never noticed the nail holes until he had filled the bucket; he arrived back, late, sheepish, and tried to explain. Miss Abigail lambasted him, but it was nothing to the day when she

60

discovered the dead geraniums. I had watched them wilt and droop and had read the terrified puzzlement in his face and wide-open mouth as he frequently went to examine them.

Francie Curry had opted out too. He also had land to succour him and the certain knowledge that he would be received into the fold of his brothers the day he finished school. Francie was a chip off the old block. I lost count of how many brothers he had. The Currys were an independent republic and a brotherhood of unity and fraternity. They sought little friendship beyond their own border. They lived in the twin bonds of land and family and from dawn till dusk filled their republic with the sounds of their labour.

School was the only place the Currys had ever performed in the public arena. It was a necessary aberration, borne as if it were a precept of the church. Francie was Miss Abigail's undoing: she never bested him for she was powerless in the face of his total acceptance. She threw her repertoire of insults and analogies at him and he absorbed it as pleasure. He was beaten and he held out his hands as if receiving gifts. The greater the tirade, the larger was his smile; it spread across his face like a warming glow.

The only homework Francie Curry did was

sums. To those he brought an invention that was profound in its simplicity and brilliant in its practical application. It never varied, never wavered and long after Miss Abigail capitulated, he continued to use it. He simply thought up four numbers, thought of four more and placed them underneath the first set. He drew a line and, for a total, put down the first four numbers that entered his head. He did it all meticulously, row after row spreading in his copybook, without blot or blemish. After each sum and exactly in line with the previous one, he wrote a large O. That was the symbol for incorrect. A 'glugger' Miss Abigail called it — the Irish word for an egg that would not hatch.

Francie never played any game in the playground. At the corner of the wall that separated the girls' section from the boys', he stood alone. He would never talk about Miss Abigail; she meant nothing to him. I would sometimes seek him out, mostly when one of my schemes had gone wrong and I had been given the cold shoulder. He had very little conversation, but he would show me his hands, have me feel the weals and calluses as if they were notches on a gun butt.

I discovered another side of him and it existed only outside the perimeter of the school. Once I explained to Miss Abigail that

I had been late coming to school because I had been chased by Liston's puck goat. In truth, I had been back in Cussen's fox-covert checking my rabbit snares. Miss Abigail delegated Francie Curry to act as my bodyguard, coming and going from school. It meant a detour for him and when he accompanied me along the route to home, he gave vent to an explosion of swear words that amazed and left me envious. He had words I never knew existed and let them loose with an ease of expression and a familiarity of usage that could have been developed only within the fraternal bond.

We were indeed a motley crew: sons of farmers, daughters of labourers, offspring of tradesmen. You wouldn't have recognised the social strata by looking at us. We wore clothes like a uniform. Our short shapeless trousers came to the knee and stopped exactly there. Anything below, the merest fraction above, drew castigation and ridicule from Miss Abigail and classmate alike. The power of convention was immense, no matter how tall a young lad may be — Francie Curry was a case in point — he could not wear long pants until he had passed through school. Francie looked like an import from the Austrian Tyrol or a British infantryman in the Africa Corps.

The pants we termed an 'everyday'

trousers, which meant that it was the same garment we milked cows in, thinned turnips, skated in mudslides, romped, fought and played in. It would be discarded only when there was no fabric left to patch or the smell finally became noticeable, even to impervious nostrils like ours and, I suppose, Miss Abigail's.

We wore ganseys tucked into our pants. The gansey was a utilitarian garment. It was also a towel and a handkerchief. Our noses dripped like faulty faucets and the turn-ups at the sleeves were stiff and discoloured from constant wiping. The Sunday shirt was worn throughout the following week. Underwear was unheard of. I wore pyjamas for the first time when I went away to college and then only because the college clothing list specified it. We were Spartans; pyjamas would have been anathema to our ways, a symbol of decadence.

We suffered from ailments and infections that now seem to have passed into oblivion. Ringworm was a common occurrence. We picked it up from cattle, especially calves, and from gateposts and pens and cowstalls. My mother waged her own personal war against hair nits. They were always about, recurring when she thought she had exterminated them. She would grit her teeth and shiver when one was discovered and once a week or more she would trawl the girls' tresses with a fine-toothed comb. She had no mercy. Every nit was an enemy and was placed for execution on a piece of newspaper and ground to death with her thumbnail. With us boys, the enemy was on a suicide mission, traversing a barren desert country. Our hair was cropped to the bone; there was no hiding place. Such cropping too was part of the uniform. It was said to make the hair grow strong and plentiful. Blood poisoning was almost as common as ringworm. We were constantly picking up cuts and scrapes and ignoring them. It was part of the Spartan image.

Roger Flavin was the epitome of that tough, lean and hungry youngster. He would eat grit to demonstrate his hardiness and come deliberately barefoot to school in all weathers. I can still see his legs dangling from his bench, scarred and wounded, with an ice blue hue. He shivered involuntarily and gnashed his teeth when he stood up. Once I saw him put three marbles between his lunchtime slices of brown bread, making what he called a marble sandwich; he washed it all down with a pint bottle of goat's milk. Goat's milk was just the man for the bones, he used to say.

Roger would walk into the field that held Reidy's Hereford bull and his concubine herd of young heifers. He would paw the ground in mock imitation within twenty feet of the bull, make horns of his hands against his forehead and pretend to charge. The bull ignored him. But Liston's puck goat was having none of it. Roger had to dive into a patch of nettles to escape. He missed one whole week of school, raved like a madman with nettle fever and when he returned, he was wearing his boots.

Roger Flavin developed a unique art form. He pricked the back of his hand with a safety pin, carving the initials of his first name when the scab formed. We treated that with awe. It was the sign of a true Spartan. I asked him to do mine. He seemed taken aback with the request and then asked, 'How do you spell Tom?' We called Roger the whittle man. He bit his nails to the roots and picked at the quicks and could boast that at one stage he had a whitlow in every finger.

Chris Hartnett imagined himself to be Billy Conn, the prize-fighter. He would walk up to you, put up his guard, feint to the left and cross with the right. His older brother, home from England, took him for a real haircut to Jim Aherne, the barber in Rathkeale. The walls were covered with photographs of famous boxers; every one a different stance, a different pose. Chris learned everything he knew about boxing in the hour he was there and learned that Billy Conn was training to fight Joe Louis for the world heavyweight crown.

We were all Billy Conn fans; there was an Irish connection somewhere and he was the chivalrous white Lancelot against the black pretender. Who knows but there might have been as much Irish in Louis' pedigree. The fight had been over two days before we heard the result; there wasn't a radio in the parish then and no one got a daily newspaper. Though Billy Conn lost, we elected him victorious in defeat. He was robbed; the referee was in the pay of the Louis camp; Louis had a horseshoe in his glove.

Chris assumed the persona of Billy Conn, throwing his shapes and feints and combinations like a salutation. There was Chris, watching himself in the reflection from Miss Abigail's flash lamp, crouching and shuffling. Going down the white road after school, he would halt suddenly and do a skipping routine. When he was finished that, he would take a stick from the hedge and strike himself along the buttocks as if he were urging on a horse. He would gallop down the hill opposite Nonie Hynes' house, kicking up spumes of dust from the white road.

We all did that. The practice had lately come into Coolcappa through Jack Hayes' cinema in Rathkeale. I had never been there, but the lore of the Wild West had infiltrated the school: Tom Mix and Hopalong Cassidy, Roy Rogers, Gene Autry, the singing cowboy. They were the forerunners of a new vogue of influence and, according to the parish priest, boded no good for the pure ways of the Irish.

Chris once stole a pencil from my brother John. It had purple lead which my father called puce, pencils he called cedars. There was a fancy chrome cover protecting the writing end. My father had found it near Greaney's cottage when he was accompanying my Aunt Hannah home to Lisnacullia. John demanded it back and Chris challenged him to a fight where the victor would claim the pencil. It had all to be done in the tradition of the fight game; a neutral venue at Mangan's Cross, a second in each corner. I worried about the fight for days. I was John's second. But however tough Chris was, he had only a minor reputation compared to his brother Jack. He wasn't even afraid of Miss Abigail and I think she deliberately backed away from a direct confrontation with him. He had wrestled the chair rung from her when she had once tried to beat him, raised it above his head as if to hit her and muttered words like 'bitch' and 'sow', loud enough for us all to hear. She never bothered with him after that, saying that she would not lower herself.

What worried me most was the rumour that the fight was a set up and that it was really me whom Jack was after because I had ratted on him to Miss Abigail. We were early at Mangan's Cross; Chris had been kept late for farting during the Angelus. I heard shouts of 'Hup there, Trigger' before he came round the bend of the road; the stick flailing at his hindquarters when he came into sight.

Jack took charge of the fight preliminaries. Normally there would be taunts and jeers, and several questions like, 'Are you as tough a man now as you were last week?' There would be none of that, Jack insisted. Both fighters would stand at either side of the line he had drawn on the road, put up their guards and come out fighting. But he did have the right to intervene and he looked at me with deadly intent. It was natural for brother to defend brother, which was very unlikely in this case, because Jack and Chris were forever rowing. But it was also natural for a brother to share in the victory and turn it into a rout of all the opposition.

Chris dropped into a crouch and shuffled, blowing through his nostrils like a racehorse.

John had no such pretensions about style. He let fly with a straightforward thump that came up from his midriff. It crashed through Chris' guard and hit him on the nose. Chris burst into a fit of crying. 'He hit me, Jack. He hit me.'

Jack intervened, as was his stated right and intent. He came straight for me, telling me that he was going to destroy me forever and that I would never again carry tales to Miss Abigail. I didn't have time to ponder on that because another haymaker from John, hallmarked with the same lack of finesse, took Jack on the point of his jaw and stretched him.

We waited in case there was any more fight left in the brothers. I was all for hightailing it out of there and making the most of what, to me, was incredible luck. Two blows, delivered with ferocious accuracy by a kid who had never been in a fight before and didn't understand what 'put up your guard' meant, had to be something of a miracle. But the Hartnetts didn't think so. They had the utmost respect for him thereafter and total suspicion of me. It was Ally who sowed those seeds of distrust. He suspected, but could not prove, who had holed the water pail and killed the geraniums. So he set Jack Harnett on me. I was Abigail's informant.

We played hurling in Dunne's field. We could muster a full team and played the game with an intensity that bordered on frenzy. We played with a sponge ball and any piece of wood that roughly resembled a hurling stick. Most common were lengths of hazel and blackthorn cut from the fox covert on Cussen's land.

Kieran Dunne was our goalkeeper. He was a wizard until the opposition taunted him and his team-mates blamed him. Kieran would make the most impossible saves, but the more he made them, the more likely he was to miss the soft ones.

'I could have saved that one with my eyes closed, Kieran.'

'Kieran, you wouldn't stop a bag of mangolds.'

Kieran had a very short fuse and vented his anger against the rock that served as a goalpost. He broke many a stick that way and made several trips for replacements to the covert in Lissochola. When he was playing well, he was most susceptible to a taunt. With notions of invincibility, he would make a sally outfield, dribbling the ball because the hurley boss wasn't large enough for him to do a solo run. He never made it upfield and when he was dispossessed, it was a simple matter for the opposing player to strike the ball into the empty goal.

'You great big looradhaun, Kieran.'

There was something of the prima donna about Kieran. Wordlessly, he picked up his gansey, which he always placed on the stone that served as a goal post, and marched off. He would return only if he was apologised to. I made many a trip to his house, a delegate from the team, carrying words of suppliance and future good intent. I would find him sitting at the corner of the kitchen table, his crooked stick beside him and his gansey at arm's length. I pleaded and after several emphatic 'no's and vigorous headshakes, he would pick up the garment and march silently ahead of me to the field. The gansey was a tool of his art, a ploy of gamesmanship. When it was placed on the stone, it had the effect of lessening the space between the goal markers and he placed it with the optimum advantage.

Few of us had real hurleys. Ally Rafter cut down the handle of his father's hay-slide and looked like a young Goliath wielding a giant scimitar. We improvised, restored and repaired. Con Enright and I went regularly to the Bog field in Rathkeale where the adults played the game in deadly earnest. We were like greyhounds in the traps, waiting for a hurley to break. Then we hared across the pitch, trying to outwit and outrun a dozen other youngsters. Acquiring one piece of a broken hurley was useless; the pieces had to match so that they could be spliced together again. Left of my vision as we faced the field was my responsibility, right was Con's. The more earnest the encounter of the older lads and deeper the spleen between the teams, the greater was our harvest of broken hurleys.

John Joe's father was a carpenter and his older brother, Mick, an apprentice to the trade. They had the best of equipment and if a suitable piece of ash could be located, with the grain running straight and then arcing, a body could do a deal with them. A good piece would make half a dozen and one of them and maybe two, if you were a negotiator, would be the reward for supplying the makings. I knew every likely ash tree growing on my father's land and further afield. There was one particular ash growing out of the earthen bank on Absalom's Island. It was a natural and, when mature, I would be negotiating with John Joe. But I made the mistake of showing it to Billy, my eldest brother. It matured but then suddenly disappeared, leaving a stump plastered with cow dung to camouflage the recent cut. I learned a long time later that Billy and the Clacker Kelly had felled it, one Sunday in August, when the rest of us were at the pattern day in Barrigone. It made great hurleys, the Clacker later told me. They sold a couple to Paddy Maumb, three to the Mullane brothers. That single tree funded excursions to dance halls and marquees, as far away as Croom and Kildimo.

The Clacker was the Casanova among the young men of the parish. He had a shock of blonde hair and a handsome tanned face. He was a worldly man and mixed adroitly a trio of interests: hurling, drink and women. But he was forever short of money and on the lookout for a scheme that would fund some aspect of the three.

Dunne's field on a summer's evening was a cacophony of noise and the endeavour of raw passion. The hurling sustained me during the day. It lifted my soul in the eternity of turnip drills and tempered my spirit in a field of mown hay. I would dream about it, create visions of glorious movement; invent ploys and plays that would never mature in the helter skelter of frenetic chaos. There was no pattern to our play, no strategy. Once the ball was in play, we all chased it, haring up and down the field like tribal warriors. The crooked sticks were primitive clubs; the clack of their encounter like the muted sound of a distant battlefield. Then, in the midst of all that passion, a whistle would sound from Dunne's yard.

The Dunnes responded as if the whistle had an hypnotic effect on them. The moment it sounded, whatever the fervour of the game, or the intensity of the fight, they trooped home. They supplied four players, including the indispensable Kieran. No one else wanted to play in goal; outfield was where you could show your skill. When Kieran departed, the game died.

The whistle was blown by Mary, who had been reared in a home for waifs and illegitimates, and had been sent out to service in her teens. She loved blowing the whistle on us. She would appear in the yard with deadly intent; it was her moment. Once when I was going home early, she came onto the yard with the whistle. The ball was lost and they were searching the hedge that bounded the white road. She waited until they had found it before she blew.

Miss Abigail disliked hurling. It led to fighting and swearing and had degenerated into decadence since the beautiful Cuchulainn had invented and mastered it, in the halcyon days of the Red Branch order. Even were she to like it, there was only a patch of rock for a playground and the risk of injury was too great. Anyway there was nothing manly about it, she said, and we would be better employed in our free time mastering the art of conversation and reflecting on our saints and patriots. She had a passion for historical heroes: Tone and Emmet, Oliver Plunkett and de Valera, the current keeper of the flame. She taught us that there was nothing finer than to spill one's blood for the Dark Rosaleen, the personification of Ireland, free, pure and holy.

Once, before a general election — the school was used as a polling station — she made us declare our parents' political allegiances. She was all for de Valera, the greatest Irishman alive or dead, and anyone whose parents did not share her opinion, was segregated to the end of the room and forbidden to mingle or fraternise with the Fianna Fáil elite. It made for some very strange bedfellows, sons and daughters of labourers and small farmers, children of servants, parading temporarily in her favour. We were of the opposite following: our political allegiance was founded in the hardships of the Economic War and was anathema to hers. We were traitors — West Brits and lackeys of the crown.

In the lore of the school, the small field

across the road was the real playground. It was ours by right, but church and school had given it to old Ned Barrett so that he could graze his donkey and cow there. I never knew why he was so favoured. At the top end of the playground there was a verdant patch that had a rockery in the middle and was yielding and safe. But that had been donated to Jack Roche, the parish clerk; it was out of bounds for us. Even to cast an envious eye upon it was enough to get Miss Abigail railing: the parish clerk was close to the priest. When it came time to mow the hay and harvest the patch, a working party was sent out from the classroom.

It was really a small chore, but it took hours to finish and the party reported back to us that Roche had a turn of phrase and a range of experience far removed from the expected saintliness of one so close to church and priest and God. His stories and expression were adapted by his listeners and adorned the whispering and the innuendo of the boys' playground, especially the sixth class. I wonder if Miss Abigail had the slightest notion of what went on in the playground and how removed our conversation was from her idealised concept of saints and patriotic heroes. Our language was sprinkled with the same kind of analogies she used, but with an overt sexual explicitness. We had rhymes, stories and expressions which would make the heroes of the pure Gael turn in their graves.

As I was coming home from Clare,
I met a woman with fair hair.
I asked her to come behind a rock,
to give her a tip of my bantam cock.

In the other parish school at Creeves there was a different regime. They had a field for a playground and hurling was encouraged. In the summer of 1949, they challenged our school. We played them in the field where St Kieran's GAA clubhouse now stands. But it was far removed from a pitch then; it formed part of an estate recently divided by the Land Commission. A large earthen bank, still ungrassed, formed one boundary. We fancied ourselves; we had practised for weeks in Dunne's field and some of the adults, who came by the white road, and had stopped to view us, declared that we were stars in the making. We would one day wear the green of Limerick and restore the county to the glory days of Mackey, Cross and Collopy.

On such flattery are dreams foundered. They came up from Creeves in trap cars flanked by bicycles, with real hurleys and a leather ball and were missing two players. But we were creamed. There was pattern and formation to their game: backs stayed in position, corner forwards hugged the goal line and drove Kieran to a stammering frenzy. Every other minute he was retrieving the ball from the drain at the back of his goal. He never saw the bullets and he missed the soft ones. He marched off home when one of them asked where we had resurrected him. To make matters worse, one of their missing players arrived: Pakie Casey, son of Owney, long as a rake with an incongruous short pants and carrying a stick shaped like a scythe. By then Father O'Connell had appeared, lured out of the confessional box by the racket in Roche's field. We had a small band of supporters, and Peggy O'Donnell, who had the ear of the priest, said, 'Look at the cut of him. It isn't fair.'

The priest had come to the same conclusion and mistook Pakie for an adult encroaching on a boys game.

'G'out of that, Casey, and leave it to the youngsters.'

Pakie walked off crestfallen. The priest's word was law. He mounted his bike and cycled away. The truth was that he was a genuine part of the team; he was still a pupil in Creeves, and younger than some of his team-mates.

It was a black day. They were light years ahead of us. To cap it all, they had a team song, which they rendered with great gusto as the calvacade drove off. Gerry Hennessey led it, driving his mother's rig of white pony and glistening trap, the whip in its brass socket like an antenna. He was like a young charioteer. We still heard them as they went by Mangan's Cross, now launched into 'McNamara's Band', interspersed with whoops of raucous superiority.

It took weeks before I had the will to play in Dunne's field again and the passion that dominated my mind for the game was never the same. It failed to lift me in fields of mown hay and the routine of never-ending work. The image of the young Setanta was buried forever in the massacre of Roche's field.

5

My mother piloted our world like a ship's captain. We were all her crew, including my father, who had long ago settled for first mate. She was the first to rise and the moment she set foot on the flagged kitchen floor, she was pitching into work and organising her crew. As long as I can remember, there was a serving boy in the house and at times a serving girl as well. That was how the tradition described them, though they could have been as old as forty or as young as sixteen.

The first to be called on deck were the paid members of the crew. In the year that followed Johnny Murphy's death, my father built a porch at the rear of the house, shutting off the arctic winds and the curious animals that had terrified my childhood. Half the porch was used as a scullery and beyond the dividing wall was the serving boy's bedroom.

The features of those serving boys have long faded except one, called Ruck. They all had a singular hatred for rising early, which evoked stern disapproval from the ship's captain. She would call again and again, be answered with muffled assurances from the room off the porch and be offered a litany of excuses that were as improbable as they were inventive. One was in the act of tying up his laces, another saying his prayers, the most ingenious asserting that he was out in the yard, though the voice came muffled from beneath the bedclothes.

She set the fire, building it from the embers every morning. I was the one whose duty it was to supply the kindling for the morning fire. It was like a regal imperative: at a moment's notice, even if it was dark, I could head for a place where there was kindling to be found. I still do it. When I walk by hedgerows and see decaying wood, I find myself marking it down as a source. Old habits, especially those founded on anxiety and mockery, die very hard in me.

My father, like his hired hands, was a very bad riser. But in flagrant contrast with the others, his little oddity, as my mother excused it, was not only accepted but indulged. Before the breakfast was ready, tea was taken to him in the bedroom and he was given a summary of the weather conditions. She rarely told him it was a beautiful morning because that might foster qualms about his lying in. By then she would have had two hours and more of hard physical work behind her. She milked most of the cows; the fastest milker amongst us could never compete with her. The milk tankards were loaded on the cart; the serving boy despatched to the creamery, calves fed and the squawking fowl loosed into the yard. 'Bloody hens,' my father used say, 'a man can't have a minute's peace with them.'

When he finally arrived in the kitchen, my father became transformed. He was a hive of activity then and muttered his impatience with our tardiness. As a young man, he would tell us, unlike the layabouts that ranged round his table, that he would have a row of manure spread on drills before his breakfast. That boast died when someone observed innocently that the breakfast must have been very late.

'Smart man,' he would retort. 'If you are half as smart with the books as you are with the tongue, you'll go a long way.'

Beyond the cobbled yard, he was lord and master. You could see it in the way he lengthened his steps and in the rigid set of his jaw. He brooked no interference, asked for no advice and we had learned to offer none. I never thought I was qualified anyway: one or two withering glances had banished any creative notions I had timidly ventured. As my brothers, Michael and John, the inheritors, grew into teenagers with ideas of newer and better ways, the only time my father listened with a semblance of patience was when we were all gathered for the evening meal. The show of tolerance was for my mother because she had been tentatively suggesting that he should listen to my brothers' suggestions. He listened and did not interrupt, even nodding once or twice. But the following day he went to the fields and nothing changed. His father had done it that way and his grandfather before him. The method had been tempered and shaped in the forge of time past and that was good enough for him.

He took it as an imperative entitlement that we should follow his leadership within his domain. I never remember him discussing a work programme or allocating any chore, except perhaps to shout an order at me through the bedroom window as he passed by outside. I was never a part of the land team and so, like the serving boy, I deserved to be ordered. As for my two brothers, who would one day inherit his fields, he assumed that they would automatically initiate the supporting roles for themselves.

I had a dual relationship with my father. One was shaped in the cauldron of work, the other in the warm glove of paternal affection that briefly flared outside it when we were alone together. Both my parents loved to go card-playing to neighbours' houses; it was my mother's prime social outlet. She would talk about it for days afterwards: how the men had complimented her card sharpness, the way she wore her clothes and her hair, and how, if they didn't know different, they would never have taken her for a farmer's wife. But there were times when she was too tired to go and he wanted to get out of the house. He went rambling; the ancient custom of night time visits to favoured houses. She hated that and wondered to us how he could spend hours on end listening, as she put it to us, to silly chatter, because my father was no raconteur. She wondered most of all how he could leave her and share himself with people she had little in common with.

Sometimes, perhaps to mitigate the effect of that rambling, he would bring me with him. I was about nine years old. Times like those were the closest I ever got to him. Nights when we walked together in the darkness, making for houses in distant clumps of huddled trees that reared in the black skyline like primordial beasts. Mornings, star-bright and frosted, driving cattle to Rathkeale fair. And once, when we arrived too late for our lift in Enright's trap, walking the six miles together to a hurling match in

Newcastle West. On such fleeting moments were founded the personal side of our relationship, the umbilical cord of ties that matter most and stand out the sharpest. I was in contention with eleven others for those sparse moments, so perhaps I didn't fare so badly after all.

I would never make a farmer. It was writ in large imperious letters in the scheme of things. I was seldom motivated in the same way as my brothers by cattle and land and tillage. I could not talk the language either. I would stand there mute while kin and neighbours talked crops and prices. But I was another pair of hands, and in my parents' view and my brothers', it was right and proper that I should contribute, if only out of gratitude and allegiance.

That was another reason why I was happiest going to school. I would be called to arms when I came home but that could be balanced against the lessons. They took precedent and the evening was well shortened by the time I had strung out the homework to its limit. Before I heard of Parkinson's Law, I was practising it: work expands to fill the time available for its completion.

Saturdays and holidays taxed my ingenuity to the limit and did the same with my father's patience. I would wake on Saturday morning and have this vision of eternal turnip drills, hayfields stretching to the horizon, cowhouses to be cleaned, cattle to be foddered. I knew the work would go on as long as there was light. It was a bleak prospect, and it wasn't lightened by the knowledge that every other farmer about us kept decent hours. The Dunnes, the Enrights and the Reidys would be long before us in the hurling field and be lying exhausted on the headland by the time we got there. My father tolerated no comparison when I begged leave from the drills and the haymaking. 'If the Reidys went to hell, should we go too?'

There was another reason why I would never be a farmer. The animals that terrified my childhood continued to haunt my fears. I had none of the natural affinity with horses that all the male side of the family, even my mother, had. She would drive the pony and trap to town and be in full command of the animal trotting between the shafts. The brothers were handling horses as soon as they were old enough to walk. It was normal for a farmer's son to have such skill and if he did not, there was something wanting in him.

I must have communicated my anxiety to the horses for they behaved radically different for me. Every horse we owned, with one exception, was raised and trained by my father. He had an uncanny way with them. He could walk out to the field and they trotted up to him, offering ears to be pinched and muzzles to be stroked. The greater part of his working life he had spent in the company of horses and there was a bond between them that seemed to be laid down in some kind of joint intelligence. I never saw him strike a horse, never put but the gentlest strain on the reins.

Once in later life, when the bones had brittled and stiffened, I watched him opening potato drills in the haggard. Everything had changed then. The horse was obsolete; newer and better ways had arrived, tractors and attachments had turned days of backbreaking labour into units of productivity measured by the hour. It seemed to me watching them that man and beast, perfectly in tune with each other, were playing the last scene of the old way. My father held the reins against the handles of the plough, but there was no need for any instruction. They worked together in slow motion. The horse's hooves lifted and came down again in movements so minutely rhythmic that he was almost standing still. Every now and then his ears would prick, the head would swivel and an eye rolled backwards. It was as if he were listening and appreciating the constant flow of affection that emanated from the hands and the words of his master.

'Good horse. Good boy. Up again now, Paddy. There's a good horse.'

Paddy was the last of the line; he was twelve years old then. He had been bred from a draught Irish mare, in a year when practicality took precedent over my father's preference for breeding hunters. Paddy Lynch in Rathkeale kept a thoroughbred stallion in his yard, an animal called Polyfane, who had won the supreme award in his class at the Royal Dublin Horse Show. We had notions that Polyfane's line would make our fortune, but they seldom went right. They sickened or didn't form well and when we calculated the time and expense of looking after them, we turned a very poor profit.

I made those trips with my father to Rathkeale when the mare was ready to be covered. I was always apprehensive because once we got to the yard, all hell would break loose in the boxes. There was a teaser stallion in one box, harnessed in such a way that he could not perform. While he teased and worked himself into a futile frenzy, Polyfane reared and kicked in his stall. He was a beautiful animal, almost blood red, whose coat gleamed like polished veneer.

The horses came up to my father in the

field and nuzzled him. They led me a baffling dance. My only way of catching Paddy was to offer him oats in a basin. He watched me with a malevolent eye while he nudged at the oats, but the minute I went to slip the winkers on or grab him by the mane, he bared his teeth and swung viciously at me. My father would not believe it, so I invited him to see for himself. But Paddy that day was as docile as a pet lamb and even lowered his head when I went to slip the winkers on.

Bill O'Donnell had more perverse experiences than mine. He lived in a cottage built on a roadside corner of one of our fields, and he worked as a platelayer on the Limerick to Tralee railway. Bill would arrive in the yard some Sundays to borrow Paddy and the cart to fetch firewood. Both of us went to catch him, me with the basin of oats, Bill with the winkers. The horse would grab a mouthful of oats and then gallop away like a charger, nostrils flaring, flatulent explosions rending the air. When we followed him to the next field, Paddy had disappeared. We went to field after field in futile search. I finally abandoned the job and crossed through a hazel thicket, shortcutting my way to Dunne's field. I was almost through when I saw the horse. Only his head was visible in the covering of briars and hazel and so intent was he in watching the hapless Bill going from field to field, that he had not heard me approach. Bill would talk about it for years and my father would smile at the telling and perhaps bestow himself silently with some of the credit for the horse's uncanny behaviour.

But he would not smile when someone mistreated one of his beloved animals. Hugh Lacey was another neighbour who sometimes worked for my father. I had been dogging his footsteps for a year or two, watching him lay his rabbit snares, admiring the way he baited a patch of stubble ground with grain to lure pheasants there. My admiration for the man was founded only on his expertise as a hunter. Lacey was a vortex of conflicting characteristics. Around my father he was full of servile acknowledgements: gratitude for the work and the milk, the vegetables and the flitch of bacon; affection for the offspring of those who bestowed the gifts. He shook off the pretence in my presence and spoke in the begrudging whine of the oppressed and the exploited. He hated all farmers, all employers. They sucked out the marrow from the bones of the poor and grew fat and sleek. And if I ever opened my mouth to expose him, he would loose his ferret upon me when I was asleep.

Lacey and I were sent to Rathkeale to bring

home a salting barrel. Once out of sight of the house, he stood up in the body of the cart and lashed the horse to a gallop. He was transformed, as if the opportunity to command the horse had freed all his pent up rages. We went down Wall's hill at breakneck speed, leaving a dust cloud in our wake. Lacey stood with legs splayed, his face contorted, a slipstream of curses fading behind us, the whip hand flailing. I knew, coming to the bend at Benson's Cross, that we would never make it. The horse went down in a blur of misshapen confusion, the cart slewed, the rending shafts cracked like cannon shot. I ran all the way back for my father and told him, for the albino eyes of the ferret terrorised me, that the horse had shied. But my father had only to gauge the violence of the crash and see the lacerations on the horse's chest to know.

'You will never, Lacey, not the longest day you live, drive a horse of mine again.'

Time and again, in the aftermath of that incident, we were visited by the gardai, auditing unlicensed bulls. Gates were left mysteriously open and the cowherd had wandered on to the road. A son of Polyfane went missing for days. When I later admitted the collusion of my cowardice, my father gave me one of his withering looks and told me that he had known all along. Did I take him for a fool? More serious than the hurt to the horse was the hurt of betrayal, of a son in cahoots against his father.

★ ★ ★

I hated it when he directed me to drive the team. Most of the fieldwork then was done by a pair of horses. They taught me an early lesson in group behaviour: how members of a team respond differently than as individuals. Both behaved in a way that was out of character. The mare, when working alone, would refuse to pull when the strain went beyond her limit. In the team, she pulled more than her share and quickly lathered up. My father would look at the slack swingletree and conclude that I was favouring the other horse. The mare's son had exactly the opposite traits. He would pull until he dropped, but in the team he was indolent and awkward. I thought he did that deliberately, exploiting that same equine intelligence that had so frustrated Bill O'Donnell. He brought that deviousness to an art form when we acquired the red mare.

The red mare was given to my father in lieu of an outstanding debt. Our neighbour John Shaughnessy raised race-horses and I thought that the red mare was as well formed as any of them; coloured like old mahogany, with sleek limbs and symmetrical lines and a head held high in haughty grandeur. She had plumbed the depths when she came into our yard because we had need only for common workhorses. If my father had been in his right mind, she would never have stayed. His reasons were partially correct and therefore difficult to counter. The man who owed the debt was emigrating with his family and, much as he disliked the settlement, it was as good as he could get. But the real objective stood in Paddy Lynch's yard in Rathkeale. Polyfane and the red mare would beget the supreme hunter.

It was not to be, however, because she never produced a foal. Then my father reluctantly decided to break her. He sent for a man named Davoren whose boast was that he could ride anything with hair on it. Davoren was a former jockey with a colourful past; they said he might have been a good jockey if he didn't have that crooked streak. He was a small dark-visaged man with crooked legs, darting eyes and hands that never stayed still. I saw him as the bowlegged wrangler in the Wild West novel intent on breaking the spirit of the untamed stallion.

I prayed for the red mare. I wished that she

would break the dark-faced jockey and wipe the leer from his thin-lipped mouth. I watched him from the kitchen window, saw him clinging like a gnome when she reared and plunged, hitting the ground in shock waves of splayed feet. But Davoren clung on and pulled violently on the reins, laughing when he struck her with the whip. He left after three mornings. There was too much blood in her, he told us; she would never make a workhorse.

But my father persisted. He borrowed training tackling from John Shaughnessy and took on the role of the wrangler. It saddened me as I saw the mare trying to cope with the restraining gear. It held her head high and made her walk with shortened steps. The bridle bit hurt her mouth and she would go down on her forelegs and try to push it off.

No matter what time it was when he returned from the fields or whatever the weather, my father would see to the horses first. He stowed the tackling on wooden pegs in the outhouse and then rubbed down the horses with handfuls of twisted hay. He watered them before turning them out in the fields near the house. In long dry spells the well dried up and we youngsters rode them to water in the stream that bounded our land. The first instinct of workhorses when turned loose is to roll on the ground. But they would never do that with a rider aboard. Except Paddy. When I was riding him, he rolled in every patch of red-baked earth from the gate to the stream. When I led him, he followed like a lamb. It seemed that every twisted trick in his mind was reserved for me and I still wonder why I keep a set of his irons in my woodshed. Perhaps my father was being devious too when he gave them to me years after the horse had died.

'Take those and look after them. That horse liked you.'

With the red mare it was different. She was honest in spirit since she was high born and grand. I hated to see that spirit being broken and her heritage being humbled. I ached for her when she wrestled with the training harness and rejoiced when I was told to take it off. Sometimes, before I turned her loose, my father told me to put her to the ring. I made her trot the perimeter of a circle formed by twenty feet of rope. It was always after supper and I knew my father was watching from the window. Every now and then I encouraged her to canter for I loved the way her limbs flowed like liquid muscle, the ripples that shimmered under her coat, her languid energy. He would rap on the window to bid me slow her to a trot.

She became a reluctant workhorse. She plunged and reared when we yoked her to the cart and smashed the shafts against the gable wall. We put her under the plough with Paddy and he exploited her honest spirit, letting her take the greatest share of the strain. She would plunge again, the plough handles would fly in the air and my father would berate me for a fool who could not do a simple thing like driving a pair of horses.

We broke her. We took the hauteur and the grand lineage and humbled her with swingle-tree and common tackling.

★ ★ ★

The government put a compulsory tillage programme in place when I was eleven. A man came into our yard in a shiny black car. He had a notebook and fountain pen in his hand and his manner was the pompous self-importance of the minor official. He told us which fields to plough and wrote it down in the black book. He recorded the dates when he would return to check, and warned about penalties for non-compliance. I would see his face thereafter, pinched and unsmiling, whenever government or the law intruded on our lives.

My mother and I took a train to Limerick

from the railway station at Ballingrane. It was to be a momentous trip because I had never been to the city before and had never been in a railway carriage. There was a notice above the stationmaster's window, in large capital letters. WE ARE NOT OUT OF THE WOODS YET. GROW MORE. It made no sense to me, especially when I misread the capital G for a C. It was about compulsory tillage, my mother explained; the government was ordering us to grow more, not crow more.

Every time there was a mention of compulsory tillage, we became shrouded in a pall of gloom. My father hated the idea. It was backbreaking drudgery with scant reward, because the government controlled the prices. God how I hated it. That notice and the thin-featured man with his arrogant manner sat in the railway carriage with me, shadowed me through the streets of Limerick and spoiled my day.

My father kept me at home from school to help him. I could never understand that decision. I was merely a supporting hand in the scheme of things, yet I was the one kept home to drive the team. We started when the wind blew, a bitter east wind that caught us square in open fields. We made bodices of waxed brown paper and wore them next to our skin. My hands dried and the constant chafing of the reins wealed my palms. When the hands bled, I wrapped them in flour bag cloth — no self-respecting farmer's son would wear gloves.

Paddy exploited the willing spirit of the red mare and slackened his share of the swingletree. The mare plunged with the exertion of the strain and the plough handles reared time and again. It was my fault. The mare walked in the furrow and Paddy walked in the virgin margin. He wandered a meandering line and dragged her out, and again the handles bucked. My father would nurse his wrists after every jolt and focus his pained eyes on me. He gave me that headshake, pursed lips and blackened brow that criticised more than words ever could. At the lunch break we would hear the schoolchildren at play; their laughter made my misery soar.

My father would look back from the headland and review the finished line of turned sod. In some things he was a perfectionist, especially those things against which his standards could be measured. He rated himself highly as a ploughman and central to that skill was what he called straightness of the eye. There was never a furrow opened in a new field unless he could get the line right. He would hang a rag on a stick at one end, place another in the middle, and a third in line with both at the far headland.

We ploughed against that first straight furrow and ribbon after ribbon of turned sod ran true thereafter to that opening line. I could not handle the team to his perfection and he would mutter and fix those beetled brows of complaint on me when he looked back. Once I ventured that it didn't matter if the furrow was crooked; it would all look the same when the field was tilled. I got the sibilant sound of annoyance and the sharp intake of breath. What was I talking about? A neighbour, even a stranger, could come into that field, he said, and what would he think of the crooked furrow?

My father had a motto that he was fond of quoting. 'There's a right way and a wrong way of doing something. The wrong way is always wrong and the right way is always right.' I am a disciple of that dictum now and have been from the time I understood its import. It has to do with the dignity of work and the expression of self in however trivial the task may be. I see it in the action of a mason who stands back from the stone he has just placed and removes it because it does not please his eye.

Our father used drive us to distraction with that philosophy. Perfection took time and yet we were the forerunners of a modern era that would worship at the altar of speed. That dichotomy was never more evident than in the hayfield. Making hay was a fever. When the hay was ripe and the weather was fair, it raged all round us in an infectious flurry of work. The hurry, which was a symptom of the infection, paid scant token to my father's quest for perfection. According to him, the butt of the haycock should be laid with care. The hay that formed the perimeter should be chosen from the top of the swarth where it was driest and laid down without twist or tangle; that would keep the butt from unravelling when the hay was winced on the hayfloat. My brothers built the butt on the pile that the tumbling jack had drawn and would smile and shake their heads when he railed about it.

He fussed about the completed haycock while they were building another. He raked it down as if he were a sculptor and he was repairing the damage committed in its making. Then he fixed the ties against the slope and the prevailing wind and walked away so that he could view it from another angle. Often he would take me with him and we would work alone, building haycocks that were models of construction. I would be shown, again and again, how to use the pitchfork so that the prongs were set in the right direction.

We worked in great periods of silence, my father and I. The silence was deepest when we went ploughing. Sometimes I thought we were all alone in the world and nothing existed beyond the hedgerows that bounded the field. I wished my life away, longing for the events that would break the silence and ease the drudgery. I watched Paddy's ears; he first heard my mother's call for the midday meal. So acute was his hearing that she would need only to come out to the cobbled yard and call in a voice a little above normal. His ears lifted and straightened and then he stopped dead.

But even that harbinger of a little comfort was fraught. The red mare plunged when the strain came on the swingletree. I grew adept at reading clouds and the sun. I would watch the shadows in the fields and decipher them like a sundial. I prayed for rain — for a deluge because my father would throw a jute bag over his shoulders and work on through showers and cloying mists. Back towards the west, in the hill country behind Kilcolman, grew the first slanting pillars of rain between cloud and land. I wished that they would settle overhead us and send drenching falls cascading down those pillars.

It reminds me now of a story in *Twenty Years A-Growing*. When the fierce storm thundered in from the sound, it terrified the youngsters in O Suilleabháin's house. Pray to God, their father advised them, and put your fingers in your ears. It didn't help, because God had his fingers in his ears too. I prayed to God so many times that he would make the weather unworkable. He kept on ignoring me and when I had doubts about invoking His help in such a traitorous way, I laid bare my concern in the confessional. It was spurious, the priest said, the implication that God had his fingers in his ears; spurious and akin to blasphemy. I should seek out and be grateful for every opportunity of suffering. It would make a man of me. I was building up a store of credits, mortifying the flesh and shriving the soul. I should take my punishment like a soldier and pray no more for such convoluted petitions.

I walked home, along the mass path through McAuliffe's' field and decided that I would pray no more but neither would I suffer, because I could not reconcile the virtue with the pain. I would escape. From now on, escaping would be my grand design. I would employ every strategy already known and invent some new ones.

If my father knew that I prayed for rain, he would have seen it as treachery. One summer, hay was felled in the field with the two beech trees. We had gathered it into rows by the afternoon and were taking tea on the headland. You could see the air shimmering in the lea of the hedge; the sky was cloudless and the cattle were running from the warble fly. We would stay in that meadow until the dew fell.

Someone brought God into the conversation and another remarked on His awesome power.

'If He wanted,' I suggested, 'He could make it rain now.'

The silence hung like the shimmering air. One of my brothers observed that it was blasphemy to say such a thing.

'But He could,' I foolishly persisted.

'I wouldn't put it past you to ask Him,' my father said. He threw away the dregs of the tea and rose suddenly, as if impelled by some possible league between the Almighty and me.

'He could make it rain, though.'

'He could,' my father agreed, fixing me with that severe brow. 'But if He does, He hasn't much else to do.'

On the Monday after my visit to the

confessional, the ploughshare struck a rock. The handles flew and the red mare plunged. We dug around the rock and unearthed a boulder that the crowbar could not budge or the sledgehammer dent. We left it there as a monument to our puny efforts; it became a monument to a grave concern. Two feet down we had discovered a clutch of seashells. They could have been buried there only by human hand, my father suspected, by an evil hand, which wanted to take the fertility from our land. There was pishoguery at work, an evil spell, and he was silent all day.

My uncle, Paddy Enright, came to inspect the boulder and the shells. He declared that the boulder was granite. It was mystifying, he said, why it should be in limestone country. The shells were another matter. We were miles from the sea, but he didn't believe that they were a portent of some evil at work. He too had ploughed up shells and nothing bad had followed. For many weeks afterwards my father added a special intention to the trimmings of the rosary. The trimmings were requests and pleas for favours that were added to the basic prayer, and quite often took longer to say than the rosary itself. When she was tired at night and my father had announced his intent to say the rosary, my mother would exhort him, 'The bare five decades, now Michael, keep the trimmings for another day.'

Had I known then the simple answers to those twin puzzles, the rock and the shells, it would have been best to hold my counsel. Because who would have believed me? We were well aware of our landscape and lived in perfect harmony with earth and mother nature, as do all simple people who depend on and live off their bounty. We never questioned because there was no need to question. God, in His infinite wisdom, had created all things. It was God who sent us the weather. It was God who ordained all, who caused the ripened seed to be wafted in the wind and deposited in a sheltered place to root. God made the mountains and filled the seas. Not a single factor of our lives, not even the blinking of an eye, happened without His command and wish. Such was the granite boulder in limestone land. It was the hand of God that had put it there.

The granite boulder was an erratic. It had been gouged out from its natural terrain during the Ice Age and swept along in the glacial flow. Once, millions of years before, a warm shallow sea covered all the land, the land of Kilquane and the land of our neighbours and all that later became the island of Ireland. The sea creatures died and calcified on the ocean floor. Limestone strata formed. Then the seas dried up, the ocean floor became the land that we now stood on and that my father and I ploughed. And so we had clutches of seashells for the ploughshare to bare. It would have been heresy to proffer that simple explanation. It was allocating to natural causes a power of creation of which only God was capable.

I will be thankful forever to the granite boulder and the clutch of shells. It would be many years later before I could place them in the evolution of natural science. That I would have to discover for myself because it was never taught in the school and the college I attended. It was anathema to our thinking of God the creator. When I began to fathom the landscape around me and could relate it to the material I read in books, it was like the whispering of a great and awesome truth. I had answers. I had reasons. And the fields, the little valleys and the low hills that filled the horizon behind Kilcolman were the first glimpses of a wonderful discovery. I was and am forever a child of that landscape.

6

Jimmy Barrett, our neighbour, came into the yard and told us that the war was over. I had no idea of the import of that news, no more than my brothers who worked alongside me or the hired hand who was at the rear of the barn, packing the hay against the galvanised iron roof. He had one of the worst jobs a body could be allocated. It was airless back there; the dust hung like a pall and swirled in the shaft of light that issued from the front opening. I was in the front opening. It was like standing on a ledge, on all sides the packed hay towered over me. I took the hay that was pitched to me by the person on the ground and cast it backwards to the hired hand.

I thought no more about Jimmy Barrett's news. The sweat ran into my eyes and the hayseed clung to the sweat at the back of my neck and worked its way down my spine. I was hot, itchy and miserable. There was no respite. The hayfloat arrived from the field with a new load of hay before we were halfway through the previous one.

★ ★ ★

I was nine and a half years old when the allied troops rolled into Berlin, in 1945. All over Europe there was wild celebration. They danced in the Paris streets and were drunk on the sidewalks of Amsterdam. The English Channel was a cacophony of hooting sirens and the traffic ceased to flow on New York's Lexington Avenue. In Kilquane, our own place, it was business as usual. The celebration, like the great war itself, passed us by.

We never took a daily newspaper then, only the priest, the creamery manager and the schoolteacher did so. Miss Abigail poked fun at us for that and ridiculed a primitive community that wouldn't spend a few pence on a daily paper. But then she would say that it would be a wasted exercise anyway for no one could read it properly. She used tell us about a neighbour who often visited her house. He would pick up the paper from the kitchen table and go through the pages as if he were reading it. Some words and phrases were familiar but foreign place-names and war terminology were beyond him. He would study the pictures that accompanied the script and make the comment; 'By God, but they're at it there'.

We took the local paper every weekend. All the knowledge of our world was supplied by the *Limerick Leader*: deaths, marriages and engagements, accounts of law cases, details of sales and auctions, the price of cattle. Far away there was a war. It raged all over Europe and out in the Pacific Rim. Now and then word filtered through from wireless sets in Rathkeale: we heard about Dunkirk and Arnhem, about Burma and Monte Cassino, but the information came garbled as it passed through the five mile communication chain to our home. We were affected only by the impact the war had on the economy of West Limerick. Petrol was rationed, but that bothered us no more than would a plutonium shortage. Only the priest owned a car.

Cigarettes were also rationed and it drove my father to distraction. His favourite brands, Gold Flake and Craven A, were in very short supply. In their stead came foreign pretenders, Passing Cloud and Camel; they were, he said, like smoking turf dust. For years we had bought his cigarettes from Ma Daly's huckster's shop, always in packets of ten. It was his way of economising; the twenty packet gave him false notions of plenty. His ration, in the war years, was five Wild Woodbines a day. They came in a small paper packet, were known as coffin nails and were a poor substitute compared to his beloved Gold Flake. But when all fruit fails, welcome haws, he would say.

My father would go through the Woodbines before the rosary was said, about ten o'clock at night. Then, if there wasn't a standby supply, we suffered. This placid man would undergo a total change of character. He became tense and short-tempered. I felt that during those periods he was alert to every opportunity that gave him an excuse to vent his spleen. Everything was wrong: the draught coming under the front door, the lack of heat from the fire, the rate at which my mother burned peat. And of course us children. He would shout and bark, aim a cuff at the nearest offending body and fume with clenched teeth at the snigger that followed when he missed. A few moments later he would marvel in cynicism at the owner of the snigger, who didn't know what the nine counties of Ulster were.

He expected preferential treatment from Ma Daly. Her cottage was built on our land, and when she died it would be allocated to Bill O'Donnell. Every evening I took her a can of milk and, less frequently, a cabbage and a small bag of potatoes. It was my mother's act of charity and I had been appointed the sole bearer of gifts. No one else

111

wanted the task. But those gifts rated very low with Ma Daly. Over the years the charity had become a duty and she would pass acid comments on the soapy nature of the potatoes and the slug-ridden heart of the cabbage. 'Ye're picking them specially for me. Any kind of rubbish will do oul' Ma.' There was a masculine sculpture to her facial features and her voice had a deep base sound. Ma Daly had never been a beauty.

My father believed that she used the cigarette shortage as a ploy to cultivate new custom. She had boxes of cigarettes under the counter and tempted the stranger with them, knowing that the custom of the regulars was secure. They wrangled at a distance, through me as the intermediary. 'Tell her this, tell her that', my father went on; 'tell her I know her tricks. Jack Mac got twenty Craven A twice last week.'

Ma snorted at the accusation. 'That same Jack Mac's a hoor's melt. Tell your father there's no man coming in to this shop can ever say I wronged him. Tell your father that for me and tell him this as well: I wouldn't give his spuds to the hens.'

My father would sometimes visit her; he would go on a winter's evening and sit by her fire. They were like brother and sister. She gave him the best chair, wiped the seat with her apron and then brought out a cushion from the inner room. She sat opposite, keeping her head to one side as he talked, as if to hear better every word and inflection. When I was there, she would swing around to me during a conversational lull and tell me what a fine person my father was. A grand man, she would say, a grand plain man. Next day he was trying to kill her with bad potatoes and sour-tasting milk: 'You wouldn't give it to wan of them Hottentots.'

One would never know that Ma Daly kept a shop. There were no jars or packets on the window, no name over the door. I never saw any delivery being made, apart from the People's Bakery van. The bakery was owned by a family in Rathkeale, who also ran a grocery shop. Perhaps they supplied everything. You would know immediately you passed Maggie Barrett's house near the school that there was a shop within. There was a white enamelled sign fixed to the gable end, writ large in the native tongue, proclaiming that she was licensed to sell stamps.

The shops were in stark contrast: Ma's had the ambience of a speakeasy; Barrett's was garishly evident. In Maggie's shop, there were framed advertisements on the wall above the dresser. A pair of ragamuffin kids, ecstatic pleasure on their faces, whiffed at the glorious aroma of Bisto gravy. A lady in a 1920s dress, her bonnet laid on an ornate table, drank from a cup of Ovaltine. And a sailor, framed in a lifebuoy, smoked John Player cigarettes. The window ledge was filled with packages of the trade, hiding the rock formation beyond it. At one end of the counter was a collection of glass jars, left within easy reach, because they contained the penny sweets.

The driving force behind Barrett's shop was the old man Ned, that same Ned who grazed his donkey on the grounds that should have been the school playground. Ned would live in your ear and was wise to every chance to turn a shilling. In the winter he cut and split hazel rods which were used as fixings to keep the thatch in place. He trimmed ashplants and sold them to drovers. In the Emergency, when paraffin was rationed and at times unavailable, old Ned made candles. He used a mixture of wax and tallow and his product hissed, spluttered and burned down to the sconce in record time.

Once he put a notice on the front gate — CABBAGE PLANTS FOR SALE — but he had misspelled the last word as 'sail.' The Gander Walsh, who had a weather eye out for Maggie, blotted his copybook when he ordered 100 plants and asked the old man to send them down by river.

I never saw Maggie smile. When I entered the shop at night, she got up from the chair beside the fire and withered my intrusion with a look of annoyance. Did I know there was a war on? Did I think I could land into her shop at any hour of the day or night? And why didn't I go to Ma Daly's shop where my father had his ration entitlement? She was as fearsome as the denizens of the night.

Maggie had no gift for small talk and tapped her fingers against the wood of the counter when I struggled to remember the list of messages. But I misjudged her because later I would find that her severe exterior masked a well of human kindness.

My eldest brother was riding a son of Polyfane near the village of Ardagh when he was struck by a lorry. The horse was put down and my father, after an agonising debate with my mother, decided to sue. We were frightened of the law; it was beyond our experience, the word itself held an ambience of dread. We lost the case; the judge ordered costs against us. We sat in serried silence around the table when we heard the judgement, each to his own foreboding.

Outside, the wind lifted the battalions of rain and flung them against the back door.

Into our distraught kitchen came a weather-swept Maggie Barrett. She sat between my father and mother and spoke out loud her revulsion of a powerful law that had played us for simple pawns. What she did most of all was articulate the pain my parents were feeling and share their misery, for misery loves company. It was never forgotten. My mother stored it and it became a landmark reference for the inaccuracy of superficial opinion.

The rationing of tea hurt us most of all. We drank it at set periods every day and any opportunity between, first thing in the morning and last before bed. We used it to celebrate joy and sorrow and to break the monotony of our ritual routines. In the late 1940s the government removed the luxurious indulgence of the habit with a tea ration. It was based on head-count. We were high on head-count — the ten children and our parents were all qualifiers by then — but it was not enough.

We had then a hired hand; a 30-year-old 'serving boy' called Johnsey, who came from a family larger than ours. He should have brought his ration of tea because it was an explicit condition of his hiring. My mother spelt it out to him in simple but imperious terms, but she hadn't reckoned with Johnsey.

However strong the command, however dire the consequences, Johnsey thwarted her at every turn. When she rounded on him, he would adopt a hangdog expression. His eyes would glisten, the set of his body would crumble, and his face, like an erring sheepdog, had an abject, piteous resignation. She could not handle it and the minute he saw the resolve weaken, he launched into a flurry of verbal tail-wagging.

'Honest to God, Missus, as true as God is in His heaven, Missus, you'll have my ration of tay tomorra.'

Like tomorrow, the tea never came.

'Christ God, Missus, I shouldn't take the holy name in vain. But I clane forgot.'

Miraculously, when she had given up all hope, the tea arrived. He presented her with a *toisin*, a container shaped from a twisted piece of newspaper, round at one end like a funnel, tapered at the other. It was filled with tea — far more than she had expected. When she told him it was too much, he reminded her of all the times he had drunk tea at her expense and wasn't it well coming to her. It continued morning after morning. He came into the kitchen as she woke the slumbering fire and made his presentation. He leaped to a pinnacle in her admiration. Weeks later, my father thought he heard a noise in the kitchen and came out quietly to investigate. There at the mantel-board was Johnsey, filling his *toisin* from my mother's tea caddy. My father solved two mysteries simultaneously: the generosity of Johnsey and his family, and the errant pages of his *Limerick Leader*.

Because of our large family, it was assumed that we were better off than most. As a result, there was more tea drunk in those days of shortage than ever before or after. Whoever came to the house — relative and friend, stranger and wandering tramp — was offered and expected the ritual cup. I remember an insurance collector who called almost every week, though the premium was due monthly. He was partial to my mother's scones and would embark on a paean of praise the moment he sampled the first morsel.

He had a falsetto voice and a range of mannerisms and topics that leaned distinctly on the feminine side. We sniggered at his curious ways and especially the way he held the cup with the little finger extended outward and then dabbing his lips with a frilly handkerchief. My father imagined him spreading manure or helping a heifer to birth. My mother criticised the laughing and the aspersions. We were creatures of our convention, she told us: the only way we had of coping with difference was to ridicule it. It was a profound observation for her time and place. It is still.

Nonie Sheridan was our most exotic caller. There was no one else quite like her. She was a relic of a tinker race that had settled in Rathkeale. Nonie hawked trinkets and Fair Isle cardigans, cards of wool and spools of thread. Long before she arrived, her coming was heralded. There were little brass bells attached to the pony's harness and they tinkled her movements once she came within range, past Mangan's Cross. The space between the bells until they resumed again measured the success of her call. I knew from the time space and the bells where she had called and where she had made a sale. I wasn't the only one who listened. My mother went into the kitchen and moved the kettle to the boiling ring. My father appeared from nowhere and found a reason to search for something in the outhouse.

I watched the trap make the turn of the lane at a place we called 'the wide part'. Once there had been a house there and we thought that ghostly reminders of the past were still present in the crumbling stones. I would skirt that place in the darkness for my father had once seen a white lady flit through the stones of the gable.

Pony and cart were resplendent. The

harness shone in the morning sun, and there were flashes of yellow painted along the length of the shafts, on the wheel spokes and round the perimeter of the axle hub. The gig swayed with every undulation of the rutted track and the bells tinkled. The cart seats were back to back, the driver held aloft the silver-topped whip like a ringmaster at the circus.

We never knew what the driver was: the husband or an employee. He was dark and swarthy, and he always wore a neckerchief under a collarless shirt. A profusion of chest hair spilled over the neckerchief. He looked more pirate than gypsy. It seemed that his only function was to drive and wait.

He guided the pony towards the hay barn and helped Nonie to dismount. Then he pulled out handfuls of hay, stuffed them into a sack bag and fixed it beneath the pony's head. He never asked permission to take the hay. The ritual of Nonie's visits were long-established. Later he would take the sack from the pony's head, fill it again and move it to a spot in the barn so that his back would be comfortably propped. He selected a wisp, tested it against his tongue and began to chew like a ruminating cow. He settled down to wait.

Nonie wished a blessing on the house and

all within. She looked old and worn and the history of her age was clear in her leathery face, like rings on a tree trunk. Her face resembled a relief map. Each jaw had a deep weal like a scar and out from each one ran a network of wrinkles as if they were rivulets, feeding the main artery of the weal. Her high protruding forehead stood out like a mountain range and her mouth was the great lake that irrigated the delta of her chin. When she spoke, and especially when she smiled, her face erupted as if some seismic activity had taken place beneath the surface of her facial landscape. She smelled of must, old age and camphor.

Nonie brought her own tin mug. It was copiously large and cocked a bountiful snoot at the scarcity of the time. The folds of her shawl covered her basket of trinkets and before she sat on the horsehair couch, she moved the folds aside. It was all so dramatic offering us a sneak preview of the contents. Then she produced the mug and laid it at her feet. We vied to be the one who would collect it and take it to the range where my mother's hand was hovering over the teapot.

'Three spoons of sugar and the 'laest' drop of colouring.'

Nonie's request became a catchphrase in our house. My father used it most. When he and I visited the Connors sisters it became a ritual. They knew his habits exactly but he would always be asked how he liked his tea. It was merely the cue for the response. 'Three spoons of sugar and the laest drop of colouring.'

The pair of sisters laughed uproariously. That catchphrase lasted until the eldest one went to a home for the aged and then it died, as if it could flourish in our collective presence only. I heard it only once since, seventeen years ago. I was walking out of the graveyard in Kilbrathern where we had laid my father to rest. I am almost unknown in that place now and behind me a couple of old men were talking about him, unaware that I was his son. One remarked that he had done a deal with my father at Rathkeale fair and they had gone into Ward's public house to seal it.

'I called for a ball of malt,' the man said, 'an' then I asked him how he liked it. You know what he answered?'

'I do,' the other man nodded. 'Three spoons of sugar and the laest drop of colouring.'

Nonie was worth all the tea in China. She was our ship to port, bearing the gossip of her circuits' trade winds. My father used say that a magpie couldn't lift across a hedge but she knew about it. It was all part of her technique: she was a natural saleswoman. She played my mother like a maestro at a keyboard; she traded her against neighbour and child. I once saw her sell my mother a blouse and a Fair Isle jumper, well past her price range, because Mrs Nolan had bought two of each and she was living in a cottage. She cleaned out a month's egg money with that gambit. She handed trinkets and ribbons for my sisters to feel and admire and was so taken by the delight and expectancy on their faces that she offered them as presents, 'if it be a thing that ye can't afford them'. And all the time she kept up her commentary of gossip. She drank from her tin mug and shoved it forward for replenishment.

'Put a hot drop in that for me, *a stór*.'

'The woman at the cross was showing again and the last one still not weaned. A Roche wan from the New Road had run off with an old fella and he twice her age. Here, girleen, feel the stuff in that drawers — like pure velvet.'

When my father arrived, there was a noticeable change in the tenor of her conversation. He was a new audience. There was banter now and ribald innuendo. My sisters sniggered with embarrassment and my mother averted her eyes.

'There's this ould fella in Rathkeale, Michael. Ran off with a young wan. She won't feel the ould age creeping up on her now, hah.'

My father attempted to engage her in repartee, but came off second best. Nonie had been married twice and he would suggest that the husbands had died from exhaustion. Then he would wonder: what was the real purpose of the swarthy fellow, who was now reclining in his hay barn. She would snigger and cackle, then make a casual observation about the size of our family and conclude that my father didn't spend all his time sleeping. My mother would look daggers at him when he tried to engage her in verbal swordsmanship. Later she would ask what had brought him into the kitchen and did he have nothing better to do than swap smart talk with an ould wan who could run rings around him.

Nonie usually arrived about mid-morning. It was a time when my mother had baked. The cake of fresh brown bread was cooling on the windowsill and wafting a delicious odour out through the door and around the perimeter of the yard. It was like the scent of blood to a school of sharks. In deference to the visitor, Nonie received the first cut and the choicest, more crust than bread. It was still warm; the butter melted and gave the bread a hue of fine filigree gold. The old woman made a receptacle of her lap, spread her legs and draped the long black dress across them. In that way she harvested every crumb. She collected them all in her fist, rolled them into a ball and sighed with satisfaction when she had swallowed it.

As the food supply improved, we saw the old woman less. By then the swarthy pirate had disappeared and she drove herself. Once my father tried to ask her about his disappearance, but she pressed a nicotine-stained finger to her lips and made a clicking sound with her tongue.

'Now, now Michael, curiosity killed the cat.'

In the latter days, that spark of intelligent sharpness had deteriorated to a razor-edged cynicism. My father would stay in the fields and my mother would be treated to an outpouring of invective towards those of our neighbours who had lowered Nonie to the status of beggar. We were struck off her list when my youngest brother Connie and I unyoked the pony from the trap, ran the shafts through the barred gate and tackled the pony anew at the far side. We had this vision of a perplexed Nonie trying to figure out how the pony had managed to drag the cart through the bars. She saw the prank immediately and wasn't amused. She let loose a torrent of insulting abuse, most of it focused on the man who had begotten those whelps of childer. It was no wonder, she concluded, that a harmless ould woman would be treated in a fashion akin to physical abuse. No wonder, when you took into account the dirty mind of the father.

I knew that day, as I watched her ride away, that she had gone out of our lives. Sometimes in the quiet of mid-mornings, I would hear the bells coming past Mangan's Cross and slow to make the entry to Connors'. An hour later I would hear them again as they faded into the distance. We had once been the last port of call on the perimeter of her voyage. We were now struck off her route and the intimacy of our lives was being fed out in confidential morsels, to new audiences on the ring of her travels.

A distant relative of old Nonie's, a man called Jumbo, took to the tour around the same time as she was waning. He had a gangling, misshapen body, and resembled a walking scarecrow with his flapping clothes and his angles and limbs askew. Jumbo had the lingo of the town and tried to parade it as smartness. In contrast to Nonie, he drove my mother wild since she could see no virtue in his clever talk. It was said that he took to tramping the country so that he could sell his own rations.

The middle and index fingers of both his hands were stained to a burnished bronze from constant smoking and, because he smoked his cigarettes to the very butt, there was a blackened spiral on the fleshy part of both thumbs like the burr on a piece of walnut veneer. He had a catalogue of clever phrases and worked them into the conversation in context or out.

'They're selling mahogany gas pipes inside in McDonnell's hardware.'

'The cops raided the Central Bar and a man escaped by climbing up a down pipe.'

'Right, said she, and he never wrote.'

We heard them over and over again and with every one the shrill cackle that followed, as if he had just invented the phrase and was marvelling at the ingenuity of it.

Rumour had it that Jumbo had a tail. It was a freak of nature, a mutant aberration from evolution's past. Because his shape was so angular and because the clothes draped from his frame, we could never establish the truth or scotch the rumour. We would examine him from all angles, make him bend over so that the appendage would be thrown into relief, but all to no avail. Because we couldn't verify the existence of the tail, we concluded that it must be present.

Jumbo fancied himself as a draughts player. He was the reputed master of the town of Rathkeale and all places within the rim of his circus. He liked to play for money, but there were few takers for that was a very scarce commodity. So he would play for tea or any other rationed item that he could trade for cash. We had recently acquired a draughts board — a battered version that an uncle had presented to my mother with a great show of magnanimity, as if it were the original of its kind and worth its weight in gold. My brother John took to its challenge like a duck to water. He was good at maths and had the skill of abstracting the permutations, rather than working them out through trial and error or committing them to memory.

Jumbo sent out a challenge. It came by way of the Clacker Kelly, who had adopted town ways and spent every free moment in Rathkeale. The Clacker had seen both Jumbo and John at play and concluded that there wasn't the man born yet who could live with my brother at draughts. We thought at first that we were being set up: the Clacker was a converted townie and those fellas liked nothing better than to dupe their rustic cousins. He, and my eldest brother Billy, devised the game strategy. The match would be played over three games; the wager on the first two would be half a crown each. John would barely scrape home in the first; Jumbo would win the second game easily. Then Jumbo would offer to double the wager on the third and final game. Five shillings was a lot of money: on a game of draughts it was madness.

The first two games went according to plan. I watched Jumbo's face as the third game progressed. A smug hue deepened his features like a patina on old hardwood. The hue became a leer, shot with slivers of purple as John lost three men and Jumbo looked set up for a king. Then the brother wiped him out. He took him with a single man from the back line, diagonally across the board, including the piece that would be king. Jumbo panicked. In a knee jerk reflex he poked a piece with a nicotined finger into the maw of a lurking killer and lost the majority of his remaining troops.

It had to be a fluke. You could see the realisation of that dawning on Jumbo's stricken face. Little flushes of colour appeared here and there like dabs of powder as he recovered his composure. Somewhere he had made a stupid mistake; it was the only answer.

'One last game,' Jumbo offered. 'Another

half crown on top of the five bob. Seven and six. Are you on?'

John nodded. They began the fourth game slowly as befitted the enormous wager. The colour returned to Jumbo's face. Then John pushed a piece between two of Jumbo's. Whichever way he moved, it was trouble: a loss of two men in one direction, the other way led to a crown for John. Jumbo sacrificed the two pieces and John brought out his new king like an Assyrian chariot, ripping Jumbo to pieces. He cleaned him out again and this time the first wan streaks of shock had barely settled on Jumbo's face before the rush of sudden anger swept everything aside like molten lava.

Jumbo threw the board in the air and kicked it as it fell. He knocked the pieces to the ground. I remember one black counter spinning through the back door and then rolling on its edge before it was submerged in a pool between cobbled stones. 'Bastards. Smart shite hawk bastards,' Jumbo raved, as he darted out the back door. He was like a puppet, jerking this way and that in anger. I wondered how all those jerking limbs would find their way back to the mother body.

Jumbo returned a few weeks later, all smiles and obsequious gestures. He came bearing recognition of his debt.

'There's your seven and six. Gimme back a florin for luck and we'll call it quits.'

John agreed on the spot. When Jumbo had stormed out, he had written off his winnings as a bad debt.

Jumbo came a few more times, to sit with John in the solitude of the barn and learn. It was the best thing that ever happened him, he said, being wiped out like that. It was like the cowboy films, he told me. However fast a gunslinger might think he was, there was always someone better; the same with the draughts.

I don't know how much Jumbo learned from John but it must have been valuable because his reputation grew around his hinterland. Yet he never played John again, nor came into our kitchen to trade his rations. I saw him many times from afar; at fairs, gymkhanas and coursing meetings. By then he was a hustler for a three-card con artist. I once saw an enraged man, who knew he had been duped but couldn't prove it, catch him by the throat at a coursing meeting. The man drew back his fist to smash him and Jumbo shrieked for the whole world to hear. 'You wouldn't hit a cripple, would you?'

We never discovered if he had a tail.

★ ★ ★

The end of the war heightened the threat of the Soviet Union. Even when Germany was jackbooting its way across Europe and the blitzkrieg was falling on London, we were never filled with the same dread. There was this strange ambivalence in our rationalisation about Hitler; he might be a friend to Ireland. We could never demonstrate that in cold pragmatic evidence. But we would make tenuous references to it, like *The Asgard* and Roger Casement and the possibility that Lord Haw Haw might be a friend in court. Deep down there were some of us, perhaps many, blinded by history and England's sins, who would rather have the jackboot than the bulldog.

We had a terrible dread of Soviet Russia. For me, and thousands of my ilk at that time, our fear owed most to the religious connotation. Miss Abigail was a die-hard republican, but even the British and the Protestants were preferable to the anti-Christs who ruled Russia — those godless disciples of the devil incarnate. Before that, it was a simple contest between ourselves and the black followers of Henry VIII as Abigail used call the Church of England. But contest or no, we had the advantage. We would always overcome because God was a Catholic.

There was a scenario Miss Abigail used

conjure up to define that contest. It was something that she had developed from Miss James' original concept. Suppose a new tribe of heathen pagans had been discovered in some part of darkest Africa and word was filtering back to us both, Ireland and England, about this new market, ripe for conversion. It was imperative that our missionaries should get there before theirs and it was our responsibility to pray that that should happen; not alone pray, but support the cause with hard currency. There was a black baby collection box on Abigail's desk. When you dropped a coin in, the black head inclined, as if to say thanks. Abigail was forever promoting that box. Each of us brought it home in turn because, apart from Abigail, the whole school could hardly muster a single coin. When it came back, she would rattle it and then gauge its weight against its previous state. She would shake her head and sigh her disappointment at the representative of the home where it had spent the night.

'This poor black babby's neck will never get a crick in your house.'

* * *

My father hoped that the end of the war should bring the end of compulsory tillage. It was a hated scheme and was seen merely as a half-baked imposition. I remember our neighbours arguing about it; my mother used liken the intensity of the debate to what prevailed during the Economic War. When de Valera's government stopped paying the land annuities, the British responded by banning the import of Irish cattle. We couldn't sell our calves and had to slaughter them because of feed shortage. We were paid a hide bounty for the skin of a slaughtered calf. The Economic War left deep-seated enmity in its wake; it divided our community more than the Civil War had done. My father would never forget the calf slaughter, and placid as he was, would bridle when someone praised de Valera's stance.

Like so many of his contemporaries, my father had a variety of skill and artisan knowledge. He was stonemason, thatcher, carpenter and gardener. When cattle died, he would conduct his own post mortem. I marvelled at the way he used the skinning knife, and he would tell me that he had had lots of practice during the Economic War.

Compulsory tillage remained policy for many years after the Second World War. During that time the horse reigned supreme. In spring, new fields, which had never known a ploughshare, were reddened in the bitter

134

east wind. I would hear men calling to horses from every direction and watch for the squadron of gulls rising above the hedges that pinpointed the working team. I used climb up to the ventilation square in the gable of the hay barn and spend hours watching half my known world, all points east and south, turn on the axis of its daily grind. I could see over the hedgerows and the clumps of trees, the low stone walls of the former tenant and the high stone walls of the indolent 'quality'. Most evenings I watched the train, bound for Tralee, leave a ribbon of smoke, like a bulbous centipede, atop the hazel thickets around Ballingrane.

The ventilation square was like a view from the mountaintop. When one of our neighbours died I counted the number of funeral carriages from that window. I harked for the sound of the hunting horn, when the hounds drew Magner's fox covert. From there I could exactly place the location of gull squadrons as they settled over ploughteam and ploughman. Jimmy Barrett was like St Francis in the high field, birds wheeling round his head.

I knew them all and their horses, and the names of the fields they worked in. Overhead the starlings dived and flew parallel with the red ribbons of earth; they climbed and peeled off, then suddenly broke, littering the sky like the scattered debris of a terrible explosion.

Jesse, Paddy Enright's sheepdog, sat in the headland by the gate and waited for its master. The first smudged fingers of darkness smeared the sky above Lisnacullia Castle. Once, when I searched the cumulus cloud over Harold's Wood, I saw the face of God. It was smiling at me.

7

We heard little about the events that shocked the world when the war was over. It was years later before I read about war crimes and death camps like Auschwitz and Belsen or realised the full horror of Hiroshima. I remember most the sudden rush of imports and the availability of things I had never known existed. My older sisters, Mary and Kathleen, had heard that there were oranges and bananas arriving in Dublin and it was only a matter of time before they found their way to our backwater. But wonderful as these fruits were — the sisters painted mouth-watering descriptions of taste and smell — they were nothing compared to chocolate, an exotic sensual indulgence.

At that time we rarely visited the town of Rathkeale. Only when we children needed new clothing, or when some broken item of farm machinery required replacement, was the trap pulled out and the pony tackled. On one such occasion my sisters were victoriously influential, for my mother bought items of absolute luxury: a brown paper bag of oranges and a single Crunchie bar that would be allocated by lot when the supper was over. I won the draw and learned in the immediate aftermath that, in fact, I had lost. They circled me like wolves, wheedling and pleading and then issuing threats and blackmail. In the end I received less of the bar than if it had been sliced into ten equal parts.

The advent of those luxuries after the war changed our shopping pattern forever. Up to then the word 'shopping' was barely in our vocabulary. The nearest comparison was the odd trip to Tommy Hanley's shop in Creeves. A body could buy most things there: groceries, hardware, animal feed, binding twine, coal. 'Almost everything from a needle to an anchor,' his slogan said, and if he didn't have something, he would offer to order it. Our neighbour Pat the Dog bought everything there.

We called him Pat the Dog because that was an expression of his. Many people in our community were likewise nicknamed. He used it to describe an occasion when one was forced to behave differently to the original intent, to pat the snarling dog, instead of kicking it, because the owner was watching. Pat the Dog would cycle home from work on a Friday night like a laden camel. There was an oilskin message bag hanging from each side of the handlebars, a larger one dangling from the bar and the carrier was heaped like a small trailer. I can see him battling against the wind and the bike wobbling as he came up the hill by Mick Harrington's cottage.

There was always a pig's head in one of those bags. Pat's wife Moll, and his two sons, hated the sight of it. Those shifty-looking eyes, embedded in the skin folds, and the ears in tufted patches of hair, were enough to make a woman sick, Moll said. Worse than that: eating pig's head and relishing it, as her man did, was the next thing to cannibalism.

Pat the Dog's house was a frequent stop on our rambling route. Late of a winter's night, when hunger returned, that pig's head was a delicacy, and no aspersions on our uncivilised mores would stay the grasping fingers. My mother and sisters, like Moll, had moved forward too in gentility, away from the coarse and the common. Pig's head was outlawed in our house: it was revolting and savage.

Every now and then my father would come home from the fair in Rathkeale with a sack full of meat from Hogan the butcher, whose calendar hung above the fireplace. It was always his last call before he headed for home and at a stage when he had visited several public houses. My father was not really a drinking man, and after a few whiskeys he was like a straw in the wind. My mother maintained that the butcher took advantage of his befuddled state, but confused or not, deep in the bottom of the bag, and therefore first to have gone in, was a pig's head. It created a gender division in our house: the women turned up their noses and we males poked fun at convent-imbued posh.

A year after the war ended, when I was eleven, I became the messenger boy. At that time I was full of confidence. A line of patter and knowledge had evolved from my progress at school and from my reading, I understood most things that went on around me. Though I was small for my age, I was more than a match in repartee when the smart ones poked fun at me. I was in the prime of self-belief and didn't know it. Out on the world's horizon, forces were gathering; the outriders were galloping over the nearest hill. In a very short time my self-esteem would be swept aside.

Every Saturday morning I set out for Rathkeale. It was five miles away and mostly I did it on foot. There was one bicycle in our house and that was in the sole possession of my eldest brother. Anyway, it was many sizes too big for me and in a permanent state of wreckage: the pedals were worn down, there were no brakes and there was an emphatic buckle in the front wheel.

In the beginning, I looked forward to those trips. I set off with oilskin message bag, the message list in my mother's copperplate pinned to the lining. I saw myself as a pioneer in the mode of the American West, heading off into strange uncharted territory, not knowing what hostilities I might meet on the way. I would meet buffalo and wolverine, silver fox and grizzly bear. Perhaps the Comanches or the Mesquileros would be raiding out of the forests in the Massey estate.

Paddy Mangan, who worked on Colonel Cripps' stud farm, was responsible for most of that. He let me read the Western books which the Colonel loaned to him, and my head was a whirl of sounds and smells, of mesas and prairie and heather, splinters from the imaginations of Frank Yerby and Zane Grey. I believed those stories. I thought the cowboy was as natural a part of his landscape as the ploughman was of mine. All Indians were savages; all white pioneers were cast in the image of God and the perfect Christian. Like the white missionaries in Africa, they carried the banner of civilisation against dark forces. *In hoc signo vinces.*

I had no responsibility for money. My mother ran a grocery account in Martin Culhane's shop in the square. She oversaw that account like the chief clerk in a counting house. When she was a young married woman that account had given her sleepless nights. It had been growing, unattended, like a monetary cancer, before she arrived in Kilquane, and it took her years to get it into manageable shape.

Nothing stays simple for long. After a few Saturdays, my journey became known and men and women waited for me, their youngsters keeping watch behind windows and half-doors. In the immediate periphery of our own bailiwick, I was young Nestor who went to Rathkeale every Saturday, fortune's messenger thrown in a route that no one had travelled with frequency before, except the Marshal.

Once a week, in winter, Marshal McMahon, whose first name referred to Napoleon's military hero, came out from the boglands near Carrickerry with a laden cart and sold peat from door to door in Rathkeale. He had a ten-mile route and everywhere favours were expected of him. He delivered and they expected more. They queried the change he brought back, so he stopped. He sat up there in the high seat that jutted out from the creel of turf and greeted everyone he passed with the interest of a neighbour. Every time they asked him, he had the same answer: 'Don't do no messages for no one no more.'

I thought I was smart but they used me: I was mere putty in the hands of hoary old codgers.

How I would have loved to offer the Marshal's response to Mrs Morrissey, who was upon me before I could get the feel for the white road in my wellingtons. She had a tongue like a rasp and an eternal war in her mind about the inequity of the world she had been cast into. Bloody farmers, of all sizes, were a law unto themselves, tramping down decent people whose only crime was to be living in a council cottage. Poor as she made herself out to be, she would have the price of half-a-dozen lamb chops wrapped up in paper. She produced that wrapping from one pocket of her bib and when I had digested the instruction, searched in the opposite pocket and found another wrapping for me.

The paper contained a different set of orders. I was to go the clerk in the bookmaker's shop and have him transfer them onto a betting slip: doubles, trebles, and yankees and accumulators. If, by any chance, and she had obviously calculated that the chance was very probable, I was refused entry to the counter, I was to wait until some adult I knew and could trust would place the bet for me. It was a hell of a directive and, naive as I was, I accepted it. The truth was I was afraid of her and the tongue that would skin a mule. She knew exactly what her winnings would be if either of her permutations came up.

That was a pattern I would see time and again in that part of the world. People who had passed through Miss Abigail's regime and were, according to her, as thick as two boards, could work out to the nearest decimal the most intricate calculations when it came to betting and odds. I had to find a way to deal with Mrs Morrissey, because otherwise I would spend hours on the footpath waiting for someone to place the bet. So I took the shortcut across the fields until I came to Mangan's Cross, thwarting the sentinels at the windows.

Beyond the cross I would encounter the Harolds, father and son. For years they had lived without a woman in the house; they had nearly grown into the same person and almost the same persona. Jimmy was 30 years younger than his father was, but the only distinction between them was the facial difference of ageing. They spoke like each other, the same words, the same inflections.

Both were acute introverts: they would avoid rather than associate with anyone. My father said that they owned one pipe and most of the conversation that passed between them was an argument about its use. Years later, when the father had passed on, I came across Jimmy one day, cutting thistles in an isolated field. He was singing and I listened, amazed, by the singer and the song. Not only could Jimmy sing very well, but the song he was singing was as much out of place as if he were singing an operatic aria.

I have heard the mavis singing her love
    song to the morn,
I have seen the dew drop clinging to
    the rose just newly born.

As I listened, I wondered too at the marvels of uniqueness and beauty that suddenly appeared in the strangest of places. The minute I made my presence known, the singing stopped in a sudden gasp, and a small wave of bronzed embarrassment crept over Jimmy's face. They were a twin enigma, father and son. They presented no face to their neighbours by which they might be probed and evaluated. We knew nothing about their personalities.

Once, Con Enright and I were sneaking along by the hedgerow, with Con's new airgun, looking for an unwary magpie. At the far side of the hedge, the elder Harold was drawing home on a cart — the residue of hay left behind by the hay float. It was a humid sultry evening and the midges were swarming in waves in the shelter of the hedge. We poked the airgun through the hedge and fired at the fleshy part of the horse's hindquarter. The elder Harold took little notice when the horse reacted to the first pellet but when we had fired some more and the horse was plunging between the shafts and the tackling and harness were creaking and humming, the old man cast about him in utter puzzlement. He took off his hat and went to beat off the invisible horseflies. He searched under the neck collar for something that was biting into the horse's flesh; he stood with his hands on his hips, incredulity all over his stance, as he contemplated the contradiction before his eyes. His staid fifteen-year-old horse was behaving like a cooped-up stallion on a diet of oats. Then he took off his hat, crossed himself and said a prayer.

Everyone who passed the Harold house was noticed. There was a high wall in front and the passer-by would never be in vision for longer than a few moments. But the shadow of somebody passing always registered on the scale of their curiosity. When I looked back, I would surprise the son or the father peeping round the pier of the gate. The face alone would be visible and it would duck out of sight when I looked.

A hundred yards from the Harold house there was a quarry, which was used only when the County Council was servicing the roads thereabouts. It was the source of two events that continually come back to remind me of that time and that place — one beautiful, one a breaker of myth.

My Aunt Hannah and I had taken tea to her husband in the hay field which he had leased from old Jim Kelly. We were walking home in the avenue between the wire fences that the Land Commission had lately erected. When you plucked the taut wire, it set off a musical vibration which strummed like an enormous guitar. We were listening to the sound, Aunt Hannah and I, and our faces were set in the direction of the stone quarry. Suddenly, over the blackthorns that hid the quarry from our view, came this dense black cloud, funnelling over the hedge, and then spreading out to form a gigantic clover. But the wonder was that we both saw the rising cloud before we heard the sound of the explosion. Neither of us associated the noise with the shape that was forming. We watched for long moments as the clover shape lost its resemblance to a gigantic shamrock, leaving shreds like torn pieces of black crepe paper as it unravelled in the sky above the Shannon.

In the heel of that same year, one Sunday, when I was nearing my ninth birthday, I chased into the quarry hunting a rabbit. I was alone except for the dogs. There was a ledge of limestone jutting out from the rock strata and there, underneath the ledge, oblivious to my presence, were a man and woman in a frenetic state of copulation. The man I knew well; he was a neighbour, with a wife and several children. I knew his wife too; enough to conclude that the woman lying beneath him was not she. I stood there in shock and then the man lifted his head and looked at me. He mouthed a couple of words and made a rude sign with his splayed fingers. I knew enough to realise that the words and the sign conveyed the same meaning.

I whistled up the dogs but lost all interest in the hunt. It wasn't finding the couple *in flagrante delicto* that shocked me. Neither was it the fact that I knew the man to be the epitome of upright behaviour, a pillar of the church and confidant of the priest. What bothered me most was that instinctively I knew I had exploded the myth and the mystique of birth; the lore of cabbage heads, storks that journeyed in the night and the occasional sunbeam. My suspicions about the lore were well founded; I had grown up, surrounded by animals, and had watched their behaviour. I knew where young animals came from. It was all apparent now, the man and the woman, the cow and the bull. There was no myth, no magic, no heavenly transport.

Once past the Harold home, I broke into a trot. I could trot for hours, as could most of my companions. I had read that the poor black people of Africa would think nothing of running twenty miles to a church and back again. To the Zulu and the Ethiopian warriors, and the tribes on the banks of the Niger, running was more normal than walking. I started to practice that. I ran to school and home again. I timed the run to Maggie Barrett's shop and could tell to the minute what time I would reach home. I ran to bring the cows to the milking and to call my father from the fields when dusk fell.

I was into a loping canter by the time I reached Ned Wall's house, because I was afraid. The thatched house was hidden by a privet hedge and by a huge lilac, both grown out of control and spreading along the north gable. It was very much like a cottage from the English school of rural landscape painting. Some years ago, a wooden splinter had entered Ned's eye as he was chopping firewood. He had neglected it and the ensuing corruption spread across his face like a loathsome fungus.

On a summer's evening, when we opened Moloney's field for the mowing, Paddy Enright sent me into the house for a cup of water. Ned Wall was sitting in the gloom at the fireside and billowing smoke was wafting around the room. Everywhere was smoked: the walls, the chair backs, the small windows. The chimney breast had a browned patina that looked like old cracking parchment. But it was the sight of Ned Wall in his backless chair by the fire that set my heart racing and filled my nights with ogres and monsters. His hands and the good side of his face were smoked like the bacon flitches that hung on our kitchen wall. Around him the smoke eddied, and out from the smog this face turned to me, glistening in the slime that covered it and pulsing in the deep-pitted wounds. One side of his face had rotted away.

He had half a mouth and a single nostril. He handed me a cup of water and asked after my father and mother. The remnants of his lips turned the words into sibilant whispers. I poured the water into our tea can before I offered it to my uncle, lest the cup be contaminated by its owner's putrefying flesh.

Ned Wall used play the flute. He played traditional music, mostly slow airs. It was unusual because we were a community of little traditional culture. The fact was that we looked down on those values, as did the people a hundred years before when they were revoking the Irish language. Native music and dance were redolent of poverty and peasantry. I remember an aunt giving an account to my mother about a dance she had attended. It was a *céilí*: she spoke with disdain about the sweat-filled room, the primitive steps, the wild uncultured whoops and, above all, the thunderous impact of hob-nailed boots on the floor when the dance ended.

I listened to Ned Wall's slow airs on summer evenings. He brought the chair to the flagstone that bordered the road and played in the great stillness. There was a wonder, a haunting loveliness to the *Lament for Staker Wallis*, as there was to Jim Harold's *Annie Laurie*. I heard snatches of it in my sleep. It followed me by day and I heard it in the quiet of shimmering hedges. I heard it when I was far away and it made me yearn for the sounds and the warmth of home. It reminded me of the blackbird that sang in the apple tree in the orchard, and which sang with such a passion and homage to existence, as if it were the only blackbird in the world and the only one so endowed.

There is no evidence now of the Constable

cottage and the wild privet surround; nothing to remind one that a house once stood there, and that a man with a corroding face played spine-tingling music in the stillness of an evening. Twenty-five years ago, when we were returning from a visit to Kilquane, my wife May and I searched amid the briars and the wild hedge until we had found the stunted lilac. An offspring from it now grows in our back garden. It is always slow to flower and quick to shed and we suffer it only for the tendrils it outstretches to a distant past. Sometimes, in the early fall of twilight, I think I hear music from the corner where it grows.

I ran past Tom Flavin's house. It was thatched too but unlike the normal pattern, there was no door on the side that faced the road. I had visited there once, delivering pork steak and black puddings, and they had kept me for tea. The house was populated by adults and the conversation was full of child talk. A sister passed a slice of bread to a great hulking brother.

'There now, pettens. Say who's good to Jimmy?'

'My little Lena is, my own lil' Lena is good to Jimmy.'

The Flavin family and ours had once pooled their labour. Two rows of potatoes had been planted in the Grove Garden when the call came for dinner; a row for the family and a row for the pigs and the fowl. The seed was glistening in the sun, waiting for its cover of farmyard manure and soil. The eldest Flavin stood in the headland with his hands on his hips, looking back at the morning's work.

'If they come,' he said, 'they won't come, and if they won't come, they'll come.'

His neighbours thought he spoke in riddles. And so he did because old man Flavin was given to a complicated phraseology. But my father liked such deviations and, as we struggled in turn to master the complexity of language, he would test us with that conundrum. I failed the test, failed it for years, because my father and those older than me had resolved that each one in turn should figure it out alone. It was my mother who shone light on the puzzle, as indeed she had done with all who had gone before me. Old man Flavin was afraid of the crows, especially the greys and the scalds. If they lighted on the field during dinner when there was no one to whoosh them away, they would eat all the unprotected potatoes. By the time I had figured out the puzzle I disliked old man Flavin and I galloped past his house that had no door to the front.

If I had time and the weather was favourable, I would take to the fields opposite

Flavin's and follow the meander of the stream. It had just gone gurgling under the arch of the stone bridge. This was the same stream that sourced itself half a mile north of Kilquane, crossed the road at Whacker Roche's and sometimes in winter and spring flooded his plot.

Whacker Roche had lassoed a trout one summer's day. He had snared it with a makeshift loop of twine, worked under a stone. The Whacker brought it down the Long Road, in an enamelled pan, and showed it to a group of us who were hurling in Dunne's field. The pan passed in wonder from hand to hand; none of us had been that close before to a creature of the water. The Whacker kept the trout imprisoned on the windowsill until he found it, one day, stiff and lifeless. For hours the Whacker and I had rested our arms on the windowsill, pondering and marvelling at the little creature in its lacquered prison.

The stream bordered Enright's pound — the acre of land where the cattle watered and the cows were milked. When the stream flooded, it encroached on the pound, and when it receded, it left a muddied patch which dried in summer and looked like the picture of a watering hole in Kenya which I had seen in a religious magazine called *The*

Far East. Con and I found a little silver fish marooned in a mud-pool. It was a minnow, his father told us, but more wonderful still, it led us to the discovery of the minnow habitat in the stream.

There was a pair of pine logs laid side by side, spanning the stream, and forming a crossing to the other bank. Directly underneath, in the silted bed, was a shoal of little fish. We had crossed that log bridge a hundred times: we had fought duels on it, we had raced over it and lain to rest on it, and we had never seen a minnow. Now they were darting from bank to bank with incredible dexterity. They were sending out puffs of silt like a thousand miniature bombs. They were everywhere and we had never seen them before.

We tied lengths of cord to the necks of jam jars and trapped the minnows. Hannah gave us a glass bowl. As with Whacker's trout, we placed the bowl on the windowsill. Hour after hour, we watched the wonder of movement, that great miracle that nature and evolution had wrought on living organisms. I can still feel the soothing warmth of mud through my toes, smell pungent watercress, hear the seething buzz of clay like an army of crickets as it dried beneath the sun. It was the summer of the minnows. Con and I were a pair of tow-headed freckled kids, sun-tanned on lower arms and below the knees, skirting furtively by the blackthorns because there was work waiting in both our homes. I think of us as barefooted Huckleberry Finns, with glass jars slung from pieces of twine, heading for Moon River.

Where I came to the road again, there was a tiny thatched house built against the great wall of Magner's estate. You would never know there was a dwelling there, if it weren't for the column of smoke, because the roof was beneath the level of the wall. This was Aggie Butler's house. I had first seen her when she came into the short aisle in the church where our family pew was. I had never seen anyone so old. She was older than Nanna, who lived in Barrett's house next door, and who scared me as she passed the kitchen window. Nanna dressed in black and seemed to have a miniature face beneath the rim of her bonnet. What I saw had the death-like pallor of waxed skin and when she passed the window I thought some ancient messenger from beyond the grave was coming to take me away.

Aggie Butler had none of that grim-reaper appearance. She had the look of someone astray in the head and who loved every moment of it. Her hair was like a wig of

156

sheep's wool, randomly laid on her head, so that it seemed to be in a different position each time I met her. The hair grew out of her scalp in yellowing tufts. It was like what Synge described in *The Well of the Saints*, 'White hair stickin' out like a bush where sheep would be leppin' a gap'.

Aggie's speech was like her hair: it came in wild spills of words, followed by spells of quietness. In the silence, she looked at me with the tilted quizzical face of a bird, as if the manner of her expression had exploded the words into space and she was waiting for them to reform and return. She cackled as much as she spoke. She would hop from one foot to the other when something struck her as funny and deserving of a jig of merriment.

I knew Aggie was harmless. My father used say that, should the truth be known, she was as sane as the rest of us; saner perhaps, because it takes a special acumen to reduce one's lot to a state of comedy, to laugh at a ridiculous world and think it hilarious. Perhaps it was deliberate, that abandonment of convention; the ultimate treatment for life in all its strange convolutions.

Aggie loved to talk. She would fix her taloned old fingers like a vice around my wrist and make me a prisoner of her chatter. The hens and the bantam fowl scraped and pecked in the cropped grass on the road's margin. People used speculate at the oddity of it. It was madder than all things about Aggie Butler because in front of her half-door were acres upon acres of the Magner estate. It stretched as far as the eye could see, bountiful and secure behind the high wall, yet this raddled old woman chose to feed her fowl on the public roadway and therefore had to maintain a constant vigil over them. But there was method in that behaviour because otherwise people would pass by without a word. Everyone who passed — callow youth, rider on horseback, carters going the road to mill or market — were forced to halt their journey, while Aggie poured forth her strange madcap cackle.

In my mind, I twinned Aggie Butler with Nonie Hynes, who lived in the shadow of the church. Nonie used tell me about the fairies; the little people, she called them — 'impish and vindictive little hoors' they were — who scampered up and down her slated roof and robbed her sleep. We hid in the long grass in Kenneally's meadow and threw pebbles onto the roof. Eventually her vexation would overcome her deference towards the fearful little ones; she would rush out from her kitchen and pour a tirade of abuse upon her invisible tormentors on the roof.

Of Aggie Butler's house now there is nothing left, not the slightest undulation to show that an old woman had lived there. She brought me in once; a sweltering day in June, as I came weary and parched from the town. She wrapped her taloned fingers round my wrist and shooed the hens and bantams through the gate before us. I was given a drink from a firkin with a wooden lid, and the water tasted like a distillation from God's own well on the very day of its creation. She poured it from a ladle into a mug which was decorated with a red horizontal stripe. There was a hint of gun-barrel blue when the water sluiced from the ladle and it was shot through by the glint of sun piercing the smoke-coloured glass of the window. When I left, she presented me with a dozen rabbit snares and a rickety goldfinch cage.

'Take them away, son. Far from catching rabbits or trapping birds I be now.'

We came out to the road again, the entourage of hens and bantams squawking and fighting. The gnarled old fingers tightened on my wrist and she cocked her head.

'Whist,' she said, with a note of fear, 'is that the booze of a motor I hear?'

The old order was changing; the world was spinning on a different axis, turning to a new antenna, seeking out strange signals and movements. The motor car was coming. Soon they would come by the white road, and leave dust trails like Hopalong Cassidy's horse. When that happened, old Aggie Butler would close the wooden gate and move her flock to the safety within. And then, until their time too expired, callow youths, horsemen and carters would pass by unnoticed.

On the evening of a beautiful autumn day, Con and I were cycling to Jack Hayes' cinema in Rathkeale. A young rabbit — what we called a grazer — almost ran under Con's front wheel, and in its frenzy, trapped itself beneath the lowest bar of Aggie Butler's wooden gate. We caught it and Con carried it into the cinema, hidden under his jacket. When the audience was in the grip of the film, we let it loose. A few minutes later there was uproar; the audience rose as one, screaming and panicking.

''Twas a rat,' a young woman said; 'a great big lad of a rat. I seen his eyes glinting up at me.'

Another said that she had felt the sensation of the rat's tail brushing against her nylons. Jack Hayes' torch streaked erratic beams in the darkness. It never occurred to him to turn on the lights, and by the time someone did, the cinema audience had fled to the footpath across the street. He appealed to his patrons to return; he had searched, he said, 'high up and low down' and there was 'neer' a rat in the house. The audience formed a queue from the street to the box office, demanding a full refund. Hayes tried to negotiate, arguing that the film was well into itself before the thing, if thing it was, got into the cinema. It would be recalled in folklore as the night of the rat.

I went along by the great stone wall of Magner's estate. My father had a story that the estate had been won in a card game from the previous owner; an impoverished Blennerhasset. He was gracious in defeat; wishing that the new owner would have luck with it. Blennerhasset was a gentleman, and it was honourable to be gracious and noble in adversity.

The stone wall I walked by had been built by our ancestors. A man and his labour, his horse and his cart, were valued at the rate of threepence a day. The estate wall was the landlord's folly — a mixture of oddity and ostentation. It served no protective purpose because the landlord was the supreme power. But it served to shut off the manor seat — the manifestation of old England — from the rude scrutiny of peasants. Every estate had its enclosing wall, and every peasant outside thought it the height of eccentricity, because in reality, it kept the landed class in more than it keep the peasantry out. I would always hear how odd the so-called quality were: their high stone walls, the avenues of elm, the stands of beech, the eternal feats of horsemanship, the incessant quest to relieve the boredom. We farmed part of an estate which once belonged to the queerest of them all: old 'cracked' Absalom Creagh and his man-made fishpond.

There was a manor house in the east of the county, near my mother's birthplace. She brought me to see it once and explained that, mingled with the strange ways that boredom induced were common human frailties. The manor-seat was set on low ground; people going the road, on foot or on horseback, could barely see its magnificence. So, at intervals, the landlord had lowered the wall and had set in iron railings, to create intermittent views of his wealth and glory.

Those were days when the horse was king. It applied to them all: draught horses, plough horses, high stepping cobs, hunters and thoroughbreds. The Magners and the Cusses, who were cousins, rode to hounds. They visited each other frequently, always on horseback, passing by on the road that bordered our land. It seemed to me then that they were the victors of life and were sharing the spoils. Their horses expressed it as their riders did; sitting up there in postures of grandeur. It appeared incredible to us then that adult people, oblivious to a world of labour and drudgery, could ride the white roads in prime work time and be so set apart from the common herd.

We never envied the Magners, the Cussens, or any of the other horsey families. It was simply so ordained by God, who in His infinite wisdom had granted a saddle to one and a shovel to another. But I admired from a distance, the pageantry, spectacle and romance that surrounded the landed people. I saw Clive of India and Rhodes of Africa in the horsemen who passed our humble way. The glory of the Raj was in the foxhunt, the ethos of genteel nobility in the great houses and their ballrooms.

Though well removed from it, I probed at the outskirts of that lifestyle. I was obsessed by hunters and thoroughbreds and I would watch for hours the cartwheel that Shaughnessy's race horses formed, under the shelter of the chestnut tree. Sometimes, the cartwheel would break away like the Arab stallions in Duffy's circus, and go galloping headlong in the lush acres of Absalom's old stomping ground.

I had found a stirrup in the wall of the Creagh house and another in an outhouse in Lisnacullia. I polished them till they were gleaming like silver amid a collection of rusted iron. On Slugaragh road, when the foxhunt had passed, I found a broken martingale. I repaired it and when no one was looking, I fitted it to the chest of the red mare and imagined us both, she in resplendent tack and me in redcoat and jodhpurs, trotting crabwise to the meet in Riddlestown.

The foxhunt fired my blood and lifted my heart. It did the same to most youngsters I knew and many an adult too. When we heard the hounds and the distant bugle sound, Miss Abigail would give us leave to follow the hunt: Con and I, John Joe Meade, the Dunnes, the brothers Wilmot. It was marvellous. We chased all day, opened gates for ageing gentry and handsome women. A man with a red face and a gold pin in his cravat threw two half-crowns at me when I helped him remount. It was a small fortune.

I have a collection of sounds lodged in my brain evocative of those times. When they float free, on sleepless night and black days, they plunge me into a mixture of pleasure and sadness. I hear the honking of a skein of geese passing over our house in a rimy November landscape; mowing machines whirring in early summer; a vixen crying in the dead of night. And always to the forefront of the collection, the bugle call at morning and the rising swell of beagle tongue.

We never realised then that we were witnessing the demise of rural ways. It never occurred to us either that the next generation would judge us against new standards and ideals and find us wanting. We saw as natural the dictum that all creatures, other than humankind, were placed in the world for our use and benefit. I snared rabbits and knew of whole families who depended on them, for food and for money. Pheasants and wild duck were delicacies; a succulent diversion from the constant bacon. I saw nothing amiss when the hounds ran a fox to death because the species preyed on our fowl stock and caused us grief. In time, I reached my own conclusion about blood sports — put away the gun and the fishing rod — and wild horses wouldn't drag me now to a hare-coursing meet.

Foxhunting will die. It was dying when I followed the hunt across moor and parkland. The era of gracious living in splendid houses: the luxury of indulgence, the disport that brightened the boredom, all that is no more.

It was ebbing away in my time; castles were falling and cabins rising. The Romans had a phrase for it: *sic transit gloria mundi.*

I hear these words in ruined manors and crumbling high stone walls.

8

Beyond the main gate of the Magner estate, I was once again in dragon country. It was the dividing line between the comfort of familiarity and the apprehension of the unknown. Immediately beyond O'Brien's Cross I encountered my greatest danger: a youngster, three years older than me, who lived in a whitewashed cottage enclosed by a tumbledown picket fence.

We had chased after the same broken hurling stick during a match in the Bog field. He had had a three-yard start on me, but I got near enough to trip him and grab the pieces, as he slithered, in his Sunday suit, on a streak of cow dung. The boy, whose name was Paudge, was round and fat, but he had a face like the Christ child in the stained glass window in Coolcappa church, innocent and angelic. Paudge would come at me in a headlong rush as I passed his house, the child-like features belying his deadly intent. He charged like a rampaging bull from behind the picket fence. I usually escaped, such was the clumsiness of his attack, but I would be reduced to a quaking jelly by the likelihood that those great red hands might one day wrap around me with the embrace of a boa constrictor.

Later, when I was able to borrow a bike, I took the turn almost parallel to the ground and had a fair head of speed built up when I flew past Paudge's gate. We would trade insults at a distance, exchange swear words, pull faces, until he tired and turned for home, wiping the sweat from his glistening brow.

Then he acquired a dog; a brown and white Jack Russell on three legs. It seemed that its only purpose in life was to listen for my coming. I had no sooner turned the corner when the barking started; short staccato yelps that would fuse into a cascade as I came nearer. As I rounded the bend, there was the dog in the centre of the roadway, spinning a dervish whirl in its excitement. The useless leg, drawn up to meet its haunch, was beating like a drumstick. That Jack Russell had a demented appearance as if it were a lone canine crusader in a world where every enemy looked like me. I could hear the gnashing teeth and feel the fanatic intent as it set itself for the charge. Paudge egged it on from behind the picket fence.

'Good boy, Roger! You're my good little dogeen.'

I always stopped on the bridge over the Deel. It was roughly halfway and I had earned a rest. In my mind, the Deel was the Mississippi and any minute now a steamboat would come round the turn past Dore's Hole. The Deel was a clear waterway then uncluttered by drooping sallies or mid-stream rushes. It was West Limerick's main aquatic artery. It sprung far away in the foothills of Castlemahon and wound its way through Geraldine territory and landlord demesne until it poured into the sea at Askeaton, the greatest Geraldine stronghold of all. I harboured a notion that I would search for the source of the Deel as Livingstone had done for the Nile. I never made the exploration because when I started to fish, it diverted me in the opposite direction. But I would get to know every turn, swirl and eddy between Rathkeale and miles downstream, far below the weir at Newbridge.

A year or two before, when my father had sent me in from the fields to search for twine in the pocket of his jacket, I had found a fishhook impaled in the underside of the lapel. He was unable to explain convincingly where the hook came from. I suspected that the jacket had had a previous owner because my father was never a fisherman. He claimed to have tickled trout under stones in the stream bordering our land. I didn't believe that, for one look at the stream and its girth — parts of it I could jump across — was enough to suggest that he was having me on again. But I learned later that he wasn't because other people of his generation told me the same story.

I took the fishhook, and like Wandering Aengus in Yeats' poem, I cut and peeled a hazel wand and hooked a worm to a length of black thread. That simple action killed my obsession with horses, horse irons, and bits and bridles. We became like soul brothers, the Deel and I, yearning for each other's company. The river spoke to me in song. It read to me from the book of its landscape, whispered words of wisdom to me, told me the secrets of its journey. I was never much of a fisherman either, because the whisperings and the secrets distracted me.

On summer evenings, when the sun went down, a group of us made for the Deel. It was said that there was a depth of ten feet in the middle of Dore's Hole. It was as black, as my father would say, as the hobs of hell and when I rounded the bend, and saw the malevolent sheen on its surface, and heard the rheumy suck as the flow swirled under the banks, it filled me with foreboding. None of us could swim. We foundered around the black hole, lying on sheaves of rushes, arms and legs pumping like Hallinan's threshing machine. We looked like reptilian mutations adrift in a world of skewed evolution. All that summer we neglected the hurling, and the noise of our pleasure brought more and more youngsters to swell our group.

Then a threesome of young women arrived one evening and stood gaping at us from the bank. We had no swimming gear on. The women were ten years older than we were, more vocal and self-assured, and they demanded equal rights to the black pool. When we refused and dared them to do something about it, they went behind the bushes and emerged in bathing costumes. It was the closest we had come to female nakedness in its early flowering of maturity. Everything changed with a suddenness that was palpable. One moment we were full of sniggering innocent bravado, the next dumbfounded with open-mouthed shock. The women slithered down the bank and their bathing costumes were pulled askew. Dark hidden places were revealed with a frankness that sucked the breath out. Our eyes had rested on the forbidden fruits and the crime of looking, as our priest would later conclude, was a heinous indulgence. Then the other realisation hit. We were stark naked beneath the black water and nothing separated us from the scrutiny of those hussies except a sheaf of rushes. This must have been the way that Adam felt in the Garden of Eden. We scrambled out in our grass skirts and went home in silence. A few amongst us confessed to the priest. The blame and the verdict fell on all of us. That black hole was an occasion of sin and we were ordered to forsake it. The rushes grew rampant around the perimeter of the pool, the bushes closed off the entrance to the black water, and we swam no more in Dore's Hole.

Sometimes in heavy rainfall, the water reached the apex of the twin bridge arches. I walked through quickly then because the rush of water unnerved me. It came round the bend with an awesome power: tree branches, dead animals and earth tufts borne in its watery grasp. My mother had a rhyme about Brian O'Linn, a kind of rustic Finn McCumhaill, who turned adversity into comedy. I remembered the same verse every time I went over the bridge and especially when the river was in spate.

Brian O'Linn and his wife and wife's
  mother,
They all went over the bridge together.

The bridge broke down and they all fell
  in,
We'll go home by water, said Brian
  O'Linn.

When the river flooded it spilled onto the road, invading Mick Roche's cottage. He had to move with his family and live with his brother Jack, our parish clerk, until the flooding had subsided and the dampness dried out. Mick was a short man with a shock of wiry white hair and twinkling blue eyes. He was forever mooching about the yard, brushing on lime-wash or leaning on the handle of a spade. Mick would bring me into the kitchen, put the kettle on and trawl me for news about Jack and his neighbours.

Roche's house was the farthest outpost in my territory. I had a passing knowledge about a man called The Count, who had a big house in the dip behind the hill. He used ask me to bring messages: a pound of sausages from Binchey's and wire nails from McDonnell's hardware shop. I was instructed to leave them at Mick Roche's house. I was never offered a reward. Something must have gone amiss in his relationship with the Roches because, when he asked me to bring him a ball of wax-end from Brandon's saddlery, I was to leave it for

173

him in a hole in the high stone wall that stood over the entrance to his avenue, like the opening to a mountain pass. He gave me four pence, three for the wax-end and a penny for myself. It was a paltry sum, even in those days, and I had to wait two hours until Brandon decided to deal with a rustic youngster. I left the wax-end in a different hiding-place to the one he nominated. It eased my conscience and made me feel that was I was a match for people like The Count and the harness-maker.

I thought about the wax-end twenty years later and went to look for it. By then, change had swept utterly over my route to Rathkeale; land had reverted to landlords' tenants, and the great houses were crumbling and decaying. The Count was dead and so was Mick Roche and not for years had a youngster walked that road bearing messages on a Saturday morning. But the ball of wax-end was still there. It disintegrated when I touched it and a lift of breeze carried off the residual ashes. It was like a cremation of all that had gone.

★　★　★

If I were lucky, and if I had timed my journey well, Miss Daisy would appear shortly. Like myself, she went to town every Saturday but, unlike me, she had transport. She drove a pony and trap — a grey pony the colour of limestone, which had two speeds only; slow and dead slow. But it didn't matter; that trap was the height of luxury. There was a tartan rug to place over the knees and the seats had cushions. Even more wonderful: there was an oilskin cloak that fitted into the shape of the seated body, and was fixed to the wood of the backrest with brass studs. It saved the tartan rug from wind and rain and kept the lower body snug and dry. My father's trap cart had none of those accessories. When it rained, water sluiced from the knees down to the floor and a puddle grew that sometimes reached the ankles.

I thought Miss Daisy was the epitome of a Victorian gentlewoman, like the pictures of characters I had seen in my mother's books. I could imagine her seated in an elegant drawing-room or a literary salon, taking tea in fine bone-china and the little finger of her right hand sticking out from its fellows. I pictured her as a study of decorum and good manners. But the painted fingernails belied the images. So too did the streaked cosmetics that raddled her cheekbones as if she had wiped her face with her hands when she was baking. I heard the gentility in the refined way she spoke; the concern when she asked after my mother and father and the small sounds of sympathy she made when something was amiss.

'Dear, dear, dear, dear,' she repeated in time to the sounds of condolence. If the condition was serious enough, we would say a decade of the rosary and when we were finished, she would say, 'There now, that's grand. God will take care of it.'

Every now and then the pony broke wind. Daisy took it as a personal affront, as if the animal had chosen to embarrass her in front of company.

'You bold boy! You bold, bold boy! Have you no manners at all? We're not alone, you know.'

Most of the women I knew of Daisy's age — probably middle forties — would simply take no notice of a defecating animal or the forerunner of flatulence. It came with the familiarity of living and coping with animals, humans included. In fact, breaking wind was regarded as a healthy sign and would be cited as perfectly natural behaviour, if there was a complaint. Doctors recommended it; my father had that in rhyme from a member of the profession.

Wherever you be, let the wind break
  free,
For houlding it caused the death of me.

Miss Daisy was very sensitive about language that did not match the gentility of her spirit. She reprimanded me for using the word 'bloody'. It was common and vulgar, but not nearly as awful as the soldier's word then doing the rounds. I should promise her, she pleaded, that such a word would never pass my lips. I was totally ignorant of it, I assured her, which wasn't quite true. Chris Wilmot had used it in the playground and Miss Abigail had flayed him with the snowdrop switch. It was fortunate, Miss Abigail said, that he had uttered it in the playground. If he had used in the classroom, she would need to have it blessed. It was as bad as that.

'How will I know it when I hear it'? I asked Miss Daisy.

Her features screwed up. Particles of rouge became shipwrecked as her jaw ruminated.

'I hope you never hear it,' she wished for me, 'but in case you do, the word begins with an 'f' and there's a 'k' at the end.' It was on the tip of my tongue to ask her how she had heard it, given the genteel world that she sought and moved in.

She chided me for using that commonplace

177

expression of rural vernacular; sounding the diphthong 'ea' as 'ae'. We pronounced meat as mate, cream as crame, heat as hate, and so on. It was uncouth, Miss Daisy said; a sign of rudeness, it distinguished the ignorant from the educated. I had heard Miss Abigail and the school inspector having a heated argument about that habit. He favoured Miss Daisy's view. Miss Abigail pooh poohed it as modern rubbish. That particular pronunciation, she insisted, was part of the noble Irish inheritance, its roots deep in the civilised antiquity of the Gael, in language, poetry and culture.

Every time the pony broke wind, Miss Daisy feared the worst. Wind-breaking was the primer for excretion, and if that happened, it would be deposited in the body of the cart. Our technology hadn't found an answer to that problem, though my father had once attempted to deal creatively with it. When he was replacing the body of the creamery cart, he had cut a hole in the wood, directly in the line of fire. While his solution didn't stop the deposit entering the cart, it could be got rid of without fuss.

When my father suspected that the pony was about to relieve itself, he put downward pressure on the tail so that the excrement would be kept out of the cart. Miss Daisy

178

tried the same approach when the flatulent staccato signalled the danger. It was such an incongruous gesture; the fingers with their rings and painted nails, pressed desperately against the tail, and her averted face convulsed in a lacework of disgust and horror. She seldom succeeded, because the natural force exercised on the tail was greater than Miss Daisy's desperation. We were visited by the full load.

'You bold, bad boy! You bold, bold, bad boy!'

We stopped to clean out. Miss Daisy had a cut-down besom under the seat and we brushed the pile through the little entrance door at the rear of the trap.

'Promise me now that you won't do that again. Promise now, you hear?'

The pony seemed to nod at the admonition and Miss Daisy smiled. If the natural order held good, she would be home before the pony had the urge again.

We came to a place called the Stony Man. The road made a 90-degree turn as it faced towards Rathkeale and the other branch went down the Dark Road and into the territory of the Palatines. They were originally from the German Palatinate and had been persecuted by the French during the 100 Years War. Following their plea for sanctuary to the

British, they had been settled hereabouts by Viscount Southwell of Rathkeale.

At the crossroads, there had once been a forge. The smith had an artistic bent: he had fashioned a niche high up in the cut-stone front wall and set a statue there. It represented his craft and perhaps resembled him. The stone blacksmith, in steel-blue limestone, was sculpted in a contemplative mood. One leg was relaxed and the point of an elbow was resting on the plateau of the anvil. The Stony Man, as we called it, gazed out interminably on stone-walled fields, on dairy herds and half-bred hunters. This was Golden Vale land — the vein of fertile green that stretched, according to Miss Abigail, from Golden in Tipperary to Shanagolden in County Limerick. It was the land flowing in milk and honey that the Normans had craved and the English had subdued and enclosed.

This was landlord country and it was dominated by the spire of the Catholic church. It was right and fitting, the parish priest explained to me once, as we sped that way in his motor car, that the spire, which represented God's power and presence, should rise above those trappings of puny power, planted by foreign idolaters. I wanted to say that the church spire too represented triumphalism, but he was an austere and

180

domineering man and brooked no disagreement.

Some years later, I had served mass when my sisters were getting married in a double ceremony. The priest asked me to stay behind and accompany him to the wedding breakfast. Once into the car, he launched into a tirade about my parents, especially my father, who had arranged for the taxi which had taken the sisters to the hotel. There were hundreds of good Catholic taxi-owners in the country, many in our own locality, and we had to go and hire 'a black Protestant' from the town of Rathkeale. We know that black Protestant well: he would come into our kitchen and break bread with us; he would seek my father's permission to shoot over our land, something that other neighbours would not dream of doing. It was never an issue that he served the same God in a different church; it was never a consideration when my father hired his taxi. But it did become something of an issue for my father in the aftermath of the incident. He worried until sense was prevailed upon him. It was so much nonsense. On such silly petty polarities are sourced generations of hatreds and suspicions which pass for denominational zeal.

The Stony Man marked another boundary in my journey to the town. I had long passed the landmarks of familiarity. Now I was entering the strange environs of another world. It was like entering the Appian Way. The road was wider and tarred. We were encountering the outskirts of Rome: better land, larger holdings, two-storied slated houses with avenues and lawns, ornate gates.

From here, a network of roadway circled a large holding that was now the Massey estate and, before that, had been but a fraction of the Southwell demesne. We went, Miss Daisy and I, and the steel-grey pony, in muted deference by the stone wall that enclosed that vast acreage of land. We passed the main entrance. It splayed out from Corinthian stone piers; two on each side, so that the wall between seemed to be poised like a raised wing that would at any moment take flight. Such was the angle of the splay; calculated and proven like a geometric hypothesis, that the main house was not visible from the prying eyes of a curious peasantry. Adding weight, and even dignity, to the expression of power and privilege within those walls was a pair of stone lions on the inner pier columns, each with a raised foot, looking outwards over the plain in everlasting vigilance. It filled me with awe, that spectacle of pomp and eminence and its inherited right to strut through life with one foot raised in a lavish gesture of class and regality.

When I was on foot, I would peer in through the gates and hope to catch a glimpse of life within the walls. Miss Daisy always pulled up too, but we never saw beyond the gate-lodge. The winding avenue curved away through the fields, studded with great beeches, and lost itself like a wandering brook past a flurry of little bends. Privacy was hoarded here as if it had been ordained by some kind of preservation order. The children of the gate-lodge played in the dust amid the hens and the bantam fowl and looked just the same as other children on our side of the wall.

Con and I, hunting pheasants, once breached those walls. We went in from the Dark Road side, one Sunday morning, when the Massey family was at church service. It was a mere symbolic gesture because we met a man outside who immediately recognised our intent — the guns and the dog were obvious — and he told us that we were on a suicide mission. The great house had a telephone which was linked to the police station and at the first shot the police would be alerted by the retainer in charge. Smart as we thought ourselves then, it never dawned on us that the police in Rathkeale didn't have a motor car and we would be long gone by the time someone cycled out. We scuttled over the wall, fired at a pheasant that was well out of range and darted back to the road again. We had made the gesture.

Sometimes the lifestyle of 'the quality' would escape from behind those high stone walls and halt temporarily, with startling nearness, in some inconsequential place. We were taking the midday meal on a Sunday when a jeep pulled into the front yard. Out stepped a man wearing plus fours, a tweed cap and a yellow waistcoat. He and his party were going to shoot the snipe grass in Stackpoole's bog field and he wondered if the children would come down, beat the grass and drive out the snipe.

Four of us went, including my sister Tina who was next in line below me and a willing party to many an act of devilment. We walked into a scene that was redolent of upper class England and replicated in the far corners of The British Empire. Bentleys, Daimlers and Austins had parked on the margin of the white road. Women sat on shooting sticks with tartan rugs over their knees, and waited to be served lunch by the liveried butler and his assistant. Great baskets of food were laid on the ground. Men were opening wine bottles or standing around in indolent knots, white-gloved hands twirling silver-topped walking sticks. They could have been at Ascot, in the recess of a bay window that fronted tiered lawns, or strolling the Strand on a summer day — Burlington Berties.

We flushed out of the snipe. The shooters potted them as the birds zigzagged over the white road. Some of the women, with their sixteen-bore shotguns, were better shots than their men. We beat the bog land a couple of times because the snipe who had survived the first fusillade returned in their confusion to the marsh again. The butler and his assistant collected the fallen snipe and counted them in pairs. He entered the number in a red notebook and gave it to the man driving the jeep. The entry would go into the archives and would form a little memorial in the annals of some great house. 'March '53, at Riddlestown, spring snipe shoot. Eleven guns, 73 brace. Prime guns: Brice-Eddington, Major, and the Dowager Serena Morehampton'.

The butler threw all the snipe into a canvas bag and presented it to Tina. And then there followed a wonderful thing. He put his uniform cap on the ground and they came, one by one — major and dowager, colonel-of-horse and lady mistress — and they tossed coins into the cap: half-crowns and florins and the odd shilling piece. We thought we would never be poor again.

Here behind the high gates and high walls everywhere, the seeds of empire were nourished and nurtured. Every male, even those that might one day inherit the manor and lands, were bundled off to English public schools, which polished the sheen of aristocracy into leadership sparkle. This was the born leadership concept emanating from class. Those young men, imbued by the nobility of war and the responsibility of position, would serve and die, and mostly die, wherever infantry trundled, cavalry charged or ships engaged. The great houses were the seedbeds of empire like offshore stud farms. Wherever they pitched their tents or raised estate walls, the landlord class and its offspring saw themselves as the epitome of all things British. But they were never quite regarded as such, either by their counterparts in the mother country, or by the institutions of empire. They were tainted, rather discoloured, by their arm's length association with the mere Irish. The mother culture, however, accepted and demanded as duty due the ultimate contribution, obedience unto death. Go into any church in Ireland where the landed aristocracy worshipped and read their life offerings to empire on white Carrara plaques. With Clive in India, Rhodes in

Africa, Gordon in Khartoum, they followed and gave their lives.

Once when the wind and the rain clawed at the message bags and made the ends of my oil coat flap at my knees, a Bentley purred up beside me. I was just abreast of the old workhouse on the outskirts of Rathkeale. The driver beckoned me into the passenger seat and told me he would 'fetch' me to the gates of Stoneville. The instant he closed the door, I was in a cocoon of comfort and wealth. I could see my reflection in the trimmings of burr walnut that gave the interior of the car the panelled effect of library walls. It was the most luxurious seat I had ever sat in; I could smell Probert's polish from the leather and hear a faint creak as if I were riding on a saddle.

The driver spoke with an accent I never had heard before. I found it difficult to decipher the words for they seemed to swirl in his mouth like pebbles and then slide through his lips in treacled smoothness. By then I was in a boarding school and when I told him that I was studying Latin and Greek, his face brightened. He asked me for my surname: it was Greek, he told me. There was a famous man called Nestor, whom Homer had written about. He was old King Nestor of Pylos, ally of Menelaus and Agamemnon in the Trojan War and renowned for his wisdom. I could see the disappointment on his face when I told him that the name was Irish. We talked about Athens and Sparta and the great war against the Persians. When we came to Stoneville, he drove straight by, out past the Stony Man and across the bridge over the Deel. He had been to Thermopylae and had seen where Leonidas had died with his little band of Spartans. There was a statue to Leonidas, he told me, and beneath it the inscription; 'Go traveller to Sparta tell, that here obeying her, we fell.'

He left me out at the crossroads by Magner's main gate, telling me that he was going to Altavilla, another great house, and he was sorry he couldn't talk further with me. Perhaps we might meet again. I went towards Benson's Cross and when I looked back, he had turned the car and was heading towards his own place. He had brought me farther than intended, done a good deed for a youngster studying the Classics who, perhaps, reminded him of classrooms and playing fields in some quiet corner of distant England. I wondered what it was that had made him tell me a fib about Altavilla; perhaps he was trying to find a plausible reason for bringing me that far. Pity we never met again.

* ★ ★

We journeyed on, Miss Daisy and I, along the length of the stone wall and the overhanging trees. Horses grazed in the fields, yearlings cavorted in the expanse of fertile plain, herds of pedigree cattle stood still and munched. We came then to the marvel of science that was closing the doors on a dark past. A decade before, perhaps more, electric power had come to Rathkeale. It was almost as significant to rural Ireland as the invention of the wheel, though it would be many years before electricity came to the house where I lived. Nothing changed our lives like the 'electric' did, even if, in the beginning, it was just another way of providing light. In time it powered the radio, cooked our meals, milked the cows, and ushered in the twentieth century.

Beside the crossroads, where one spur went on to Askeaton, they had built a powerhouse; the force for all the bulbs and wires that lit up the town of Rathkeale. I thought it looked like a space-age station. It was a complex of cables that ran a network of engineering intelligence all round the building. The glass disks and their bulbous companions were the cells of some superior knowledge. But it was the hum, the ever-present vibration, that awed me the most. It was energy, communicating a unique language to the superior few who understood it. The hum pulsed and flowed and when I closed my eyes, made me feel that I was a time traveller in one of H.G. Wells' novels.

When I was alone, I stopped and listened for that hum. It both frightened and exhilarated me. Stories abounded about the electric. It was fraught with danger, the folklore said; 'no man who didn't know the ins and outs of it should go next or near it'. All around the powerhouse there were warning signs; zigzagged miniature lightning bolts proclaiming the danger within and without. But the ever-present hum fired my imagination, and shot it forth into swirls of questing curiosity. Around where that powerhouse stood, little had changed in two centuries. The horse was still king; men mowed with scythes and toiled with spades and pitchforks.

I remember thinking about those things again, seven years later, when I got off the train at Ballingrane after an interview for a job in Shannon Airport. My father was waiting, holding the pony by the head, because the hiss of steam would scare it. He was talking to Julius Shepherd, whose ancestors had come out of the German

Palatinate and settled thereabouts under Viscount Southwell. The Palatines had brought with them the long-faced spade, the idea of planting in drills, the craft of grafting fruit trees and growing cabbages.

Some years before, a firm called Pierce in Wexford town had developed a horse-drawn mowing machine. It would be obsolete in a few years. And in its passing it would take the draft-horse, the long-faced spade and the making of hay trams. A dramatic change was sweeping the land. I had come that day from a place where aircraft landed and men spoke diverse tongues. But those two men, my father and old Julius, who once represented different cultures, were as rooted now and alike as peas in the shared pod of tradition. I watched old Julius with his wagging finger and animated gestures; my father nodding. Neither of them had yet heard the hum. Nor would they hear it if they were asked to listen.

The railway passed under the bridge where the straggle of town houses began. The railway is gone now, and a new roundabout diverts the traffic beyond the bridge. The railway station and its outhouses have been converted to an industrial park. I have deep affection for that old railway line. Before I ever sat in a carriage, I used climb the eastern column of the hay barn, look out through the ventilation square in the galvanised iron, and follow the progress of the steam engine as it went between Ballingrane and Rathkeale. A lot of its progress was visible because the land was flat and the main cover was hazel scrub.

My mother loved travelling by train. She brought me with her when I qualified for whatever selection process went on in her head. We took the pony and trap to Ballingrane and, as we left the house and until we passed the first bend of the lane, she wore the expression she had cultivated all morning — reluctant compliance with a trip she would rather not make. Out of sight of the house, my mother's face brightened. She sang snatches of song and her feet tapped to its rhythm. At the station, Old Julius Shepherd materialised out of nowhere, raised his cap, and untackled the pony. When my mother entered the carriage, she underwent a dramatic change, because now she was visiting those places that all her reading imagined, travelling in a foreign country, taking the *Orient Express* to exotic parts. In those days the carriages were wood panelled; there were pictures of great houses and magnificent vistas fixed to the panels. She studied them intensely and read the captions aloud. Then she sat, leaned back, and closed her eyes. The beginnings of a smile crept from the corners of her mouth and spread like a warming glow across her face. I thought again how beautiful she looked.

The steam engine was the fastest mode of transport we had yet experienced. My father never shared my mother's love of rail travel because he had a dread of what he called sacrilegious speed. There was no need in his world for headlong disregard for life and limb. His neighbours would have agreed. I got a lift once from John Madden and his grandfather in their ass and cart. When we passed the hurling field, a train came hurtling round the bend and, though it was slowing for the station, the young lad's face was alive with excitement.

'There's speed for you,' he kept saying; 'boys, that's speed.'

The old man had his hand over his eyes.

9

Every Sunday morning Mick Harrington took the shortcut to mass. He came by our front yard and his coming had the accuracy of a timepiece. The first mass-bell rang as he stopped and looked in our window. He wasn't curious; it was simply to determine if we were up and going about our preparations. One morning we had slept out; a faulty alarm clock had lost time during the night, and when we arrived at church, the mass had reached the final prayers. To make matters worse, my father led us all the way to the short aisle where the family pew was. Our collective embarrassment was savoured by a congregation entertained by our discomfort. It would be talked about for days, not because we were late, but that we had trooped up the aisle as if in defiance of the priest, who had no tolerance for lateness. We made as much noise as a column of infantry; the priest stopped the prayers and withered us with his glare.

The blame was laid squarely on my father and, he in turn, chided Mick Harrington. How could he have passed the house and not warn us? Surely he had seen the activity around the farmyard and could judge how far behind it was. So every Sunday afterwards, Mick would stop for a moment and look in the window.

It was a minor miracle that we weren't late more often. My father was like a feudal bishop being vested for mass. He got out of bed at the last moment, and from then on the focus upon him was intense and methodical. One of us fetched collar and collar studs and presented them ready to fasten. Another polished his shoes and a third pulled the stockings on my father's outstretched legs, fitted the shoes and tied the laces. All the time he sat in the armchair, ordered the sequence of the vesting and muttered his irritation when the sequence went awry. Invariably he discovered that he had forgotten something after we had left the house: the rosary beads, the handkerchief, or the coppers for the church collection. One of us was to blame.

Because Mick Harrington passed by our front yard and kept an uneasy watch on our time keeping, we developed a distant affinity with him. It was distant because Mick was reticent and shy, especially in the company of women. That was a common complaint in the country — perhaps it emerged from the insularity of our lives. It started in childhood: when a strange adult visited a house, the children hid behind their mother's skirts, or peered out through windows or the cracks in bedroom doors.

In recognition of his Sunday morning watch, Mick was included in my milk round. In the beginning it was an imposition. His house was a mile away on a stretch of roadway that was sparsely populated, and resembled a country lane. Most of the land on either side had been divided by the Land Commission. In the vicinity of Harrington's, there was a little collection of houses, but not an offspring amongst the aged adults.

At the dip of the road — we called it Downey's Hollow — lived Jim Downey and his daughter Mary. They too had benefited from the Land Commission divide; they now owned patches of land throughout the parish. Old Jim Downey was forever on the move with his horse and cart; sitting up on the front with a jute sack over his knees and a look of infinite boredom on his jaundiced features. He always suffered from a runny nose; two drops constantly hung from the far points of each nostril, and never came together. Jim was dour and humourless; the most I ever got from him was a curt headshake, accompanied by a loud clearing of his sinuses.

Mary — then well advanced in years — was forever on the road too, driving her cattle from one pasture to the other, home for the milking and away again afterwards. She had a deep red face and a smile that appeared like a frozen mask. I never saw her without the wellington boots. Where the rim of the wellington met her upper leg there was a round rusty weal from the constant chaffing. Mary had a deep unfeminine voice that boomed out in the stillness as she marshalled her cattle. In her herd were cows, yearlings and young calves. The young ones cavorted; she darted here and there to bring them to order, and all the time the deep voice sounded like a far off foghorn. We hid in the shelter of the road hedge and made the sound of the warble fly. The herd took off, galloping along the white road. It stampeded up leafy laneways and vaulted the low places into neighbours' fields.

The warble fly laid its eggs in cattle hides and the larvae grew under the skin. When the eggs hatched and grew to wormhood, they bored an escape tunnel in the skin. Nature had willed in the animals the instinct to stampede when the warble fly buzzed.

By the time Mary had gathered the herd,

she was running sweat and the red face was like an over-ripe tomato. When she discovered what was happening, she appeared one evening in the front yard while we were having the supper. She stood between the small piers of the wrought iron gate — legs splayed, arms akimbo — and gave vent to a strident tirade of abuse. Then she turned and left, swinging her arms and still shouting. I met her on the road the following day and she acknowledged my greeting as if nothing had happened. Whatever salutation was offered her, be it hello, how are you, a nice soft day, Mary responded in the same way. Her face creased with the frozen smile.

'Well thanks,' she said.

We named her Well Thanks.

Mick Harrington, the Downeys, the 'Soldier' Listons, all lived on the road to Tynies. For years I thought the name Tynies belonged to a family who lived far in off the roadway. Then I thought it was a nickname. Later, in an ordnance map, I discovered that it was the name of the locality. I should have known for Pat the Dog frequently referred to it. He cycled that way to work on the railway line. It was an exposed part of the road and he used it to describe the hardship of his journey to and fro.

'There's a wind coming up Tynies and

'twould freeze the 'mebbs' on a brass monkey.'

I had often walked that long rutted track that passed as a lane to Tynies. Just before the entrance, there was a cut-stone barn and a thatched house, set at right angles to it. Mick Graney, our neighbour and friend, had lived there until he moved to a cottage near our house. He still worked the land for the owners. Like my father, he was great around horses, and took immense pride in his work. I spent a whole day sitting beside him when he was mowing a hayfield. There was a second seat on the mower because it could be converted to a reaper which took two people to operate. At the end of every swarth, Graney dismounted and examined the line he had cut. It didn't matter that no one else would see the work, or that in a few days from now, the hay would be gathered and all traces of his workmanship would have vanished. He and my father were birds of a feather. The horses were not his, but he treated them as if they were. He clucked his satisfaction to them, spoke words of appreciation and brought them water from a bucket that he kept in the cool of the hedge.

Mick Graney was a lovely man: warm, kind, and fun to be with. We played cards together in later life, went to race meetings and made adventures to public houses. I remember him most for the manner in which he looked after himself and his cottage. He was always turned out immaculately, smelling of carbolic soap, its scrubbed appearance on his ruddy cheeks. It reminded me of walking the land in early morning, when the dew was lifting and everything about that new day had the pristine scent of renewal, as if, before dawn, it had been washed and perfumed. Mick Graney kept his house like he kept his person. It exemplified my father's dictum about order and tidiness: a place for everything, and everything in its place.

My brother John, when he called to bring him to Sunday mass, found Mick Graney dead in his chair. He was sitting upright, a woollen sock in his hand, ready to pull it on. The floor had been swept, the range was glistening after a coating of black lead, the breakfast things had been returned to the dresser. A fresh white shirt was airing before the range and the polished boots were within reach of his hand.

The people who lived at Tynies kept a puck goat at stud. Most times there was a small herd of goats on our land. We turned up our noses at the milk, but ate kid-meat without a murmur. The meat was a delicacy, compared to the constant diet of home-cured bacon. As tastes and traditions changed, goats' milk went into decline. It had echoes of poverty and a strong and tangy taste that lingered long and bitter on the palette. My father took his usual futile stance on the side of yesterday's custom. It was the best milk in the world, produced the best cheese, and here we were turning up convent-trained noses at the practice of past generations. But when that same influence outlawed the killings of the kids as barbaric, he fought no war against it. He seemed to tacitly welcome it as if he had been waiting all along for the change to manifest itself.

When a female goat came into heat, I was nominated to bring her to Tynies. I hated the task. It seemed that some strange bush telegraph had broadcast my journey and people were stationed behind windows, or leaning on half-doors, as I went by. It was amazing how many had chosen that time to work in roadside fields. Mine was a passage of broad sly winks, knowing cackles and lewd comments.

'Where are you going, sonny?'

'Describe me what will happen when you get there?'

'Couldn't ye do the job yeerselves?'

It was like running the gauntlet. My heart fell to the pit of my stomach when I was bidden to stay home from school and walk the sow to the boar at Ballingrane or the cow to the Hereford bull in Rathgonan. When I returned to school the following day, it started again. Everyone knew what my absence had been for. When my name was called out in the morning roll-call and Miss Abigail enquired where I was, my brother would answer with gleeful clarity, 'There's a heifer bullin' Miss and he's takin' her to McCarthy's whitehead.'

Miss Abigail saw no humour in the titter that threatened to explode into full-blown laughter. She had made it known to my father that it was wrong to expose impressionable youngsters to such exhibitions of raw sexual activity. His response was that his son would see worse in time and what else would he expect to see on a farm? But despite that frankness, he shared the same sanitised expressions as his neighbours had, in describing the animal's condition. 'The roan cow is looking the bull,' he would tell me; or 'the sow needs to be serviced'.

It was enough to fill me with foreboding. Apart from being the butt of our neighbours' crude comments, every trip was a miasma of suffering. On the outward leg of the journey I was forced to trot to keep up; there was some odd biological instinct afoot that I could never fathom. Whether sow, nanny goat, or skittish heifer, each one seemed to know unerringly where it was so resolutely headed, even if it were a maiden voyage, or if the location was in the opposite direction from the previous time. Coming home was entirely fraught; a perverse tortuous route that would tax the patience of Job himself. High-strung heifers, obstreperous sows, led me down every deserted laneway, into farmyards to be barked at and cursed, into swamps and thistle-filled fields. Gone was the unerring instinct that had guided the outward journey. It was replaced by deliberate contrariness.

There was only one redeeming feature in those tiresome journeys. Sometimes the chore took me to Ballingrane and this was like standing on the perimeter of a different world. Those descendants of the German Palatinate were the most industrious and hospitable of farmers. When one neared their homesteads, especially in late summer, the air was saturated with the scent of ripening apples. Everywhere there was order: trimmed hedges, limed walls, houses as white as driven snow. There were no weeds in the fields, or fallen walls, or gaps in the hedges proclaiming the want of a hanging gate.

Walter Ruttle would let me loose in his orchard, bid me fill my pockets and bring apples home to my mother. There was Beauty of Bath in abundance. In the immediate territory of my homeland there was never more than a single tree and that would be raided and stripped at first ripening. The Palatine orchards grew Bramleys, Cox's Pippins, damson plums and pears. Trotting down the Dark Road, I salivated at the thought of those pears. Two centuries before, when John Wesley had come to preach Methodism, he had found those people without religion and, in his words, much given to debauchery. They converted en masse and a short time later, two of his converts, Philip Embury and Barbara Heck, emigrated to the United States and founded American Methodism. The Palatines had planted a pear tree in honour of Wesley's visit and a graft from it was still flourishing in Walter's back garden.

The drunkenness that had disappointed Wesley was no more, but the Palatines still held the art of cider making. I didn't realise then why the pitcher of amber lemonade smelled and tasted so deliciously different and I wondered why Nash's lemonade didn't have the same effect. The drink put a spring in my step and, at the start of the inward trip, made me giggle at the antics of the obstreperous sow.

In front of Mick Harrington's cottage, divided by twin-privet hedges, was a flower garden. He never cultivated it and it grew rank and disorderly. I think he kept it deliberately in its overgrown state so that the sculpted hedge would be thrown into stark relief. It was trimmed to perfection. His brother Sylvester told me that Mick used a spirit level to keep it in size and shape. He would walk me through that twinned tunnel when I left to go home and if there was a sprig astray in the sculpture, he fetched the scissors from the kitchen and snipped it off.

Mick was living a Spartan existence, alone except for his birds. There was a story that he had been given a bicycle lamp when he and his sister were much younger and living together in the cottage. The donor showed them how to switch it off and on. Later that night, Mick was drawn to the lamp again, and while he was examining it in his hands, it fell on the table and the impetus of the fall switched on the light. Try as they might, they couldn't turn it off. Finally they put the lamp in a bucket of water and left it overnight in the farthest corner of their garden plot.

On Sundays, his brother Sylvester, would cycle out from Rathkeale where he had married and been settled for more than 30 years. The contrast between them was dramatic and immediate. Syl's bicycle was the latest model, replete with airpump, dynamo lamp, and a soft velvet covering on the saddle. His hair was sleek with brilliantine oil and his plump, well-fed face proclaimed a caring wife and sanctuary from the ravages of weather and toil. Syl wore a tailor-made Sunday suit and one could see the folds of the trousers reflected in the sheen of his brown shoes.

Sitting at the opposite side of the fireplace, Mick looked more like Syl's father than his brother. His white hair was streaked with yellow patches like thawing snow at the verge of a pool. His skin was blotched and the clothes hung in angular disorder from his frame, as if he were a badly-fitted dummy in a draper's window. The brothers would sit there for hours in silence. But the moment a neighbour ambled in, Sylvester would swivel in his chair, the expectancy in his face followed by a rush of words. Mick would contemplate the fire, poke the peat sods, make the odd trip to the window to see what the day was doing and listen in silence.

That Sunday visit was a hardship for both of them. Sometimes a message would be delivered to Mick's house by the People's

Bakery van-driver that Syl wouldn't be out the following Sunday. I would find a brighter chirpy Mick sitting beside the fire, the light of anticipation in his face. He would be gone come Sunday, with Chris Tobin or his father Lar, hunting rabbits with terriers and ferret, or catching goldfinches. I met Syl one day when I dropped my message list at Martin Culhane's. He asked me if I ever got a word at all from the brother. Trying to talk to him, he said, was like milking stones, and if it weren't for the wife and the blood relationship, he wouldn't go next or near the place. Syl kept coming until the day he died, which was long before Mick took ill. I would have wagered that Syl would outlive him by a decade. One Sunday, when the rain swept in from the direction of Mannix's Folly and the wind mourned in concert, Mick looked across at the seat where Syl used to sit. He remarked to me how much he missed the regularity of the man in the chair, though devil the word he could ever get out of him, he said.

Mick was a bird fancier and I became a disciple. He had a cock goldfinch and a mule; a cross between a goldfinch and a canary. The goldfinch was called Langford because it had been trapped in Colonel Langford's field. When I saw him around those birds, I could understand how Mick's natural reticence had been compensated for. In their presence he had companionship; their song was a special language that was spoken to him exclusively, as the crickets spoke to my father. They filled his mornings with their exultation to the dawn, entertained him in the twilight hour before darkness.

Mick was the first man I knew who was a bird fancier, though it was nothing unusual. I had seen pictures of Chinese street-scenes, where youngsters carried cage birds slung over shoulder poles. When we were stretched on the grass margin at Mangan's Cross, after a game of pitch and toss, Paddy Maumb would lead us off in an English vaudeville song.

> My old man said, follow the band,
> And don't dilly-dally on the way.
> Off went the van with my home packed
>   in it,
> And I walked behind with my old cock
>   linnet.

My father said that when he was a boy, there was scarcely a house in the parish that did not keep cage birds: blackbirds, thrushes, linnets, larks — any small bird that had a range of song. It never occurred to me that there was anything wrong with the practice. I was fascinated by goldfinches, from the first time Mick Harrington had brought Langford out from the room and hung the cage in a window recess that was bathed in sunshine. There isn't a bird formed as beautifully as the goldfinch. I had seen flocks flit from field to field, perching on thistle tops, feasting on the seed. Now and then, on the roadside, I would see a goldfinch probing groundsel plants. But there in the window recess, in the morning, every detail was lighted and magnified. It was like watching the trout that Whacker Roche had snared and seeing every iota of design and colour that the natural environment had blurred.

I marvelled at the creation of such beauty: the crimson head, to the patch of ivory beneath, the tan chest feathers, the slivers of gold on the wing tips, but most wondrous of all, the three white spots on the folded wing that matched exactly, in size, tint and placement, the trio on the other wing. It would be less perfect if a painter with a draughtsman's skills had drawn them there. But magnificent as the arrangement of beauty was, it came second to the wonder of Langford's song.

Like most people who kept birds, Mick could imitate their call sounds. Only one person I knew, the Clacker Kelly, could do it better. He could whistle the calls and then fuse them in harmony with the longer notes.

Once we were crossing through Harold's Wood, making for Paddy Kenneally's house, where a hurling match was being broadcast on the radio. Beyond the boundary of the wood there was a lone blackthorn bush, and as we came by, a flock of goldfinch passed overhead. The Clacker hunkered down beneath the bush, motioned to me to do likewise and whistled the calls and part of the goldfinch song. Overhead the flock of birds seemed almost to stop in mid-air and when the Clacker strengthened the volume, they veered and came swooping down to light on the outer twigs of the bush. There must have been a hundred birds; they decorated the tree with slivers of gold and all around us were the chirrups of enquiry. They had heard and responded to the call but couldn't figure where it had come from. As the Clacker whistled through his repertoire and held them there for ten minutes or more, I could see and sense the confusion in the flock. Where was their feathered kin who had spoken their language, bade them stop, and engaged them in a dialogue that we could only imitate but never understand?

When Mick wanted the bird to sing, he

would place the cage in the window recess and whistle the call. Langford hopped from the feeding trough to the perch. Its arrowhead tail swished and then it launched into song. The song filled the room; it poured from the bird's throat in a throbbing stream of marvel. It turned the air to music and worked its way into every space of my consciousness. I was hooked for life.

There is hardly another sound that gives me as much pleasure as the goldfinch song. The loveliest piece of music I know is Shostakovich's 'Romance' from *The Gadfly Suite*, but I would be hard put to choose a preference between the two. Sometimes Harrington would provoke the birds to vie with each other, Langford and the nameless mule. They sang to a heart-pounding crescendo, competing with each other so intensely that Mick would cover one of the cages to still the conflict.

I was captivated. I pestered the old man for a bird of my own. Why did I need one? he asked, I could listen to his pair of songbirds any time I wished. And if the song wasn't enough, I could listen to the lore of the bird fancier, whose natural reticence became free-flowing, once he was tuned to his favourite subject. Over and over he told me about the time he had discovered a goldfinch nest in the crabapple tree at the bottom of the garden. When the clutch feathered, Mick put the nest in a cage and suspended it from a branch. The parents fed the brood through the bars and every other day he moved the cage towards the house, along by the hedgerow. Still the parents fed their young until the cage was hanging off the gable. He separated the cocks from the hens and placed them in separate cages, but left the female cage-door open. The parents taught the hens to fly, but continued to feed the others long after their siblings had flown. Finally, when the parents abandoned their young, he brought the cage indoors and placed it beside Langford's predecessor. The birds learned how to feed from the seed in the trough and to drink from the drinking bowl that was fixed to the outside of the bars. And they learned to sing, for as Mick explained it, it was no different from the way that humans learn to talk. The song was there all the time; it needed only the stimulus of another voice to bring it forth.

When the lore and my patience wore thin, Mick promised me he would find me a bird if I could find a cage. My father and I went to sell potatoes in the market at Newcastle West. There were standings there — makeshift booths covered with tarpaulin — and in one of them, hanging from a pole that also held rabbit snares and traps, was a row of finch-cages. Early that morning my father had given me a shilling; it was a reward for rising with him in the cold small hours of darkness and for scouting the market to get a feeling for the prices. I had sixpence left — the other half had been invested in an ice cream, but in my mind I was still rich. I was shocked when the man in the booth told me that the cages were half-a-crown each. It was an enormous amount of money. My father laughed at me; did I think he was made of money? Anyway, if he could afford to give me the half-a-crown, how could he explain to my mother that we had spent so much on a childish indulgence?

Weeks later he asked me to go with him to Andy Connors' house. I had accompanied him on such visits many times. I never liked it because I would be left sitting in the corner while Andy and his sisters held a half-whispered sibilant conversation, as if I was too fragile for its adult import. My father was a master of small talk outside his own home and could spin out trivia like a spider weaving a web. I suspected I was being used; made an ally to his petty conspiracy, for my mother frowned on those visits and I could feel that she blamed me too. We would travel across fields in utter darkness; you couldn't see your outstretched hand. He took my hand in his. It was warm and firm and its callused weals were bonds of security and little moles of affection.

But the visits were rewarding too. Before we left, the Connors sisters would go separately into the room off the kitchen, trying to make it look so casual that it was patently obvious. Each would find an occasion to come near where I was sitting, take my hand and press a little wad of paper into my palm. Andy, their brother, would rummage in his pocket as we set off across the cobbled yard. My father would protest at the rattling of coin; Andy would tell him to have sense — it was only a few coppers. When I unscrewed the paper wads in the light of our kitchen and counted the collection, I was usually one and sixpence richer.

On one of those visits Andy led us to an outhouse. It was stone-built, with a slated roof, and I could feel the warmth of the animals that were housed in one half of it. The other part Andy had converted to a workshop. I had never seen a place so tidy and well arranged. My father beamed at the sight of it. Andy rummaged behind a pickle barrel and brought out a bird-cage. He told us that he had made it himself when he was a few years older than me. The workmanship

214

was far superior to that which the huckster in Newcastle West wanted half-a-crown for. Andy had used the wood of a Spanish wine-case and the bars were cut from the spokes of a bicycle wheel. The feed-trough moved as if it were gliding over velvet; the top-frame was scalloped and inlaid.

My father told me, as we walked home, that when they were both in their early twenties, he and Andy had taken a woodwork night-class and Andy was a natural with his hands. A few years later I came across a miniature table when I was rummaging in the loft over our kitchen. It held neither screw nor nail and the dovetail joints were sublime in their accuracy and fit. It was my father's graduating project from that night-class.

Mick Harrington, Lar Tobin and I, went to the field in Langford's estate where the blacktops grew. Mick and I had cycled to Tobin's house with the mule cage covered in sheets of brown paper. I knew Lar Tobin already; he was the mason who had built our second outhouse. Between the old one and the new he had erected a fowl-house; a perfect solution, Lar suggested, for filling the space which otherwise would be an eyesore. My father had wanted to build a turf shed there, but my mother vehemently supported Lar's idea, which made him suspect that Lar was merely a conduit in my mother's scheme of things. My father's suspicion was correct.

I didn't know that trapping wild birds was then outlawed. Had I known, I probably would have shared the same aversion to that law, as did all bird-fanciers I knew. It was merely another piece of government interference, like compulsory tillage or the regulation which said that bicycles and trap carts should be fitted with night-lights. Hardware shops stopped selling birdlime but would offer instead a product called Dak, which circumvented the law because it was promoted as a rat-catcher.

The technique of bird trapping had been brought to a fine rustic art. One end of a six-inch hazel twig, the bark shorn off, was fitted into the soft core of a piece of elder wood and the birdlime rolled around the remainder. It rolled on from the tin of Dak like a ribbon in continuous flow. Nothing was left to chance. There were many bushes in Langford's blacktop field but none might suit, so Lar had brought his own with him and stuck it into the ground. The limed twigs were fitted to the thorns by the other end of the elder. The mule in its cage was placed out of sight beneath the bush and we hid under the shelter of the stone wall. If the mule would perform, he would attract a flock of goldfinch and they would light on the bush. Some would land on the limed twigs and become fastened and held there.

The mule did not perform. He was desultory and sulky all that dark evening and did not raise his voice above a tired twitter when the goldfinch passed overhead. But he did attract one — a solitary bird that seemed to be aimlessly passing by and that wheeled and landed on a limed twig when the mule chirruped. I had my goldfinch.

I brought it home in a paper bag with air holes pinched in its side. I hung the cage on the kitchen wall between two flitches of bacon which were placed there to smoke. My instructions were followed to the letter: cover the cage until the bird's fear and its wildness have subsided, fill the feeding trough with hemp-seed, put an eggcup of water on the floor of the cage with a few sprigs of groundsel, or a piece of hard-boiled egg, in case the bird does not discover the hemp-seed.

In the months that followed, I was the butt of every joke about that bird, now called Connors, after the cage benefactor. When I took off the covering, Connors was perched on the feeding trough, spitting out shelled seed in rapid fire. A few seconds later he switched to the eggcup, drank, and then sampled another morsel of egg. By now it resembled a woodpecker's borehole. I noticed something else but dared not mention it to anyone yet. The wall plaster behind the bars was dotted with tiny holes as if there was a colony of woodworm there. And on the flagged floor directly below was a little mound of gravel. Harrington had told me how birds took gravel into their craws to aid digestion.

My father started the jokes. We didn't catch that bird, he said; it had given itself up. Somehow it had reasoned in its tiny brain that a life of comfort in a sumptuous cage was far more comfortable than foraging in the wild. The jokes grew more embarrassing when we knew for certain that the bird had no song. Harrington said it sometimes happened like that. In the same way as some people were born dumb, so were birds.

I bore it all with outer tolerance and internal anger. I prayed for a small miracle. Surely it was in the power of the Almighty to give a dumb bird the gift of song. I wasn't praying for a major event, like the conversion of Russia, the sort of thing my father included in the trimmings of the rosary.

I took the bird to Harrington's house. We placed Connors between Langford and the mule and Mick inveigled them to compete in song. They bombarded Connors with song but apart from a few lazy chirrups, he was deaf to their repertoire. Amid their outpouring, Connors' head bobbed up and down as he gorged himself on hemp-seed and spat out the shells. The bird was handicapped, maybe brain-damaged, Harrington said. My father said it was a 'glugger'.

I was devastated with disappointment and seething from the mockery. I resolved to let Connors free. I took the cage out to the bawn-field where we milked the cows in summer, laid it on the ground beside a flowering thistle, and opened the door. Gingerly, as if anticipating danger, the bird emerged from the cage. It sprang to the thistle-top and dallied for a while to sample the seeds. Then it flew high to the top of a thorn tree that served as a gate pier to a field we called Hayes'. So long, Connors, I thought.

I was immediately filled with remorse. The bird may be a glugger, but it was a handsome goldfinch. It could be a good one to mate with a canary, Harrington said, if it could ever figure out what to do. Despite the unflattering jokes, Connors was a part of the kitchen menagerie, like the sheepdog, cats, inquisitive hens and the sickly calf. Every time my father spied groundsel, he would pluck a sprig, poke it through the bars and Connors would peck at his finger. My mother has accepted the gravel mound and the pockmarked plaster. The nearest Connors ever came to singing were his early morning chirrups that heralded dawn. He was as good as an alarm clock, my mother said. Somebody always remembered to buy seed and replenish the water in the eggcup.

While I indulged in remorse, there came a flitting flash of gold and a few lazy twitters. Connors lighted on the cage, surveyed his surroundings with head turned sideways, and then hopped in through the open door. He fell with gusto to gorging the seed and spitting out the shells.

And so began the goldfinch era. It was like an epidemic, affecting all around us. There was a couple of singing birds in every house, a tin of Dak and a collection of stripped hazel twigs embedded in elder holders. Goldfinches filled our conversation and lighted the routine of our young lives. We discovered the El Dorado of goldfinch habitat. West of Waterfield, in a part of the old Creagh estate, there was a field where the blacktops grew in wild profusion. The field was fallow, except for the wild birds. It was filled with linnets and larks, dunlin, seskin, and was the mecca of the goldfinch.

They came in great flocks. They would land on a bush and light it up like fairy lights. Their twittering and quarrelling set up a babel that tremored in the air like the constant splintering of breaking ice.

I can never fully explain the obsession that affected us youngsters. For me, part of it was the desire to possess a living symbol of the wild, representing the sublime beauty and the wonder of creation. But I never did capture a songbird like Langford. The nagging doubts in my mind grew bigger and frequent, but I rationalised them all away.

Then my father and I went to hew firewood, one bitterly cold day in November. The promise of snow was in the air, the sky was the colour of slate. We sawed the blackthorn into logs with an ancient crosscut but the effort failed to take the cold from the bones. A flock of goldfinch bobbed overhead, heading for the blacktop field in Waterfield. A few Sundays before, that haven had been invaded by a band of trappers from Newcastle West; one of us had given away the secret. They captured more goldfinches in a single day than we had taken in successive winters. Someone had told my father about it, and as the pair of us wrestled with the crosscut he remarked that it was wrong for birds to be captured like that and ventured that two-thirds would die in captivity.

On another day I was with Con in Lisnacullia. His father was drawing hay from Gortroe and we were working high up in the barn. Behind us was a great patch of flowering thistles. The seeds were lofting in the breeze and wafting away in their fluffy parachutes. A flock of young goldfinch, many still without the full markings of maturity, lighted on the thistles. We left the barn, rigged a small bush with the trapping gear, and settled down to wait. We didn't notice the hay float returning. When he found us, Paddy Enright was filled with anger. Small blame to him because thunderclouds were gathering above the low hills near Ardagh; their advance columns of slanting rain pillars were touching the pine trees in Leonard's Wood. Con had the good sense to walk away from the tirade; I felt it was dutiful to listen to my uncle.

It wasn't just the dereliction of duty I was being pilloried for, but more for the senseless cruelty to little birds. He sent me home and I went in shame and consternation. Paddy Enright had finished by telling me to stay in Kilquane in future. Every time I came to Lisnacullia I kept people idle. Halfway up the lane I heard my Aunt Hannah call me. She brought be back and gave me a glass of milk, a chocolate biscuit, and a great bowl of consolation. But the truth had dawned.

Connors died when I was in boarding school, in the same month that Mick Harrington passed away. By then the old man was astray in the head and would forget to feed the birds. Sylvester's people took the mule and Lar Tobin brought Langford to hang on his kitchen wall, within sight of the field in which he had been captured. I went to see Harrington during the Christmas holiday. He didn't know me from Adam; he was lying on the bed in the room where he kept Langford, a pair of dull clouded eyes fixed on the ceiling, his hands over the coverlet like parchment stretched across a framework. When he noticed that someone was in the room, he took me for a tinker come to steal. I talked to him about the birds and suddenly he seemed to remember. A flicker of light crept across his face like a sunray breaking through cloud.

'Do you want to hear Langford?' he whispered.

'Yes, I would.'

He whistled the opening notes, cocked to his head to the side and held up a finger to bid me listen.

'There,' he said. 'Now he's at it.'

The only sound in the room was the patter of rain against the window pane.

⋆   ⋆   ⋆

The goldfinch era stretches out long tentacles to me. When I hear a goldfinch song it will jerk my mind to that time, almost 50 years ago. In truth, I seldom hear the song now and rarely see flocks of goldfinch. Nor do I see their cousins the linnets, or dunlin or seskins. I walk through meadows and fields and never encounter a skylark. The order of nature seems to be gone askew.

Once more only did I own a goldfinch. I was directing a business-training course and discovered that one of the participants shared a similar rural background. When the training was over, he presented me with a goldfinch in a cage. I brought it home with the intention of releasing it; the bird had been recently trapped and could still cope with the wild. I awoke the next morning to an outpouring of glorious song that would have matched Langford. I was hooked again. But my wife and children harangued me every day; their hearts bled for the captive bird.

We took the cage into the back garden and opened the door. The bird flew first to Ned

Wall's lilac tree and then took off across the rooftops, rising, falling and chirruping. The line it flew would take it across the Shannon estuary and into West Limerick.

In another time it might have found the blacktop field in Waterfield.

10

I would never be a farmer. It was writ large in the scheme of things and no one ever queried it, least of all me. By the time I was ten, I had accepted it with the same certainty by which it had been ordained. It led me into conflict with my father because he expected me to work with similar energy and motivation as my brothers, who would inherit the land. I disliked the routine and drudgery of the work, and would avoid it whenever I could. My father was aggrieved by that, as if I were abdicating the very core of our traditional values.

When we were young, my father was lord of the farm. He decided when mowing, reaping, the spring sowing would begin. He would ask my mother's opinion but the discussion that followed, if there was one, was largely innocuous. My father allocated to himself the things he liked doing best, then my brothers took their preferences. The hired hand and I were left with the remainder, the thin end of the wedge. The hired hand obeyed with the convention of his position. I escaped.

My world was young then and filled with a

host of potential discoveries. Away to the west, beyond the boundary of Mannix's Folly, was a vast pristine territory, ripe for exploration. Down the road from our house were callows and gorse land: a fastness for snipe and wild duck, a hideaway for any youngster who had a mind to disappear. To the south was Lisnacullia and the Norman keep-tower. The tower was reached by a winding stairway with a marble column; green as the lichen on riverside stones. It crumbled at the second floor but from there all the flat plain was visible and near. Away to the east I could see the spire of Rathkeale church and the fertile rolling land of the Golden Vale.

I would lie awake in early morning light and plot my escape, listening to the riot of the sparrows that roosted under the thatch eaves. A blackbird, and a succession of its offspring, had chosen the palm tree outside the window to make a clarion to the dawn. There was a wood pigeon, cooing and thrumming in the pear tree at the bottom of the haggard. My father had a phrase for imitating the sound that the wood pigeon made: 'Take two pounds, Caitheen, take two pounds, Caitheen.'

Gradually, as the birds celebrated the dawn, the sounds of awakening came across the land. Sheepdogs barked and cows lowed. The geese and ducks in the fowl-house set up a cacophony for freedom. Jimmy Barrett's shadow passed by the window; my mother started the fire and went out to meet her round of chores. She was almost running by the time she reached the back porch.

Dawn in rural Ireland is the most beautiful time of the day. It comes out of its haze cocoon, cleansed and smelling of perfumed freshness, as if every morning was a re-creation. There were sights at dawn that never appeared again until the day died: foxes slinking along hedgerows, making for the sanctuary of their covert; cavorting rabbits in a colony, meadows blackened with crows like newly-spread manure. All the wild was abroad in that safe period before hostile man made his appearance. When I fished once at break of day on the banks of the Deel, I saw an otter and her brood. They were diving off a flat stone in the middle of the river, pushing each other in, squabbling and playing. I realised that day that I may never see the moment repeated, but I also knew that I was privileged, for few had ever seen.

But I seldom went at dawn. I rarely arose until all the others had gone from the kitchen; like my father, I too, was a bad riser. He would come to the bedroom door, lecture me about being slovenly and lazy, and contrast me with the sons of other fathers, who were dutiful and grateful, and who were long gone to the fields.

It didn't matter, he told me, that I was destined to walk a different road. While I was under his roof, I should work like the rest. I can see the sense of that now, but back then the recurring accusations of slothfulness and ingratitude only strengthened my resolve to get away. While the birds sang adoration to the dawn and Jimmy Barrett's shadow heralded the opening of another day, they brought visions of eternal turnip drills and never ending swarths of mown hay.

My mother always asked me where I was going and I told her nowhere. She then made a half-hearted plea, for peace sake, as she called it. They were busy in the fields, the weather was promised to break; I could do what I liked on the morrow. But we both knew that the petition was a ritual and she never pursued it. My father would say in the daily tirade that I regarded myself as a cut above everyone else. Far from it; the opposite was true. I felt isolated from and inferior to those who, like most of my contemporaries, had a natural affinity with the land and the rigours of its demands. That to me was the ultimate reason why I would never make a farmer, far more that the scheme that was ordained within my family. I grew up knowing little — nor did I want to know — about the lore of the land. I could not cope with its rhythms or routines. It set me apart; it brought me no solace. I could only escape.

So, most mornings, I whistled up the pack of dogs and went west. We went by the Hill field where there was a ruin of an old house. It was hidden by the highest part of the boundary wall, and the briars and bushes that had grown out of its desolation. The folklore said that a family had lived there, with the same name as ours, offspring perhaps of the original brothers who had settled the land. I had found the bowl of a clay pipe where the hearth had been and a bottle with a glass stopper that looked like a child's marble, and probably was. When the bottle was upturned, the marble fell snugly into the neck. I never believed the story that people had lived there for it looked more like a habitation for cattle and pigs. But when the records were researched, many years later, the folklore was proven right.

In front of that ancient dwelling was a large rock; testimony to my father's brush with death. He had been attacked by his bull and was helpless on the ground, with the animal's forelegs on his chest. Our next-door neighbour, Thomas, hearing the bellows of the enraged bull, drove it off with his dog and pitchfork. Frustrated, the bull attacked the rock and rolled it twenty yards from the ditch. Thomas died of a heart attack in the year I was born, while he was working in one of our fields. The field had become a jungle of ferns and low bushes and was swarming with rabbits. We called it the Ferny field. Once we had passed the ruined house, the dogs took off in chaotic abandon. I stood on the far side of the stone wall, fearful of the ghost of the man with the weak heart who had saved my father. I said a prayer for the soul of dead Thomas and another in gratitude for my father's life.

The old ruin was a great place to hide. No one ever went near it because those who had died there during the Great Famine were reputed to be buried beneath the floor. Death, burial and the paranormal were inextricably woven in our minds. Every house had its own repertoire of supernatural stories and were exported from one kitchen to another. After some hair-raising account of a dead body rising, which left us hushed and grim, I would be afraid to enter the darkness of the parlour.

For many years I skirted the Ferny field, the place where Thomas died. Yet I was never bothered by the ruined house. I hid my snares there and the short throwing-sticks that we used for rabbit hunting. There was a rusted sheet of galvanised iron lying on the ground, and when it rained, I fitted it over the corner where the walls met and shivered with the comfort of snugness when the rain pattered overhead. I sat in that spot for hours, read, and contemplated. I kept the paperbacks there that Paddy Mangan had given me. In a crevice between the stones I had hidden the most wonderful book of all, about Camelot and King Arthur and his Knights of the Round Table.

I had to hide the books because my father believed them to be a major contributor to the malaise that was affecting me. He had nothing against reading; my mother read every moment she could. That was fine, but when the books drove a youngster astray in the head, and filled him with such distraction that he never heard the questions repeatedly asked of him, it was time to call a halt.

* * *

We had a name for every field. We cut across the Grove Garden, the dogs and I, and into the grove itself. It had been planted at the bottom end of the Creagh marsh where old

Absalom had built his fishpond with the island in the middle. Long before my time, and after the demise of the Creaghs, the parish priest and his curate had lived in the estate house. They made the journey to the new church in Coolcappa, which my grandfather had helped build in 1878, on horseback or by carriage. The carriage ruts were still visible in the grove, as was a pair of ornate stone piers, now encased in the wall. In my forties, when I became disenchanted with aspects of my inherited faith, those piers would symbolise it. They were the twin portals of power and religion that had dominated our lives down the generations. When the portal that represented the Creaghs fell, how ironic it was that that power was supplanted by the church. The paradox of the priests in the estate house raised not the slightest whimper of protest, nor the timid framing of a question. My grandfather's generation was straddled with poverty. The priests, who preached the dignity and nobility of poverty, rode to church and lived in feudal splendour in the house of the landlord.

The grove was a miniature rain forest. The undergrowth was lush, tangled and barely penetrable. The dogs loved it because it held the promise of more exotic game than the everyday rabbits. At one time there were three badger setts there, outside each one a little mound of debris. 'The badger is the cleanest animal of all,' ran Miss Abigail's saw; 'he cleans out his bed every day.' And then she would add, in that acid throwaway that marked most of her observations, 'which is more than I can say for you lot or those that whelped you.'

The badger setts excited the dogs. They yelped, growled and worked themselves into a frenzy, tearing at the roots that criss-crossed the entrance of the holt. They abandoned me. Only Towser, our aged sheepdog, followed in halting indecision. Every time I looked back, he was stopped with one front paw raised. When I was out of his sight he returned to the pack.

Beech, larch and sycamore had raised a canopy over the tangled undergrowth. The grove was impassable except for the track that the cattle had worn, as they languished from the warble fly and the heat of summer. This was the favourite hiding-place of our horse, Paddy, when Bill O'Donnell tried to catch him of a Sunday. I often stayed there for long periods, hiding behind the bole of a beech, watching the display of birds and animals. A pair of tawny owls roosted on the naked branch of a decayed sycamore. I listened for the sound of a weasel hissing; our folklore was filled with stories about it. There was one about a man who had killed a weasel litter. Fearing retaliation, he had barricaded his house and closed up every possible entrance. But the weasel crawled through the keyhole, severed the jugular vein of the man in his bed, and sucked his blood. My father had once seen a weasel pack bury one of its members. He prayed that he had gone unnoticed, for those who disturbed a weasel funeral paid for it with their lives. When I was with Bill Hodge, checking his rabbit snares, we saw a weasel mesmerising a rabbit. The weasel had laid a trail of scent around it and the paralysed rabbit stood in the centre of the circle. When we had driven the weasel away, the rabbit was still motionless with petrified fear.

Paddy Danaher had died in the autumn of my eighth year. It was surprising how his cottage had survived since then. The thatch was sagging in the middle, but the windows were still intact, as was the little picket fence that surrounded his garden. The front door hung ajar, creaking in the breeze. Opposite the cottage was the crumbling ruin of Absalom's manor. Once they had occupied opposite ends of life's unequal status. Danaher's antecedents had lived there on sufferance; their duty was to open and close the manor gate, and if they weren't at their station when the carriage came through, they were threatened with expulsion.

It was small wonder, my father used say, that all the Danahers were astray in the head. The Danaher I knew must have been the epitome of them all — stone mad, as our neighbours would describe it. His white hair had stood on end, as if shot with static, but it was the eyes that terrified me. They were like those of a predatory bird, staring without a blink, boring through my forehead. Suddenly they would fill with the fire of violent anger and his hands would clench and unclench.

Danaher lived on rabbits and had fixed in his mind that all territory within a square mile of his cottage was his exclusive hunting domain. Bill Hodge was his mortal enemy. Danaher would come by our yard on his way to do battle with Hodge, and the air would be full of his fury. He cursed and swore and used that dreadful soldier's word that Miss Daisy had warned me about. He was going to murder Hodge: he would string him up by the balls, hang, draw, and quarter him and then bury him in quicklime. And if that wasn't enough, he'd bate the living shite out of him.

My father had bought hay one summer in the field next to the cottage. I was sent down for a gallon of water when the day came very hot and the hay turned crisp in the swarth. Danaher was sitting before a roaring log-fire, wearing his topcoat. The room was filled with smoke and he looked like a dervish as it swirled around his head. He sprang from his chair when he saw me standing in his doorway, picked up the fire tongs, and ran at me. 'Get the hell out of here, you hoor's melt! This is what I'll give you; the tongs across your arse.' I ran, as my father would say, like a scalded cat.

Time was when he used populate my nightmares. It was always Danaher in the central role, no matter what ghoulish drama was playing inside my head. Trolls and ogres had Danaher's profile, the banshee had his hair standing on end, the weasel that wriggled through the keyhole to suck my blood had his face. I was still timorous, peeping through the sagging door of the cottage, though Danaher was four years dead. Everywhere was covered with dust, and the cobwebs reached down from the thatch like trailing catkins. The backless chair was still beside the fireplace; a neck-collar and donkey's straddle were fixed to a batten on the chimneybreast. I could feel his presence, though I knew that he was only bones in an unmarked plot in Kilbrathern graveyard.

One year later the cottage had vanished. Someone took the stones to build a wall. The picket fence rotted back into the soil, grasses and briars grew up through the flagstones, and all that was left was a mound. I have come to know those mounds well. Every time I walk in the quiet fields I see them. There is one forming now where our house once stood. They are the graves of dead generations; the unlettered tombstones of their time and place. There will never again be houses in such locations for their time has come and gone.

In the final pages of his book about the Blasket Islands, *An tOileánach*, the author, Tomas Ó Criomhthainn, explains his reason for writing it. He wanted to give people an understanding of what life was like on the island, 'because our likes will never be there again'. Those sentiments are equally true of my father's generation and of mine. Our time too has passed; the way we lived then has gone forever.

★ ★ ★

To the rear of Absalom's manor house was a high stone wall, enclosing a deer park. That was another phase of ostentation in the social history of landlordism; when deer parks went out of vogue, they were turned into kitchen gardens. Those stone walls were the last vestige of Creagh glory and would have endured but for the ivy that colonised the mortar joints and let in the damp.

Charlie Dunne and I had fled the school playground when we heard the hunting horn in Cooltomin. We ran through the lands of Mount Henry and into the grove by the priests' carriageway. Charlie loped like a gazelle ahead of me; he had the long legs of his father and uncles, who were famed athletes in their day. As we neared the ruin of Absalom's manor house, the hounds were in full cry. We knew they would come by Danaher's cottage because the fox would head for the covert nearby. That would be its undoing: Danaher was employed by the hunt to close the entrance to the dens.

We saw the fox come up the bank of the stream and along the avenue of elms. It was nearing the end of its run: its head was low, tongue fully extended, the rib cage filling and emptying like an overworked bellows. Then it did an extraordinary thing. It climbed up the stone wall where the arched gateway had fallen, ran along the top, and disappeared into a patch of ivy about a hundred yards away. The hounds milled around the archway, yelping and snarling in disarray. The red-coated rider with the bugle in his hand asked if we had seen the fox. We both knew it would be worth half-a-crown. I struggled with my dilemma but Charlie had no such qualms.

'What fox, sir?'

The hounds continued to mill and a few riders galloped around the perimeter of the wall. Eventually the whip called the dogs to pack and they headed for the covert. We both later made half-a-crown each: Charlie opened a gate for a lady on side-saddle and I chased and caught a riderless horse. We were full of admiration for the cunning fox who had duped the hounds and we couldn't wait to share the news. But we got a very bad reaction. Few in the schoolyard had any sympathy for the fox. Someone told Miss Abigail and she put us facing the wall for one full day. We had been deceitful in the smart way we had answered the huntsman and that was worse than a lie. Deceit was evil, the product of conniving people without truth or honour. But worse, by our deceit we had caused the fox to live merrily on. He would father brood upon brood to pillage scores of fowlhouses.

I think often of Charlie Dunne. He reminds me of the bad side of rural Ireland in those days: the sundering of human blood ties, the exodus from hearth and country. Charlie left Coolcappa when he was sixteen, a raw gangling youth with long legs, going with his mother in the pony and trap to Ballingrane railway station, and from there to the boat in Dun Laoghaire. He was cast suddenly into the maelstrom of an utterly different life, without friends, contacts or privilege, because being Irish was not a reference. But he grafted and persisted, coped with the pain of isolation, and built a good life. Charlie's story is repeated a thousand times by those who went before him and went after, by kids from the Long Road and the road to Creeves, from Rathreigh, the Pike, and Coolcappa. They were pieces of flotsam coming to shore in Liverpool, New York and Sydney.

Charlie could run like the wind. I would start at Reidy's gate, he at the church gates, 50 yards behind. He passed me out at Leonard's as if I were stopped; a hare to my tortoise. I would find him sprawled on the grassy knoll opposite old Ned Barrett's shop, chewing a rib of grass, without the slightest sign of exertion. It was in his blood to be a runner. Charlie had an uncle in the Palestine police and another in the British army in Shanghai. While they were home on holidays they persuaded Jimmy, Charlie's father, to enter a sports meeting in Foynes. The brothers were hot favourites, but Jimmy, without training or technique, beat them both.

Miss Abigail had a frightful animosity towards the Dunnes. Charlie avoided most of it because he was an altar boy; he would be gone for part of the morning to minister to Father O'Connell. But his brothers who followed him, Kieran and Patrick, suffered grievously. Jimmy was a kind, patient man, cast in forbearance, but eventually the treatment of his sons got the better of him. He tore into the schoolroom one morning, the fire of battle in his face. I had never seen Miss Abigail cowed before, but that day she was speechless and wan in the presence of such anger and the threat of retribution. When she had recovered, she sought the escape route of the bully. It was all a fabrication; she had never laid a hand on Kieran, or called him the vile insulting names that Jimmy had quoted. And then she turned to me for collaboration.

'You tell him, tell him. Did I ever mistreat his son?'

I was dumbfounded. Kieran was three classes behind me but it seemed, once more, that I had been chosen to be the scapegoat. The twin horns of a horrible dilemma were being thrust at me. Part of me wanted to relate it as it happened: the insults, the beatings, the hours of vilification. But the stronger part, the fear bordering on terror, opted for discretion.

'No,' I stammered, 'you never did.'

Jimmy looked at me with compassion for my plight.

'What else could the poor boy say?'

The genes of industry were strong in the Dunnes. They emigrated and did well. Kieran and Patrick joined the British police and rose through the ranks. Between them they had more humanity and decency than Miss Abigail had to the power of infinity.

★ ★ ★

I went towards the covert of Lissocolagh, which stood like the remains of an ancient settlement in the middle of the plain. It occupied almost an acre of ground — a great tangle of briar, gorse and stunted trees. The covert was home to fox and badger, pheasant and woodcock. Around its perimeter was a network of forms and runs, woven by rabbits — so many that the grass around the rim was cropped bare in a ten-foot wide swath.

Lissocolagh belonged to the Cregans whose home was the furthest outpost in my western route of diversion. I walked by the edge of the covert. Because it had once been an earthen ditch, the young ash trees grew horizontally out of its base and then turned upwards to reach for the light. It was the place to find the makings of a hurley. This was where Kieran cut his hurling stick and worked it with an axe and a glass scraper until it became a primitive relative of the real thing.

The Cregans were an Irish version of landed gentry. They had a beautiful house set far in from the road, commanding a vista of gently rolling hills and woodland dells. So many of the great houses seemed to have that kind of placement in common: taking full advantage of vista and landscape. But it wasn't so much that their owners chose the right location, rather did they work on it, year in, year out, to embellish the site until it looked like a perfect gem of nature's handiwork.

The Cregans had a passion for horses. The half-bred hunter was the status symbol of that time and qualified the Catholic gentry to approach the margin of the planter landlord class. But they would always stand on the verge; they could ride to hounds, pay their subscriptions to the hunt, be droll characters out of Somerville and Ross, but never enter the fold. It was a twilight state because the Catholic gentry were regarded by the rest of us as interlopers, reneging on their own kind.

One day, Richard, the eldest son of the Cregan family, announced to Miss Abigail that he had ridden his pony to the hunt the day before and that a lady from the Wyndham-Quin party had chided him for wearing his Sunday suit. Then she gauged his measurements with her riding crop and promised that she would search an old closet and find him a more appropriate outfit. Every emotion that passed through Miss Abigail's mind could be read on her face like a map. We were experts at deciphering them. At first she was enthusiastic; the Cregans were distant relatives of hers, but the connotation of cast-offs sent her into a fury. The arrogance of those people, she railed, offering rags of charity to a people who had been kings, princes and poets when the forerunners of the landlords were pirates and land robbers.

But it didn't stop Richard. I saw him at the next meet in Riddlestown, wearing jodhpurs and a green velvet jacket that was several sizes too large.

Owen was the Cregan I knew most of all. He was my age, round and plump, with a perpetual smile of angelic innocence, like a Cupid's face. Owen's disposition was in harmony with his appearance; he was constantly good-humoured, as if he was perfectly at ease with the world. We were friends and had been since the day the priest had come into the school, held a whispered and agitated conversation with Miss Abigail, and then called Owen to the front of the class. Without query, the young curate drew back his hand and struck Owen with force, turning the angel's face to fragments of shock and hurt. While he had been offering Sunday mass, the priest had spotted Owen smiling and winking at a little girl in the opposite aisle.

I walked home with Owen that evening, by Waterfield and Absalom's fish pond. All day a volcano of anger had welled up in me, which frightened me with its intensity and its implication of heresy. What the curate had done was barbarous. Owen was the most inoffensive lad. What else could he be for his age and his time and place? Something was seriously amiss, I thought, if men of Christ, of love and charity, could behave like fanatics and wreak their zeal on the powerless innocent. But the strangest thing of all that day was Owen himself. He had forgotten the incident a few hours later; his smile was shining forth.

There was nothing conventional about the

Cregans and I loved to go to their house in Ardlaman. But I went sparingly, as a kind of special treat to myself, because otherwise I would have destroyed the lure and wonder of the place. It seemed that their breakfast lasted all morning. Whatever time I arrived, there would be a place laid for me. I would sit at the great pine table and wonder at the regime of the house. The family came and went like house guests; I could discern no work pattern. I knew that George, the eccentric patriarch, was still in his room and would not appear until well into the afternoon. If the animal was close to the house, he would then saddle the horse, and ride over a portion of his land. But most likely, he would wheel out the bicycle, call for his crony Lanny, and they would head for the public house in Ardagh. They shared the bike. George would cycle for a mile and leave the bike against the hedge where Lanny would find it. He, in turn, would pass George on the road and leave the machine another mile further along.

George had his own quarters in the house: a room on the second floor filled with books and tack. It smelled of old wood and smoke and, even in summer, a peat fire used to simmer in the grate. Owen's mother would sometimes send me up there with toast and

247

marmalade for George's mid-morning snack and ask me to bring down the tray with the remains of the last meal. I would find it in the corridor in front of his room. It occurred to me then that he seldom left the room, except to partake in one of his excursions to the races or the daily trip to Ardagh. George Cregan was built like an aged, overweight jockey, with pronounced bowed legs, a perfect match for his Queen Anne chair. His face was browned, like well-used leather, and two of his fingers were missing.

In one corner of his room there was an easel which held a large cardboard chart. It was filled with cut out figures of soldiers, armoury and miniature flags. I was immediately drawn to it and George asked if I would like to study it. When I nodded, he led me to the easel, remarking that I was the first person who had ever wanted to know. The chart depicted the allied forces in the aftermath of the Normandy landings. He had flagged out the beaches — Juno, Sword, Omaha — each distinguished with emblems: Union Jack, Stars and Stripes, and Maple Leaf. Hours of painstaking effort had been lavished on the chart; carving the figures, painting uniforms on the tiny soldiers, decorating aircraft and tanks.

I was amazed at the enormity of the task

and its unique endeavour. No wonder that no one had shown any interest. In our world of the daily grind, it was an indulgence in an exotic flight of fancy; a whim of the privileged eccentric with nothing better to occupy hands and mind.

George put me sitting by the fire and read to me from the book of his life. He had gone to a Jesuit boarding school and hated every minute of it — not the learning, for he enjoyed all that, but the silly discipline that the regime demanded. Except on the playing field, the students were not allowed to run. They had been compelled to walk with decorum everywhere else — corridors, stairways, the main concourse. The angels, they were told, little invisible creatures of God, inhabited those places, and unruly boys could crash into one and break off one of its wings.

George slipped out one night to skate on the frozen lake. He was caught and beaten. He ran away. In Sackville Street, in Dublin, he went up to a British army-recruiting sergeant, lied about his age, and became a soldier in the Great War. George fought at the Somme and survived it by accident. His gun-barrel exploded, severing the index and middle fingers of his right hand. The accident was real, George assured me. It was a common occurrence for a soldier to deliberately shoot off a finger, be invalided out of the army and qualify for a pension. He wandered about the towns of England in the years after the war and then came home to Ardlaman.

Ardlaman had seen the best of its days by then. George and his sons would preside over its downfall; indeed would hasten its end. He was unconventional, a kind of rural bohemian and his sons inherited the behaviour. George could not tolerate the predictability of farming; the eternal routine that ordained every day and made men a servant to its rigours.

Sometimes, in later years, I would go to Ardlaman when Owen was running it, to help with the harvest. I would have to wrest him from the bed and force him into the cornfield. In mid-afternoon, George would join us and take a turn at some of the work. And then suddenly he was gone. I would catch a glimpse of him, heading out the avenue between the trees, making for Ardagh with Lanny. Entertainment always took precedent over work. If the Limerick meeting fell on the only fine day of the month, George would go to the races. And so would Owen.

Though they walked and cycled together every day and sat in the pub for hours,

George and Lanny rarely spoke to one another. Lanny was a dour crusty man who hawked, spat and broke wind with the same regularity as he drew breath. In the beginning I wondered what George and he had in common until I realised that it was simply the public house and the bicycle arrangement that shortened the road to Ardagh. George's soldier's pension funded them both. He was well read, had words at will and they poured out in cascades when he was fortified by a drink or two. In the pub he might find a kindred soul, an old soldier or a traveller who had been to distant places that George knew or had read about.

When the pair were old, I stopped at the pub with my brothers on our way home from a funeral. George and Lanny were sitting at the same table, deep in silence. The publican told us that they had had a row, hours before, about the battle of Clontarf. George maintained that it had been fought on a Good Friday. Lanny told him he was a fool, that every Christian knew it was Holy Saturday. George brought me over to the table to arbitrate and when I agreed with Good Friday, Lanny slapped his glass on the tabletop and stormed out. We were all jumped up beyond our station, he told us as he left, every man jack of us, showing off our bit of education and contradicting decent people.

We brought George home that night because Lanny had taken the bicycle. George took us into his room. The fire was banked in the grate. He poked it into flame and banged on the floor with his stick. A few minutes later we heard the tea tray being laid on the floor outside, followed by a knock on the door. We stayed for hours while he regaled us with war stories and escapades from his youth. Then he switched to horses and one animal in particular, a mare called Hope and Glory, the best little mare he had ever thrown a saddle on. In the corner of the room, opposite the easel and the chart of the Normandy landings, he had a writing bureau with a rolled up top. He rummaged in the drawer and brought out a faded silver cup. They had won it, he and Hope and Glory, at a point-to-point meeting in Kilmallock.

I was always struck at the similarity between George and Owen. Owen could have been his father as a young man: the same free spirit and bohemian approach to life. Owen missed school regularly, sometimes for weeks on end. He would set out from Ardlaman with good intentions but be distracted by something he saw along the way. John Shaughnessy's horses especially diverted him.

They might be grazing in the field as he passed by Waterfield, or grouped around the trunk of the chestnut tree like the spokes of a wheel. Owen would stand and watch them; imagining an Ardlaman colt at Ascot, or re-living Hope and Glory at Kilmallock. Sometimes he would rush at the horses and drive them into a high-kicking stampede. He did it to hear them snort, to see their wheeling action and to watch the muscle spasm beneath their shimmering coats.

They had a strange relationship, father and son. No matter what we talked about, Owen would bring his father into the conversation. One would have thought that his father was the very font of greatness. But the core of the stories had been gleaned from other sources and embellished by Owen. They seldom spoke to each other. It seemed that Owen had established his father as his role model, in the same way that many another youngster would try to emulate some distant hero whom he had never known.

No one in that family seemed to have any relationship with George. He was the odd one, isolated away in his room. When Owen grew older, his model father became for him an object of ridicule. The distant hero became a bagatelle, and the glory days had the hollow ring of sounding brass.

The brothers never agreed. They alternated between emigrating and returning home. When Richard came back from England, Owen would be gone the following day. Eventually Richard stayed in Ardlaman and Owen took up permanent residence in London. Adulthood became a copy of his youth. He made money and lost it in that same 'come day, go day' attitude that had been formed in Ardlaman, just as he would walk away from a field of mown hay to join me in a rabbit hunt.

Owen has been dead for more than twenty years. He died in a condemned London basement, alone and penniless. But he is forever fresh in my mind. I see him sprawled in the shade of a hedge on a summer's day, his face alight with innocence, the stories of Ardlaman glory tumbling from his cherubic lips.

★　★　★

From Ardlaman I looped around by Hallinan's farm. Tom Hallinan was a Renaissance man; it was he who brought the miracle of horseless machinery to our quiet backwater. Machinery was a wonder then; the slightest advance in technology was heralded with awe-struck appreciation: carts shod with rubber wheels, the wheel plough, a machine for digging out potatoes.

I was in the queue at Gur Adams's forge when I first heard the whirr of the horse-drawn reaper in Magner's cornfield. There were seven of us waiting for service and, in a body, we crossed over the fields to see the new wonder at work. It was an amazing sight. We were, like stout Cortes, 'silent, upon a peak in Darien'. Here was a piece of equipment with revolving arms like a miniature windmill, which dropped the mown corn on a canvas sheet, took it into the maw of the machine, and spun it out a few seconds later, bound in a sheaf. It was a quantum leap. When Kilquane corn was ripe, we needed a small army of binders to work the mown row. We never had enough help so the driver had to alight at the end of the row, and take a turn at binding, until the way was clear for the next cut.

Dinny Lynch was with us that day at the forge. He was the most amazed of all. He took off his cap, wiped the moisture from his forehead and said, 'Boys, boys. What will the 'hoors' think of next?'

Tom Hallinan shattered our wonder. What we thought was a quantum leap was just a short pause in evolving innovation. He brought the first tractor into our community.

It was an ugly monster with great iron wheels; they were shod with steel cleats that cratered the earth and tore up the surface of the white road. Tom was a big man, who bore his size in an awkward-looking way. But, in sharp contrast, he walked with dainty steps, as if he were constantly seeking an even spot on which to put his feet down.

Threshing days ran every mood and quirk in Tom's personality. He reminded me of the caricature face on the cover of the Mac's Smile razorblade, in vogue at that time. Viewed from one direction, the face was scowling and beetle-browed; on the other, it was smiling expansively like the man in the moon's. When the thresher purred, he was the soul of good humour and fellowship, but when the purr changed and signalled an imminent break, his face blackened. He would arrive at the verge of explosion as the break continued to outwit him, and eventually could contain his frustration no longer. Tom kicked at the great iron wheels and beat at the canvas belt that slithered like an anaconda from the tractor to the thresher.

'Bitch, you hoorin' bitch,' he roared at the thresher. 'I'll show you who's the boss.'

We took it all in bemused tolerance for threshing was a red-letter day, not to be spoiled or dampened by the antics of a volatile man.

I watched the progress of the tractor and thresher from the incline of the Clover field. The TVO engine belched smoke like a tramp steamer and roared with the volume of an angry dinosaur. Its progress was slower than a horse and cart. The wooden thresher tottered and weaved behind the monster with every shift of the ground and every rising breeze. It would take an hour to make the trip from Mrs Den's haggard to ours. By the time the thresher had arrived at the top of our avenue, and was manoeuvred into the haggard, the waning October sun would be setting behind the Carrickerry hills. It was dark when the machine was set in place and anchored to the ground, but the word would be out: Hallinan was in Nestor's haggard. The news went from house to house like a bush telegraph and men changed their plans for the morrow.

They came up the avenue; a score or more, in twos and threes, pitchforks on their shoulders. Their chatter was loud in the brisk sharp morning and the light of anticipation was in their faces. They would work hard, but the toil would be mingled with fun and the odd ribald story. There would be fresh meat instead of the usual hard bacon, frequent mugs of tea, steaming scones, a few bottles of stout.

My mother built a second fire in the outhouse to cater for the crowd and, like my father at the haymaking, seemed to be consumed with a fever of work. Her kitchen and her cooking would be at stake. She muttered to herself as she went from chore to chore, trying to remember the pattern from last year. Flavin ate no meat; the substitute fried eggs should be lightly turned so that the yoke remained runny. Otherwise, Flavin would pick at his bread, leave the egg untouched, and the criticism would filter back about the woman in Kilquane who didn't know how to fry an egg. Hynes wasn't talking to Regan, so those two couldn't be put sitting together. Donovan had a passion for jam; he would plaster it on his bread an inch thick. When he had had his fill of bread, he spooned the jam from the pot into his wide-opened mouth, as if he were a guest at a Roman orgy. Once I heard a man describe him. 'Donovan ates no butter, but you couldn't keep jam drawn to him.'

All day long the thresher whirred, the air pulsing with the vibration. The tractor belched smoke and chaff wafted in the breeze like a snow swirl. Then everything would stop when a part broke. Hallinan danced like a shaman in exasperation.

Our family had gone into threshing folklore because of the beehives. Paddy Enright had given my father a couple of swarms and he had placed them in the shelter of the ash tree in the haggard. The whirring thresher inflamed the bees; they surrounded the machine and the work team in a buzzing frenzy. Many men were stung that day. Hallinan was pierced on the lobe of his ear and on the tip of his nose. He shut off the engine, and went into the kitchen to join the casualties being treated with my mother's bleaching blue.

'Bees, bees, my bloody arse,' he kept on saying to my mother, 'I wouldn't give a rat's fart for all the bees in China.' He observed that people should stick to things they knew about and not be messing around with fancy notions. Every year afterwards he refused to set the machine until he had established that the beehives had been removed.

★   ★   ★

From Hallinans I followed the stream until it branched and formed a tiny island. I had found a nest of coot there and kept the secret. If I shared it, the word would go out, and someone would breathe on the eggs. Then the adult coot would forsake the nest, or so we believed. I watched that nest from the far bank, creeping through the fellestrumps, peeping through the triangular petals of the flowers. But some creature of the wild was watching too and raided the nest, perhaps a magpie or a grey crow. I shared in the traditional hatred for those birds. Both were scavengers. The grey crows gouged out the eyes of new-born lambs. The magpies, more devious and cunning, would also discover the hen laying beyond the farmyard and pillage the eggs. Jimmy Barrett kept a shotgun on the ledge above the front door. The moment a magpie rattled its presence, he would rise from the table and go off in armed pursuit. The English introduced the magpie into Ireland and we believed that it was a deliberate act, another calculated infliction on a hard-pressed peasantry.

The left fork of the stream took me west of Mannix's Folly. When the hunger took me, I would walk through the farmyards and the dogs announced my presence. I would be brought in for tea and a slice of brown bread. If my timing was right, I was invited to share the midday meal. That generosity was then as simple and natural as breathing. No one — tramp, tinker man, low born or high — would come within the perimeter of a homestead without being invited to break bread. If one refused, it was a slight on the spirit of the offer. I never refused because I had deliberately come that way and provoked the dogs to announce me. I had the appetite of youth's spent energy; currant cake and scalding hot tea never tasted as well as in another man's kitchen.

My parents played cards in May Den's house. All round Kilbrathern card playing was rife. They played a version of forty-five, called forty-one, because the best trump was valued at eleven. The youngsters in that community were raised on cards. I have always got great pleasure from watching the perfection of an art, no matter how trivial it may be regarded. Later in life, when I had the wit to appreciate it, I used marvel at how good those players were. No matter what turn the game took, how finely it was balanced, they seemed instinctively to know the correct card to play. All that is gone now: the card schools, the post mortems, the vocabulary of the game.

'Why did you hit me, Mick, and I going in my place?'

'Spades for slaves and let them go dig.'

'Count it now, let ye.'

'Nothing for the bonham but the jack.'

The bonham was the ace of hearts and the

jack the knave of trumps.

May Den had a heart of gold. The moment the dogs barked, she would come out to the yard and lead me in by the arm. She always seemed to be baking; her fingers were covered in dough, an eternal flour smudge smeared her forehead. I was put sitting by the fire, on a converted milking stool, and offered a steaming corner of freshly baked bread that had been cooling on the windowsill. A tumbler of Nash's lemonade followed, brought out from the parlour, and as I left, May Den would give me a florin.

I came home by Coley Well. It was a holy well dedicated to a patron saint. The word patron, in our vernacular, was pronounced as pattern. The water issued out from a rock-fissure in Egan's marshy field, and formed a crystal pool, still as if it were ice-bound. I would study my face in the water and be reminded of Narcissus, who fell in love with his own reflection. When one of us fell sick, a messenger would be dispatched to Coley to bring home the curative water. Once it had been a place of pilgrimage. I found it hard to believe that for it looked so insignificant. But I had found a letter that a youthful friend of my father had written to him from New York. He wrote about the pattern day at Coley: the circle of cobbled stones around the well where the pilgrims would walk in prayer, the rustic seats where they sat in contemplation or watched the passing parade. This little well, forlorn and forgotten, had once hosted a major event in the heyday of my father's youth.

From Coley, slaked and mindful of Narcissus' foolishness, I made my way to Kilquane. All around were the sounds of the gathering evening: voices in the distance urged cows to the milking field, sheepdogs barked. The curlews sent melancholy tones of loneliness across the flat plain. In the skyline, above Harold's Wood, a flock of rooks flew ragged formations above the pine trees. I looked for the face of God in the mackerel sky and hoped He would smile at me. I had yet to face the wrath of my father.

11

In the early days of my mother's marriage, her sister Hannah spent long periods in Kilquane. She met her future husband when she was walking out of Maggie Barrett's shop and he was going in. Hannah was laden with a jug and some cups and Paddy Enright advised her to mind the crockery. That innocuous icebreaker led to her elevation as mistress of Lisnacullia. For years, their wedding portrait adorned one shelf on the mantelpiece above our parlour fireplace. Hannah was a ravishing young woman then, sending out a glowing vitality through the sepia tone. She sat on a chaise longue and her husband stood behind, lightly resting his hand on her shoulder. I used study that picture intently. It was the one that first evoked my dislike for photographs and their fossilised representation of fleeting youth and vanished beauty.

Lisnacullia was far in from the road. It was hidden in the valley that the ice had carved millennia before. That valley flowed all the way from Leonard's house, weaving and undulating like the contours of a great serpent. I used halt in wonderment of that valley as I came the unfamiliar way by Connor's land. When I climbed the hayshed, and looked out of the ventilation window in the gable of the barn, it was flat land all round, broken here and there by clumps of trees and hazel thickets. The geography of the valley was a new discovery.

I imagined that I was the one who had found this unknown territory. It was visible only when one breasted the slope at the first gateway. Then it was all laid out below: the white house in the lowest place in the valley, the Norman keep tower rearing above it like some gigantic custodian. From Keneally's house to where the white road marked the end of the valley floor near Flavin's, the passing of the glacier was written in dramatic landscape etching. Fields folded to the southeast; the rising ridge ran the length of the serpent's back, the flat places on the ridge plateau held the homesteads, Mullane's and Costello's further on.

On the valley floor was the carved passage of a great river that had, for thousands and thousands of ice age years, flooded the plain like the Nile. The river had formed at the bottom of the glacier, and roared down the valley in times of spate, when the meltdown came. It must have covered most of the valley floor because I could still make out the original riparian boundary, far outstretched from the shallow bed that now contained its flow. When the heavy rains came, Con and I would wade across the flooded land as if it were a shallow sea. The waters teemed with life then: flocks of coot and moorhen bobbed like wreckage all over its surface; mallard and teal occupied one stretch of the shallow sea, as if the birds had agreed to a territorial covenant, flotillas of swans glided by in arched arrogance. Plover, feeding on the bounty of the overflow, covered the shoreline.

I vested Lisnacullia with an enveloping mantle of romantic chivalry and chained the image to my soul. It was Camelot. Around that time, because my school class had galloped ahead of the curriculum, Abigail ordered three copies of an extension reader called *Avalon*. For some reason, she believed she had received only two. I was able to bring the third copy home and keep it, hidden in the wire-mesh basket that hung from the parlour ceiling and which contained years of bills and receipts. That little book grew into a sesame of words and images. It lauded chivalry and honour, and our world still held association with those concepts, though there were limited occasions to practice them. It praised liberty and fraternity; great concepts which provoke men to war, but which are forgotten when the war is won.

On the first storey of the Norman keep-tower, it was easy to imagine that we dwelt in Camelot. This was the banqueting hall, with a great round table in the middle, where resplendent knights-in-armour revelled long into the night and their ladies, in ruffed finery, tripped delicately between the hall and their chambers. We had not realised then, Con and I, that the keep-tower had never been a castle; it was simply an outpost that held a small garrison and guarded the approaches to the valley. It had belonged to the MacSheehys, Scottish mercenaries known as gallowglass, who had been brought to Ireland by the later Norman wave.

The castle, as we called it, frightened the living daylights out of me. I would never go in there alone but I would hang about the walls, daring myself to enter. It was once an evil place; people had been killed before its gates. Above the main entrance, where the portcullis once had been hinged, I could see the marks of the boiling pitch that the defenders had rained on the attackers. There were great globules like petrified icicles protruding from the wall. Running like a chimney from the banqueting hall to the rock face on which the castle stood was the murder hole. We were told that people were thrown in there for all sorts of reasons; as serious as treachery, as frivolous as looking askance at a bad-tempered knight. It was small wonder that the castle was now populated with fairies and evil spirits.

I could never imagine entering the tower at night. But Con said he often did, to vet calving cows and minister to sick beasts. I wouldn't do it for all the gold in Africa. Hannah had stories about the place that would send shivers along my spine and into my sciatic nerve. Once, her husband Paddy had gone late at night to inspect a sick cow. As he approached the gate with the fearsome pitch marks, he heard sounds of revelry from the first floor. Suddenly the sounds changed to voices of anger and the clash of steel on steel. He put out his hand to draw back the door bolt and a voice commanded him to stay and state his business. He explained about the cow. The voice told him to go back and not to venture in if he valued his life, the cow would be looked after. When Paddy came back in the bright of dawn, the cow was munching happily at her stall, a healthy calf butting at her udder.

In the dead of night, Hannah said, when the wind was howling down the valley from Mullane's and the night was as black as ink, one could hear the clank of arms, the galloping of horses, and the shouts of battle borne on the wind. Elly Costello, who did odd jobs in Lisnacullia, wouldn't go near the castle, even in daylight. She said it was inhabited by a clan of fairies, who every now and then, like a swarming hive with a new queen, spread out to colonise old raths and new depressions amid the crags. She heard them playing their music as she went home in the darkness. If she hadn't blocked her ears, the music would have enchanted her and taken her in fairy-form to a distant rath.

Elly was a strange character, a little astray in the head, but harmless and mild-mannered. The only thing that provoked her was the mention of an ex-boyfriend called O'Donnell, who had jilted her. Sometimes Paddy Enright prevailed upon her to sing and as a special request to sing *O'Donnell Abu*. When she came to the line, 'On with O'Donnell then, fight the old fight again', she would stamp her foot and aim a clenched fist at whatever object was near at hand.

The first floor of the tower was reached by the spiral stairway, on steps that mail-clad Norman soldiers and servants had worn to a glittering blue-black sheen. Along the spiral was a column of green marble, fused with slivers of quartz, like blemishes in an aged skin. We thought the column was a work of art and marvelled at the skill that had crafted it, 700 years before.

Our journey always ended on the first floor, at the banqueting hall. It still held the remains of a great fireplace and opposite it, on the other wall, was the only window in the room. It looked out forever — to the hills above Ardagh and the grove of beech that clung to the horizon way away to the south. That place was called Knockaderry, my father told me. It was the place where the black-robed nanna in Barrett's house came from. I saw the grove every morning when I looked out my bedroom window. It stayed in my head like some navigational instinct, as if I were a migratory bird and the grove on the horizon was landfall. The clump of trees became a landmark of my time and place, a kind of standing stone, and it rooted me to the spot where I had grown up. It came with me to boarding school. When I woke in the morning, filled with misery and loneliness, that pine grove rushed headlong into my yearning. I promised myself that I would visit it and worship a little at the shrine it had become. The first morning of Christmas holidays, it was missing from the horizon. Someone had cut it down and I often wondered would the axeman, if he had known what it held and represented for me, have spared it.

Beyond the first floor, the spiral stairway was broken and crumbling. It didn't deter the hardy explorers, who sometimes came out to the tower on a Sunday and climbed to the top. I remember one, with a flowing crop of unkempt red hair, thin as a rail and the light of devilment in his eyes. He went up to the top of the tower as if he were a mountain goat and hollered wild Gaelic phrases in keeping with the cut of his features. He was a scholar, Paddy Enright told me, a brilliant young man from the Kerry home of the Geraldines. We heard later that he had fallen into the sea from a broken tower on the edge of a cliff. He was presumed drowned for his body was never found. I used look at his name scratched in the limestone of the door lintel and breathe a prayer for the soul of Gearoid Mac Gearailt. He must have been a little astray in the head, a youthful Paddy Danaher.

The Camelot phase passed on, and Con and I played handball in the banqueting hall. It was a kind of desecration. I thought no more of roasted flesh covered in red-hot pitch, or of the magic music of mischievous fairies passing from one rath to another. But I never placed my foot on the highest stone of the tower as the wild man from Kerry had once done. I had none of his flaunting bravery.

★　★　★

Lisnacullia was as different to Kilquane as chalk is to cheese. Most of the time Kilquane was raucous in its activity; its inhabitants came in and went at a furious pace about the kitchen and the backyard. There were rows and arguments; cattle lowed, pigs squealed. My mother rushed about in her frenetic energy, singing verses of songs one moment, shouting instructions the next.

In Lisnacullia I could hear the silence. I remember the first time I slept there, in one of the bedrooms above the main kitchen. Lisnacullia had two: one to cook and pass the working day in, the other to while away the leisure of the evening. I awoke with the sun streaming in the window. The foundation for the house gable had been wrestled out of a hillock, which now rose outside the bedroom, almost as high as the window itself. The sunrays hit the hill, flattened out and splashed into the room like the wash of a wave. It bathed everything in light: ceiling and ceiling boards, every stick of furniture and the bedclothes.

It wasn't the streaming light that struck me

the most. It was the silence. The farmyard was away from the house and here, in the brightness of morning, with the hillock like a sound insulator outside the window, the quiet was palpable. I could hear the sigh of the beech trees that bordered the field known as The Pound, hear a wood pigeon greet the morning. But it was the sound of the clock in the downstairs kitchen that soaked into my mind like a burrowing memory. I can hear it still, as plain as day, as it tocked in the downstairs room. I'll take it with me till the day I die.

House, land, and the organisation of both, ran like clock-work. You could set your timepiece by the movements of Paddy Enright. How I envied that routine, the certainty that work would finish on the appointed hour. Every evening, at the same time, Hannah sent the collie to round up the cows. When the cows were milked, the horses would arrive back in the yard. Of course, no organisation like that comes about by happenstance. It was planned and organised and was built on the early start of the day.

Lisnacullia was a reading house too. The books were stacked in order on the windowsill of the main kitchen, or arranged with similar care in the press beside the fireplace. My father and Paddy Enright had once committed a preposterous act. They had taken the day off and brought their wives to Limerick city. While the women were looking at clothes, the men strolled into O'Mahony's bookshop. Paddy Enright bought *David Copperfield* and recommended to my father that he buy *A Tale of Two Cities*. No two books could have gone to such diverse locations. I would often pick up the *David Copperfield* in Lisnacullia and marvel at its pristine state. The comparison with the other book was stark and desolate. *A Tale of Two Cities* had gone through the wringer of our philistine behaviour. The binding had been ripped off, the dog-ears loosed from page corners, there was a tea-ring stain, like a sepia-toned worm, smack in the middle of the flyleaf.

Worse than the ravages of its handling, the book had been scrawled throughout with names and notations, little renditions of our emerging egos. My father, in a rare expression of literary ownership, had written on the flyleaf, 'Michael Nestor owns this book, bought and paid for with his own money'. My mother had chosen the final page to distinguish her background from our humbler one, 'Catherine Nestor, native of Killenoughty, Tory Hill, near Croom, County Limerick'. Mary, my second eldest sister, had merely written her name and address, but on the next line after 'Kilquane' had written 'Church View'. That had its origin in the time when my aunts were unmarried and lived in our house. Letters to my mother, from family and friends, had addresses with house names, 'Rose Cottage', 'Lake View', 'Blossom Hill'. Nothing would do the aunts but to be equally as imposing. One could rarely see the church from our house; it was hidden by Jimmy Barrett's barn, by hedgerows and clumps of trees. The quest for a religious reference and the pursuit of grandeur, made a nonsense of fact.

Billy, my eldest brother had many entries; I thought them clever and effected with the flair of the most sophisticated amongst us. 'Billy Nestor is my name, and lowly is my station. Kilquane is my dwelling place and heaven my expectation.' All of us who could write featured in some expression of ego and it would continue until the very last one had made her mark. The youngest of us, suffering the lash of Miss Abigail's tongue, had written, 'I am Nancy Esther Nestor, I'm the smartest of the lot, I'll show that strap Miss Abigail, I'm no scrapings of the pot'.

I have that book still. I read it, not for Dickens' towering tale but for our story.

The Sabbath in Lisnacullia was honoured

to the letter. I never knew the Enrights to work on Sunday, no matter what the weather. Every year, the sudden whirr of their mower would transfix my father, when the noise wafted across Kelly's hedgerows. For the first time, it seemed, he was aware that summer was upon us. Our fields weren't ready for the mower: they hadn't been enclosed in time and were still short of full growth. We hoped and prayed that the weather would come good when we were ready.

God has His fingers in His ears again because we were still haymaking in early August. Every year my father bought meadowing. He waited, interminably it seemed to us, for extra growth, and invariably the black clouds rolled in from the horizon, carrying their Atlantic deluge. We had warned him about the frivolous nature of August weather, but he steadfastly ignored us. There was one particular time when we were at work at the bought meadowing in Donovan's field, beside the road. A few days before we had turned the swarth into grass cocks because the day came wet, with a cloying mist. Now we were shaking them out again, turning the discoloured hay to the sporadic rays of a weak sun. People went by on the white road; the world and its mother, except us, were going to the pattern day in

Barragone. We were labouring like swains at a task that was at best only repetitive containment. Most likely it would rain and we would have to make those grass cocks again. The passers-by shouted greetings at us and wished God's blessing on the work. Their salutations were laden with the bonhomie of selfish complacency because their hay was safe in the barn. My mother was with us that day and she promised that come next year, if she lived for it, we would never again be shamed in August. But my father had a strategy to counter her vow. The next year he bought meadowing in a field that was far from the road.

How I hated Sunday work. It was the one day that I could never escape and that made it worse. I was cornered because that morning of religious practice kept us together. My father would make the announcement before we left for mass and never took his eyes off me as he spoke. Sometimes, I used to inveigle Hannah to ask me down to Lisnacullia and primed Con to fill out the details of the ruse. It worked only now and then because, loyal as she was, Hannah would be loath to scheme against her own kin. My brothers, who saw no reason why I should not share the burden of Sunday labour, watched me like security guards.

There was another thing about Lisnacullia that was even more phenomenal than the dedication to the Sabbath. On Mondays, about mid-morning, when she had the front kitchen to herself, Hannah would bring yesterdays clothes from the bedrooms and put them in readiness for the next Sunday. They were brushed, cleaned, creases ironed in, a fresh handkerchief replaced in her husband's jacket pocket. But here was an extraordinary thing. The Sunday shoes were polished and left waiting in gleaming splendour in the press beside the fire. I never saw Paddy Enright, his son or daughter, Bridie, polish a shoe. In our house my father was the only one for whom the shoes were polished, and usually by me. For the rest of us, searching for the tin of polish and finding it empty or tracing the last known whereabouts of the lone moth-eaten brush, were the bane of Sunday morning.

The press beside the fire in Lisnacullia was also an airing cupboard. The books that Hannah stacked there were warm to the touch. The press smelled of luxury and comfort: the tinge of camphor that mingled with the warmth gave out a scent of lilac. It must have seemed a vermin paradise to the field mice that found their way in there. But paradise veiled the hell of sudden death.

Hidden by the very shape of its improbability and camouflage was the most ingenious mousetrap. It looked, felt and smelled like an ordinary lump of wood. Four holes, widening into tunnels the diameter of a florin, led to a morsel of cheese where the tunnel ended. But just before the cheese, and hidden in a groove in the perimeter of the tunnel, was a sprung noose of fine-wire. The noose was held in place by strands of thread which prevented the mouse from getting at the cheese. The mouse chewed the thread, triggered the trap and was garrotted by the wire when it whipped upwards.

Hannah checked that mousetrap first thing every morning. In May and June, when it must have seemed to the mice that they had struck pay dirt in the airing press, all tunnels would be occupied with the hapless dead. Four more would follow during the night, and then the trap would lie idle, as if the truth about paradise had infiltrated the vermin world. Like most young fellows of my age, I was taken by the art and construction of the invention. When Hannah was out in the yard and I was alone in the kitchen, I would take out the block of wood and examine its demonic technology.

My reputation as a drone had taken deep root in Lisnacullia. I was never asked to help in the fields unless I volunteered and in normal circumstances I was unlikely to do that. Paddy Enright knew full well that if his son and I were thrown together, one of us would lead the other astray. When it happened he banished me from the yard and eventually extended the ban to anywhere around the vicinity of Lisnacullia. Hannah mediated on my behalf. Her husband compromised: if I wanted to keep Lisnacullia on my escape route, I should confine myself to the kitchen.

I used think that I was alone, in a world without humans. The clock ticked on the wall beating eternal harmonics into my memory. The swallows and the martins twittered in a discordant line on the wireless cable outside the window or screeched like keening women above the broken walls of the keep-tower. The wood pigeon cooed in the beech tree that grew out of the Pound field wall. A dog barked far away. All those sounds added to the silence: took it and shaped it into an intense depth, as if they were the bastion walls that enclosed it. I looked up from the book, suddenly conscious that the silence had risen all around me like lightened air and I was adrift in the wallow of the calm.

Maybe it was that same silence, that oasis of enclosed tranquillity, that beckoned the migratory birds to Lisnacullia before they reached other ports of settlement. Hannah brought tidings of the migrants' landfall on her visits to Kilquane. In the gathering darkness of early November frost, the wedge of greylag would settle on the overspill of the river, filling the air with a language that had echoes of snow-capped mountains and great oceans far away. The geese honked as they passed over Kilquane, but they were airborne then, flying the air thermals and the draughts far up. Above Lisnacullia the honk of the skein was deep-throated, full and apprehensive, as the flock circled for landing. Later days would bring gunshots in the darkness and in the early dawn. Near Rathkeale, in a place called Ballyanlin, the gunshots were a barrage. A smaller colony of Palatines had been settled on the banks of the Deel, on land that bordered on commons and the river's flood plain. They had been bivouacked in Blackheath Common in south-east London in 1709, while the British government and Queen Anne debated what to do with them. Someone had the idea that, instead of shipping them to the New Deutsch colony in America, where the German emigrants yearned to go, it would be more economical and expedient to ship them to Ireland. They were Protestant, expert farmers; they would make ideal colonists in a country that needed role models in tenantry and religion. Viscount Southwell of Rathkeale took the greater share and settled them on his estate; about 3,000 souls, with their rags, seedlings, and traditions, and each man with a gun bequeathed by Queen Anne. For 200 years those guns sounded on the flood plain of the Deel. The barrage went into the folklore: 'the 'queen annes' were at it this morning.'

'Swallow' was for us a collective name and included swifts and martins. They arrived in late spring, navigating through that incredible technology of instinct, which homed them to birthplace. The outriders of that African odyssey seemed always to find Lisnacullia, days before the migrating army located its resting places. The swallows are in, Hannah would tell us.

The effect on my father was like the first whirr of the mower. It silenced him in contemplative focus; he tilted his head, sucked in his breath, and directed his gaze at a blackened spar beneath the thatch. Summer was upon us. Despite all the longing and anticipation, the sustaining imagery over winter days and spring cold, the season had come like a thief in the night. Fields were water-logged, spring sowing lagged behind, the grass still held the browned ravages of rampaging winter. But God, maintaining His infinite cyclical order, had sent the avian scouts to tell us that summer was marching behind them. My father dragged his eyes from the blackened spar and thanked God that he had lived to see it.

Lisnacullia heard the first call of the corncrake and the cuckoo. Hannah would announce them like a look-out from a crow's nest. We had little affinity with the cuckoo, because it was a parasite. Miss Abigail was the instigator of our disdain for the cuckoo; she had put a slant on it which reflected the webbed intricacy of her republican mind. The cuckoo was an English bird. Of course, it went off to Africa to winter, but that merely demonstrated that the bird was cute. But wasn't it a perfect living analogy for the British and how they treated us? They took our land, they made us work it for them, they threw out the true-born, and replicated themselves through trickery. Perhaps it was the experience of my own position in Kilquane that left me with an unspoken regard for the cuckoo. I admired its ingenuity; it showed me that there were more ways than one to skin a cat. I kept that notion secret because it would be a prickly weed in the seed-bed of my time and place.

The corncrake was everywhere in summer

grass. I heard it before I went to sleep. I heard it in meadow and dale and marsh. I would wake in the middle of the night; hearing it crake, filling the darkness with the ratchet sound of discordant pain. For my father, the corncrake was the true bird of summer. I remember him stopping the mower and walking the square of hay that was still standing, to flush out the birds. When I slept in Lisnacullia, the corncrakes woke me several times at night. In the riparian margins of the little stream that ran by The Pound, the grass grew thick and high. Corncrakes lived there in colonies. Their craking is the lost sound of my time and place, a forlorn memory, carrying the awful sadness of wanton extinction. In all the images of passing time and change, I find none that hurts like the concept of extinction. It took millions of years to form and shape the corncrake, to harness the processes of selection and mutation and to fix a pattern of genetic programming that would replicate itself to a tolerance that no machine could emulate. In a single generation we destroyed it, like a bulldozer tearing out the ecology of a hedgerow. Our children, from whom we have borrowed this land, will never forgive us for our mindless bombardment against the creatures who share it with us, and who, in the priorities of mother earth, are probably more important than we.

★ ★ ★

Lisnacullia will always be summer: cattle sheltering in the lee of hedgerows, shimmering air in the background of sloe bush and whitethorn, wheel marks in green fields where the hay float has passed over flush new growth. I went shortly after dawn to bring home the cows because someone was unwell. The land had emerged new-born, smelling clean and fresh like red carbolic soap. The fields that rolled down the glacial path, to the banks of the ancient riverbed, had a blue green sheen like an artist's brush stroke. Broken fragments of cumulus had peeled from the cloud body and were wafting in a lazy upbeat, heading west to sea. A roan heifer poked at a hedgehog with her nose and blew twin blasts of air to test her curiosity. The hedgehog curled into a ball and rolled down the incline to rest against the bars of the gate. I saw a pair of foxes, vixen and mate, circumnavigate the open country. In Connor's meadow, where the ripened grass had been raised into hay-wynds, the birds were feasting on the bounty of the dew. The meadow was full of birds, so many that the patches of green were like tiny islets in an ocean of darkness. Suddenly a squadron of starling took off from the meadow, trailing like a ribboned kite as it climbed. Then the crows rose, and the smaller birds and the sky above Lisnacullia was darkened with their passing.

I have seen that summer dawn for 50 years in my head. It is a monument, not to memory, but to God in His heaven and man and animal in His place of creation. What invention and scheming it would take to make that happen again, as it did so vividly in the freshness of a summer's morn long ago. There are children in this land who will never know the story or see the creatures that once inhabited that rural dawn. I was lucky and I know it, as I did that early morning on the banks of the river Deel, when I saw the frolicking otters on the stone islet.

I was never asked to work in Lisnacullia, and had it happened, I would have removed the place from my escape routes. Bad as my desertion was, it would have been doubly wrong if I voluntarily did somewhere else what I had been avoiding at home. Paddy Enright would ask me now and then what I was doing in his place, laying about, as he put it, when I should have been at home helping with the harvest. I knew by then that when one had no sensible answer to make, at least to the mind of an adult, it was better to remain silent.

I think Hannah understood or maybe she just interpreted the silence in my favour. I remember her fighting my corner when she came to visit. The world, she said, was made up of many people and different natures. My father was not at all impressed with that. Why should he pay for labour when one of his own was traipsing about the country? My father and I had become like spokes from the same wheel, but so fixed to the rim of our diverging orbits that our paths had ceased to meet. He searched for me, came to the Hill field, calling my name. I would watch from my hiding place, like the horse had done to Bill O'Donnell. I felt he was hurt; I was dishonouring tradition and duty.

I spent many hours in the kitchen with Hannah. We would bring tea to the toilers in the field and amble our way home by the hedgerows. Our world was a leisurely place then; perhaps our aspirations were mostly matched to that. But not Hannah's or my mother's. They were both from the same stock and stable and were fired by their ambitions for their children. Sometimes I think that Hannah rehearsed the conversations with me that she would later have with her husband and she would nod rapidly when it seemed that my answers reflected her thinking.

Hannah would leave me alone when she went to milk the cows. Over all the house, the silence settled again, like a lowering canopy. It hung so heavily that it frightened and oppressed me. I would walk to the door, listen to the noises from the milking, and be lightened when someone came out of the byre to empty a milk pail. All the time the clock tocked on the wall under the staircase. I was as familiar with that kitchen as I was with my own. Hannah would run in to check on the state of the fire and remind me that soon the men would be coming in for their tea.

I was beginning then to lay down the foundations which would later develop into full-blown inferiority. I had never realised that I was abnormally small for my age. Of course, I had been told so by my school peers, but a few well-chosen insults about their own physical characteristics quickly silenced their observations. But then something happened that radically altered my self-esteem. I was crossing the stream by the pine planks and met Paddy Farrell at the other end. He was about seventeen then, he was no oil painting and that day, with a sprig of hay in his crooked mouth and a shapeless hat on his head, he looked to me like a troll. His intent was obvious in the cut of his face. The moment I reached the middle of the plank, he would toss me into the water. When I wouldn't play his little game, he set to mocking me: I was the runt of the litter, the scrapings of the pot, something must have gone terribly wrong to produce me. I understood nothing about his last remark but, even if I did, worse was to follow. He had heard that I would be in the confirmation class a few weeks hence. I was too small, he said, for the bishop to confirm me. When I stood in front of him, the bishop would ask what was I doing there because this was not a First Communion class. 'My advice to you,' he went on, the sprig of grass bopping in his mouth as he spoke, 'bring a butter box to stand up on and maybe the bishop will see you.' He burst into peels of laughter and fell into the long grass at his side of the bridge, tumbling in merriment.

I told the incident to Hannah and she was furious. She salved my drooping confidence with a bottle of Nash's lemonade, and a sandwich of cream crackers and strawberry jam. She told me that the next time she met Farrell she would put a flea in his ear. Sometimes during the day she would remember, purse her lips, shake her head and say with all the outrage she could muster, 'That fella. My buck *oinseach*.'

That evening she told her husband when he came in from work. His first reaction was to laugh and wonder where did Farrell get the wit to fashion such a proposition. He imagined out loud the stir it would make when someone came out of the congregation and placed my butter box by the altar rails. Hannah fixed him with a look that stifled the bubbling mirth, but he went on to justify, in a serious way, the harsh reality of Farrell's solution. You might as well face up to it, he told me. You are small and you are going to have to learn how to take your medicine. Maybe, he ventured, it will make a man out of you.

I could always depend on Hannah for sympathy, and I suppose I milked it. She must have known more about me — hopes, dreams — than anyone. I saw myself as an extension of Lisnacullia, as if I qualified for some kind of filial affinity with the place, even if I directed it all myself. But there was, in truth, more to it: Lisnacullia was comfortably well off and I benefited from its bounty.

Some Sundays we would travel to hurling matches in Rathkeale or Newcastle West. When Hannah came to visit she would simply say that I was going. Then my father would be invited and after a few minutes of apparent deliberation, he would agree and appear grateful. I'm not sure if he ever was. My father was not athletic nor had he a real interest in any of the activities associated with it. I had never seen him cycle a bike, hunt rabbits. He never talked about hurling; I don't think, even as a youngster he had ever played the game.

The Enrights invariably went without us. By the time we got to the meeting place at Mangan's Cross or at the church, the trap car had long gone. 'Gone this last 30 minutes,' the woman at the shop would say. I was sorely disappointed, but I thought there was a spring in my father's step as he walked home. An hour before the appointed time, my father would disappear. I searched and saw him at the far end of the headland in Waterfield, scrutinising the growth of young turnips. I shouted, he looked up, and when I beckoned, he bent down again as if I were a stranger shouting a salutation. I tried to rush him through the dinner and he suggested that, if I was in such a hurry, why didn't I go without him.

It was Machiavellian behaviour. My father would rather spend his Sunday napping in the chair after dinner and then strolling by the hedgerows. It would have been so simple, it seemed to me, to say that, but it would run counter to his naive philosophy of trying to please everybody. In the end, he wound up pleasing no one but himself and he must have been consumed with the scheming that it took to achieve it. All evening I would mope about and wonder what I had missed: the rigour of the game, the clash and the fervour of man against man, the excitement of the crowd, the mad primitive melee when tempers erupted and the crowd joined the fight on the pitch. All those things happened when I was absent. Con would come home with two broken hurleys that would splice and be as good as new. One he would store in the outhouse, rubbed with linseed oil, so that it would season into supple hardness. He would sell the other for half-a-crown.

Con was the first youngster I knew who owned a bicycle. Not a hand me down, or an adapted high-nelly that drew whistles of derision when it passed the cornerboys in Rathkeale. It was a junior Raleigh, the latest model, with gleaming chrome and green paintwork that glistened like a mallard's neck feathers. I would sneak out to the shed at the gable-end and stand there admiring it. It took a long mustering of courage to get astride it, balance myself with one hand against the gable wall and imagine myself flying down the hill at the Stony Man. I felt the wind on my face, hair whipping into my eyes, I saw from my peripheral vision the blur of hedgerows as I flew past.

The bicycle opened new vistas; we were mobile. The town of Rathkeale was a mere hop away; Newcastle West, Ardagh and Foynes, a Sunday canter. It was an expression of the way we were then, that we could park it against a gable and find it there when we returned. There might be a small knot of people gathered to admire it; a passing temptation in someone's head to spirit it away, but the thoughts passed as they always did.

★ ★ ★

Summer days shortened into autumn. A second brood of house-martins, grew to adulthood in the banqueting hall of the keep-tower. The swifts shrieked in demented chorus, flew incredible aerial acrobatics, from specks above the tower, to sudden scimitar-shaped flashes between the potato drills in the kitchen garden. I read my books, talked to Hannah and brought tea to the lea of hedgerows for the toilers in the fields. Days shortened.

Along the wall of the keep-tower, in niches

and ledges designed for warfare, Paddy Enright kept his beehives. Hannah would bring two-pound jam-pots full of honey to Kilquane, glowing in autumn amber. I have a picture in my head of the kitchen garden when Hannah and I went to lift new potatoes in the mid-mornings of high summer. The light shafted off stone walls raised by Norman artisans; young breezes swayed the flowering stalks, bees hummed. The hum was the first thing that registered when I opened the barred gate. It filled the garden, perfumed the wind and took away every other noise. The hum had a sound like a mower in a distant field, lifted to an even pitch, and seemed fed with nectar fluid.

I rode the bicycle bar to the Central Cinema in Rathkeale and was entertained more by the urbanity of its owner, Jack Hayes, than by the films he showed. He was the alto sax man in a dance band and his talk was full of cosmopolitan name-dropping. Filmstars he referred to by first name — Humph, Cary and Alan. He had supped with the masters of jazz and drunk with the cream of band leaders — Victor Sylvester, Johnny Dankworth, Glen Miller, Dave Brubeck, Hoagie Carmichael. Hayes stood in the foyer of the cinema accepting ticket halves and shuffling them in his hands like a gambler. All the way up the wall to the balcony, rising in gradients of fame and beauty, hung the smiling images of glitz and notoriety. Jack Hayes cultivated the mannerisms, the smiles, the speech patterns of the stars and tried them out on rustic youths. I said something he agreed with; he nodded and smiled. 'You can play it again, Sam.' He aimed a beam of torchlight at a groping offender in a back seat of the stalls. 'Hombre, I got you covered. Another move like that and I'll fill you full of holes.'

I thought that cinema was a wonder world, full of smiling heroes and surly villains. It portrayed a lifestyle as far removed from Kilqaune as Earth from Mars. There was a Tuesday night serial called *The Phantom*, in which a faltering sheriff muddled through routine assignments; but when something more exotic happened along, he changed into cowboy gear, whistled up his white horse, and rode off to save the wagon train. He finished every serial in dire straits where death was the only conceivable outcome. Davy Mack, our cousin, rode the bicycle seven miles each way to see *The Phantom* escape. Davy was so impressed by the ingenuity of the man that he called to Kilquane on the way home, and let us into the secret, frame by frame.

Apples ripened in September. There was a

Beauty of Bath in the orchard, right in front of the kitchen window in Lisnacullia. Its smell wafted over the wall, invaded the kitchen and permeated the barn and the outhouses. The ripening apple tree brought the first hint of change: shortening days, autumn stacked in the haggard, screaming swifts with a new tension in their flying. Summer was gone, autumn well advanced, the scouting riders of winter would soon appear on the horizon.

And then I too, like the swifts, would leave that place.

12

In deference to our separated brethren, the 1947 All Ireland football final, between Cavan and Kerry, was played in the Polo Grounds in New York. It was broadcast live, at midnight on a Sunday. That broadcast overshadowed the final itself: for me and many of my neighbours, it was the first time we had heard a radio. There has always been a close affiliation between the people of West Limerick and Kerry, particularly north Kerry. Once you went west of the village of Ardagh, the tentacles of the Kingdom reached out to you: the accent, the lie of the land, the landscape and faces of men. When the footballers of Kerry won, we rejoiced. When they were beaten, we shared in our neighbours' sorrow.

I had been hearing rumours about this thing called a wireless. It was an extraordinary concept, stranger than the idea of light and energy piped into the kitchen. The people of Ratkeale knew all about the wireless. So did my brother Billy and his friend, The Clacker. The Clacker was then working with the county council. He spent most of his time in Rathkeale, drawn there, we assumed, by his cosmopolitan outlook. He could give a reasonable version of Micheál O'Hehir in the white heat of a Cork and Tipperary battle. By then the great Limerick team of the 1930s and 1940s had faded and were slipping into memory.

Kenneally's was the only house within walking distance that owned a wireless. I had heard the word first when the news of the broadcast was being trumpeted about, months before. Paddy Kenneally became like a Medici art patron, who would be bringing the first voices of a new wave intelligentsia to that quiet place. I had gone and inspected this wireless thing for myself; sidling down the Kenneally avenue on my way home from school. Kenneally was part of a group of people who gathered on the roadside after Sunday mass; he would go inside the gate that opened onto his avenue, close it, and then speak with his neighbours as if he were a prisoner talking through the bars of his cell. His house was set on a little plateau overlooking the valley that the ice age had formed.

I couldn't see the wireless when I ducked around the front of the house and peered through the kitchen window. In truth, I didn't know what I was looking for. The word 'wireless' had neither shape nor form in my mind. But I could see the cable that stretched from the rooftop of the barn, disappearing through the hole in the window-frame. According to those in the know — the likes of the Clacker and his cronies in Rathkeale — the secret of the apparatus was in the wire. The wire, they said, attracted and collected the sound as it bounded along on the airwaves, took it into the back of the set, and transformed it, through some class of a microphone, into a human voice.

The Clacker told his disciples, those of us who hung on his knowledge like rustic youngsters in a rural academy, that every sound ever made was still passing backwards and forwards in the air. Sound never died, he explained; the voices were just waiting to be rediscovered. And they would be, because the wireless was only the beginning of it. The time would come when all human sound would be plucked out of the air, and whole conversations would be played over again. The Clacker's brother, Paddy, was not impressed. He reckoned that most of what was in the atmosphere was pure blather and best left forgotten.

I am not too sure if my brother ever invited me to go with him — perhaps I just tagged along, as I had been doing since I turned eleven. Billy didn't like that at all. I would follow over the fields as he made for the Clacker's house. He would stop at every stile and loudly berate me. I had all the instincts of a sheepdog or cocker spaniel then: I stopped when he did, cowered respectfully at every fierce warning, took backward crestfallen steps. But I would follow later, and when he looked for me as he went into Clacker's house, I was stalled a safe distance away, like our dog Towser, when he wanted to abandon the hunt and join the pack around the badger sett. I had the notion that something very mature and important was happening. Why else would I be barred from entering the sanctum of the Clacker's kitchen? Why should the conversation suddenly stop when I came within earshot and scraps of paper and dog-eared photos be guiltily pocketed when I arrived?

The night was as black as ink when we crossed the High field. We had to grope in the darkness to find the iron gate at the entrance to Kenneally's. We could hear the voices of people ahead of us, the sudden squirt of laughter from a group behind; the world and its mother was going to listen to the wireless. All along the upper reaches of the avenue, bicycles were thrown against the hedge and the farmyard was a collection of trap carts like a circled wagon train. It wasn't just the match that had drawn the crowd; it was more the wonder and curiosity about this exotic new technology.

My father dismissed that infant advance of invention and science as mere gimmickry. Perhaps that was his way of managing the uncertainty that it brought. He never learned how to drive the Volkswagen when it finally arrived, or sat on the driver's seat of the tractor which had preceded the car. He was uncomfortable as a passenger. We are in loads of time, he would tell the driver — a euphemism for drive slowly.

What my father regarded as gimmickry had a far wider range than invention or advancing technology. I would ask him, the night before a fair, assuming that the day went well for him, to buy me a mouth organ or a Jew's harp. Every other kid in the school had one; many had two. I yearned to play the mouth organ. There was no musical tradition whatever in our family. It was accepted as a certainty, like a precept carved in stone, that no Nestor could or would ever sing. Once a young fresh-faced curate, recently out of the seminary and imbued with fair play, asked Miss Abigail if she had forgotten to call me, after all in my class had rendered a party piece.

'Sing? Him? He's a Nestor. He couldn't sing to warm himself.'

I never did own a mouth organ. Fol dols, my father would say; what do you want an ould fol dol for? That was the collective term in the vernacular for items of little value that usurped the purchase of important things. 'More in your line to buy a nib for your pen.'

Kenneally's front yard was a foretaste of things to come, though they would be long in coming. But already the youngsters in fifth and sixth class could talk about the wireless with the ease of familiar terminology; an uncle or some near neighbour had a wireless. Funny stories were doing the rounds which smirked at the attempts of simple people to understand concepts beyond their ken. There was a man in Rathreigh who called the wireless 'the lad in the box'. Near Tally Ho Cross, in the house of an old woman, a crowd gathered to hear the Grand National. They came again on Sunday to hear a football match but the wireless went dead before half time. 'Why wouldn't it go broke?' said the old one, 'an' a herd of racehorses galloping all over it yesterday.'

The wireless was a great mystery to me, removed as I was from the experiences of people like the Clacker or youngsters who had aunts or uncles in towns or villages. I had a false idea of what a dry or a wet battery looked like because I had taken the basic shapes from my current knowledge and let my imagination abstract them outward. It was like encountering a new mathematical problem. Of course I knew what a battery was; the classic example around and probably the progenitor of all others, was the one used in the flash lamp. 'No,' Tom Moore told me, 'you have it all wrong.' He wanted to bet me everything, 'down to his very last farthing' that he was right. Wasn't he watching the wireless every day and it sitting on the sill of his mother's kitchen window?

There it was again; another example of how deprived I was by father's attitude towards fol dols. Moore lived in a council cottage; his father did the odd bit of work for neighbouring farmers, but his son had a pair of mouth organs — a bass and a tenor, he told me, in whispered patronising confidentiality. They made different sounds, he explained; they were set in different keys and, to demonstrate, he played the opening bars of *Swanee River* on each one. They both sounded the same and when I said so, he shook his head in tolerant recognition of my abysmal ignorance. It was the same head-shake Miss Abigail had conferred on me when I once had tried to sing a song.

Kilquane was the Spartan school: the house of no frills and no indulgence for the creeping influence of gimmickry. There were two bicycles in the house by then; my father saw them both as the epitome of our headlong gallop towards modern degeneration. Billy owned one bike; the other was a high-nelly, left behind by an aunt because she was embarrassed to be seen going the road on it. My brother was then attending a secondary school near Foynes and, listening to my father, one would have thought that the bike had been bought exclusively for that reason. Any other use was a declaration of laziness and a negation of the old forming virtue of hardship. Whether else the bicycle was used for — fetching his cigarettes, delivering milk to Ma Daly, going to Lisnacullia with a message — it was all the same.

'Next thing is, ye'll be cycling to bed.'

★   ★   ★

I was conscious, approaching Kenneally's house that we were really out on the edge of the technology circuit. It would be many a day yet before a wireless predicted weather in our kitchen or sang the songs of John McCormack. But for a few fleeting moments, when the Curlew Smith sent me into the kitchen for a light for his pipe, I was able to see enough of the apparatus to engage in a second phase conversation about it. Without the Curlew, who got his name from the plaintive wail by which he drove his cows to milking, I would never have got near the kitchen. It was standing room only. The Kenneally couple, sitting at opposite hobs of the fireplace, were looking at each other with shocked perspiring expressions, as if their house and its decorum had been invaded by a plague of barbarians. The listeners were locked together in statuesque rigidity; a wave of body heat swept out the door, steam swirled like the smoke of a thousand genies escaping their bottles, in the cold air of night. The press of bodies swayed, toppled and righted itself again.

I had one look in the kitchen door and decided to retreat. It would be risking life and limb to force my way to the fire and select an ember for the Curlew's pipe. But in that moment, standing there on the threshold of a new dawn, I saw the wireless. It was a box — a fancy one at that — with a grill in the front and, beneath the grill, a dial. I was certain, though the Curlew told me I was mad, that the dial was lighted. Beneath the dial was a row of knobs and at each side of the set were the batteries. I saw at once that I was wrong: my imagination had built on a false premise.

The dry battery was conventional enough, merely a monstrous version of what I had known. But the wet version was like nothing I had seen or tried to conceive. It was a square of frosted glass, held in a metal frame, a liquid shimmering in the glass-bound enclosure. I learned something else from a neighbour of the Curlew's that would later try my patience and goodwill to the hilt. The dry battery wore out, according to my informant; 'the power went 'clane' out of it, and it had to be 'thrun' away.' The wet battery worked differently. When the power ran down it could be recharged.

Apart from that brief moment, I never heard the commentary that night. The crowd had spilled on to the front yard and the scores were relayed to those at the perimeter. There was little excitement, even when Kerry was doing well in the early part of the game. In the end, when Cavan won, I couldn't detect any sense of disappointment. We were totally in awe of the wireless, locked in muted appreciation of the miracle amongst us.

The Curlew and his neighbour held a conversation about the way things were changing, and how the world would never be the same again. It was not a good thing, according to the neighbour. Interfering with nature was like flying in the face of God; that wireless yoke would lead to trouble down the line. But the Curlew was having none of it. Anything that made life better or more enjoyable was good.

'Time will come,' he whispered, 'when the horse will lie idle in the field. The tractor will do the work of ten of 'em and twice as many men.'

Then he dropped the whisper to its lowest decibel. 'I hear tell, that they will be putting a man on top of the moon one of these days.'

'Will you talk sense?' the Curlew's neighbour admonished him; 'someone might hear you. Man on the moon, how are you, you might as well tell me that water will flow backwards up the hill. Have a scrap of sense, man.'

I think of the Curlew often. He was a wiry, garrulous man who had views about everything and who seemed fulfilled by hard physical endeavour. Hard work killed no one, he would tell me, when I strayed into one of his fields and found him breathing hard. I wonder how he felt when the tractor did make the promised appearance and was followed in time by other pieces of equipment which made the hands of toil redundant. The

Curlew visits my thoughts when I walk the avenues or passageways and see them rutted and overgrown. In the days of the horse, there would never be that ribbon of green in the centre of the avenue.

★　★　★

The wireless lore was finding its way into our community. It had its beginnings in the accounts of the Second World War and especially the broadcasts of Lord Haw Haw, the Irish-born German propagandist. Some of the youngsters at school would dash around the playground imitating the anti-British broadcasts. 'Jairmany Calling. Jairmany Calling.' It was as far as they ever got. The Clacker was a fan of Haw Haw's. He would cycle to Rathkeale when a broadcast was expected; once he told me that the great man had thanked the inhabitants of Foynes for taking care of the U-boat crews.

Very soon after that night in Kenneally's house, Paddy Enright installed a wireless in Lisnacullia. I could now see and study at my leisure, this acme of modern technology. There was a notion that the liquid in the wet battery was acid-based and if a single drop fell on one's hands it would burn to the bone. It was explained to us that acid was a bit like caustic which was used for burning off the young horn growth on cattle and we knew how painful that could be. I had been right about the lighted dial. It glowed a bright yellow once the operating knob was switched on and it illuminated an express itinerary throughout the capitals and cities of Europe. I read names I had never heard of before; there was no mention of them on the tattered old map of Europe that hung forlornly behind Miss Abigail's desk: Helsinki, Hilversum, Reykjavik, Antwerp. And there too, in the middle of all that civilised urbanity, was the name Athlone, proclaiming us European before we ever heard of Monnet or Schuman.

Billy and I went to Lisnacullia to hear a weekly programme of Irish songs called *Round the Fire*. The idea behind it was simple, but we found it profoundly effective. You had to imagine that you were in a house to which a group of singers had rambled. I could see the fire in my imagination: the open hearth, the goose wing on one of the blackened hobs. As if the hearth was a kind of pump-primer, other pictures and sounds flowed into my mind: the crackle and sigh of green logs, the paraffin lamp throwing shadows against the white-washed wall. We listened to the singing and the commentary with rapt attention and we were there in the

309

midst of it. Two songs leap from my memory across the expanse of years: a young woman singing *The Turfman from Ardee* and Seán O Síocháin, who became the general secretary of the Gaelic Athletic Association, rendering Sigerson Clifford's balled *The Boys of Barr na Sraidhe*.

The wireless was treated sparingly, as if in deference to its uniqueness. Only a handful of programmes merited the homage of scheduled listening. Paddy Enright knew exactly when one of those came on air: the news, the weather forecast, Bart Bastable, before bedtime, with *Hospital Requests*. 'When you wish upon a star, it makes no difference who you are. Anything your heart desires will come to you.' Immediately the cows were milked, Hannah came in from the byre and switched on. We would be seated for the news. That same pattern would be repeated in Kilquane, when we finally broke through the tradition of fol dols, and a wireless sat on the windowsill, its back to Mannix's Folly. When the last cow had been milked, my mother would tell one of us, 'Go in and turn on the wireless'.

My father relented. He made a great show of it, though the transition didn't cost him much. The electricity grid had been extended to the village of Croom; an uncle, my mother's brother, lived close by. By now, further steps in technology were advancing: the electric kettle, indoor water supply, an iron for pressing clothes. Then we heard of the most dramatic thrust of all: a wireless worked by electricity. Hot on the heels of that information came the news that my mother's brother had installed one.

The uncle presented us with his old set. A Sparling man from Rathkeale, whose ancestors had come out of the German Palatinate to be one of Viscount Southwell's ideal tenants, drove into the yard to rig it up. He ran an aerial from the corner of the barn and prised it through the deal frame of our western kitchen window. The wireless filled one half of the window; from then on it could be opened or closed only by moving the set. The slightest movement was taboo because it interfered with the machinery within the apparatus. It would be working perfectly until someone shifted it. When the switch-on failed to provide sound, there came the inevitable blaming query.

'Who moved the wireless?'

It was extremely temperamental, somewhat like its former owner, whose moods, his sister admitted, were impossible to time. It failed at the most crucial moments: when my father, who was set to go mowing, wanted to hear the weather forecast or when Micheál O'Hehir was due to come on air. It failed when our neighbour Tim Larkin, who was playing for the Limerick senior hurling team, had won possession of the ball.

That wireless was on its last legs when it was bestowed on us. According to the Sparling man, who in the beginning made numerous trips to the windowsill, it ate up batteries like there was no tomorrow. That was the symptom we feared, because, as my father used say, it was the most expensive endowment that ever entered the house; presents like that he could do without. Did we think he was growing money in the orchard? It would lay there, silent for long periods, blocking out the light to the kitchen, until the batteries had been replenished. I was despatched to Rathkeale, holding the wet battery in one hand, steering a wobbly route with the other. It required two trips because the battery had to be yoked to a charging apparatus for a couple of days. A dry battery cost ten shillings and the repair man charged by the hour. So the wireless sat on the windowsill, dumb and gathering dust, until my father was coaxed to fund the remedy.

Eventually, in a rash moment of opulence, we threw out the wireless and a brand new set adorned the windowsill. But only for a short time. Paddy Quin, a carpenter and stone mason, was doing work in Barrett's house and my mother had him fix a shelf on the wall, above the horsehair couch. By then our musical tastes had broadened and our interests had moved beyond weather forecasts, greyhound track results and the late-night, deep bass tones of Bart Bastable. We had discovered Europe, the Forces Network, and Radio Luxembourg.

My mother would come in from the milking, turn the knob, and the house was filled with pop music. She would change back to Radio Éireann, turn off when the news was over and not think about the radio again until my father reminded her that it was time for a repeat of Din Joe's comedy show. A very loud voice assailed her ears, telling her that the music was being despatched to her with the compliments of H. Samuel, and inviting her to send her request to Keynsham. My father decried the sound as roaring and screeching that passed for singing.

It became the war of the traditions. On one side was Athlone, with the news, weather forecasts and music that a body could listen to: lovely Irish songs and lyrics that had meaning and pathos. In opposition was Luxembourg and its foreign insidious influence. Father Lynch preached about it from the altar. Radio Luxembourg was evil. We had thrown out the landlords, the land grabbers, the 'shoneens' and the Protestants but worse was now coming in through the back door. Only this time the evil was colonising the minds of the young and innocent; aided and abetted by the ignorance of parents in this very parish. We were prostituting our holy land for a modern Gomorrah called Keynsham.

'Turn off that goddamn screeching! Ye heard what the priest said.'

We had come in from the meadow at dinnertime. We were seated around the kitchen table, the boys, the girls home from boarding school, parents and Ruck, the hired hand. We listened to the news and the forecast and then a sponsored programme came on. Guy Mitchell started to sing.

> She wears red feathers and a hooly
> hooly skirt,
> She wears red feathers and a hooly
> hooly skirt,
> She lives off just coconuts and fish from
> the sea,
> Got a rose in her hair, a gleam in her
> eye and love in her heart for me.

My father stopped eating; turned his head to one side, the fork held in mid-air. He was doubting the evidence of his own ears. This was from Radio Éireann, his beloved Athlone, the heartland of national values. One of the sisters sniggered and my mother got up from the table to switch off.

'Leave it on, woman.'

I work in a London bank; a suitable
    position,
From nine to three they serve you tea
    and ruin your dis-posit-ion.

Kathleen couldn't contain herself any longer; she held her hand to her mouth, but the laughter exploded through her fingers. Ruck guffawed and followed that with a severe bout of camouflage coughing. Then everybody was laughing uncontrollably, drowning out the Guy Mitchell song. My father laughed too, but only briefly, because for a few moments it seemed to him that we were all laughing at the stupidity of the song. Then when he realised that the joke was on him, that we were responding in unstifled merriment to his reaction to the song, he kicked back the chair and walked out.

'Turn off that goddamn wireless.'

He didn't speak to us for days. We had

laughed at the tradition that people had died for and which went back to the days of Celtic kings and gods. Then one evening, as if the silent mode was still in vogue, he had a conversation with a slice of brown bread that he was carefully buttering. There were no greater idiots in the world that those who made fun of themselves, who went aping after pagan influences from across the sea and had no idea of the wealth of culture in their own place. My father gave up after a week of silence, interspersed with the odd soliloquy to an inanimate object. Then he adopted the classic response of the long-suffering, righteous, minority.

'Have it ye'er own way. Whoever yet listened to me?'

The world opened up. Europe flooded our kitchen in diverse tongues, all of them caterwauling, as my father would say, the language of popular music. From this remove, it seems no more like pop now than does country and western sound like rock. I could then hear every word and decipher the sentiments, however trite they were. Gracie Fields, Vera Lynn, Jo Stafford, had a clarity in vocals that required little compensating embellishment.

I fell in love with clarinets, saxophones, all things brass. I kept it mostly to myself lest someone should tell me that it was far away from clarinets I was reared. But not the Clacker; he had the ear. He would drop the same names, as did Jack Hayes: dance-band leaders, purveyors of jazz in blue and trad, Latin-American sambas and tangos. The Clacker had a gramophone and a collection of 78 rpm records. I went through the collection one Sunday morning and for the first time made acquaintance with names that would light my soul in a few short years: Tauber, Pinza, McCormack, Caruso. He had every record made by the tenor Christopher Lynch. Lynch was from Rathkeale, son of the man who kept the stallion, Polyfane. They had worked together in the County Council; the Clacker maintained that Lynch had developed range and volume from singing into empty tar-barrels. The Clacker evoked the propensity of the human spirit to fly, even in the most remote bounded places. The magic of music and the nectar it feeds the soul soar far above the arid deserts that bigoted men would confine us to.

★　★　★

The wireless spread tentacles into every corner of our quiet land. It floated us off into flights of wonder, on journeys of global

317

exploration, bringing exotic mental landfalls under thatched roofs and between white-washed walls. Great wooden masts, like single goal-posts, soared from haggards and from orchards. The incoming migratory flights of swifts and swallows made rendezvous on aerial cables; the outgoing exodus of first, second, and third generations assembled there and chirruped flight plans and farewells.

The world was becoming the global village that Marshall McLuhan would later enunciate. But in its beginnings, in the early technology of wireless, it was a gentle and happy fusion. Cultures touched softly in the quiet of country kitchens, flights of wonder and imaginings rose in the currents of the airwaves, crossed boundaries into tundras, deserts, rain forests, and made landfalls in incredible cities.

My mother learned how to move between stations and restore the cacophony to the gentler sounds of Athlone. There were spare dry batteries in the airing press; the wet one was constantly on charge in the wireless shop in Rathkeale. The Sparling man came less and less frequently. We had cast the bestowment of the uncle to the loft in the cowhouse, in case we ever needed spare parts. We vied for knobs, sounds and interests, running the range of the geography of the dial. We heard of families who had solved that problem by putting a second wireless in the parlour; but we were far from that kind of ostentation — the second set was in the realm of the fol dols.

I went into Kelly's shop in Rathkeale one winter's evening, the last port of call on my message list. That shop was a bolthole. There was a couple of young girls, my own age, who were always walking the pavement when I hit town. One was blonde, with a pretty face, who averted her eyes when she passed. The other, in the local way of saying, was butty, short and round, with cascading dark hair and a face that was open and welcoming. She would look at me head-on and smile, inviting the first words of contact. The smile broadened when my gauche discomfort signalled its effect. I blushed to the roots of my hair and no matter how I warned myself to stay calm and controlled, I stumbled when I stepped off the footpath. I could hear them giggling in my wake as I fled to the shop across the street.

There was always a queue in Kelly's and that young lady with the cascading dark hair would be already there before me. I could never figure out how she had managed to worm her way in, but there she was, looking around and smiling. I let people pass me in the queue, and once when I did that, I eavesdropped on a conversation about the wireless. As I listened, I was reminded of how we had laughed when we heard about Victor Costello and his new bike. It was a Raleigh, with a Sturmy Archer three-speed. But Victor never used the low or the high gear; the middle one was good enough for him. We suspected that he didn't know how to make the change. The young woman behind the counter in Kelly's was carrying on a running conversation with a customer. They were talking about the BBC. I listened, committed names and descriptions to memory and vowed that I would never laugh at Victor again. I hadn't known that the Light Programme existed.

In our house the BBC wavelength was never used. It was a kind of subliminal influence that made us refrain from it; half-forgotten pangs of history, starkly remembered utterances from Fr Lynch's pulpit, other voices of republican hue. The Light Wave was English; created, driven and fed by a similar ilk of man and his politic, who had ground us down for 500 years. We may not talk about it any more; we would be generous and respecting to the scion of that same establishment who still walked amongst us or came to visit. We would appreciate that there was hardly a house in our community that hadn't a representative in the land of John Bull. But deep down, in the repository of fundamental wrongs, the spirit stirred for vindication and remembered.

Modern symbols festered the old sores. The English laughed at us still, poked fun at us in cartoons, reviled us on stage in caricature, and put notices in boarding-house windows telling the Irish not to apply. The wrongs that cried for vindication found succour in the political vision of our time: a land self-sufficient, comely maidens dancing at crossroads, the burning of everything British but coal. When I first went to work, the young man who sat at the desk beside me told me confidentially that the West-Brits were still amongst us. They were the lackeys who ridiculed the Gaelic Athletic Association and Irish dancing, read *The Irish Times* and listened to the BBC. There was one in particular who played cricket and rugby, the antithesis of all that was Gaelic Ireland. Such men, like Cassius, were dangerous.

The young woman behind the counter in Kelly's shop listed off a range of programmes that appealed to her. I came home, fighting the elements that were always vigorous on the return journey. The wind blew from Mannix's Folly, straight into my face; the rain ran down my neck. The kitchen was empty because it was milking time. I stoked the fire, turned my wet clothes to the flames and tuned to the BBC. I found an adaptation of Zane Grey's *Riders of the Purple Sage*. A narrator, with drawl and homespun accent, brought me up to date with the story and in the background a vocal group, called Sons of the Saddle, harmonised *The Old Chisholm Trail*. I heard the rustle of tumbleweed as it passed in the wind, the creaking of leather, the lash of the bullwhip, the clip-clop and the galloping of horses, cattle lowing for water. The fire went out and my mother, coming in from the milking, scathed me for selfish laziness.

I had stood on the threshold of the wireless legacy. We had been merely on the outskirts, barely exploring the fringes. But there was something else: I had discovered the pleasure of total focus, undisturbed by the din of activity or the babel of voices. It provoked in me a reversal of behaviour; much as I needed to escape during the working day, I now needed a way to get back in when the kitchen was empty.

From my days at the ploughing, I could read the sky. I could time the dipping of the sun or the thinning light when the sky was overcast, listen for the barking of sheepdogs or human cries moving cowherds to milking.

When one of those signals bespoke the hour, or when the flocks of rooks, like airborne shreds of tattered clothing, hied to Harold's Wood, it was time to come home.

The wet battery lasted about three weeks, if order and control were applied. I tried to win my parents' approval for a regime of common good. My mother tried but lost the promised attention in her work and its competing priorities. My father never bothered, unless the power was wrung out when he wanted to hear the forecast for the morrow. He could take it or leave it; he had done without the wireless for almost a generation. But the others would come into the kitchen and instinctively switch the set. Then they would walk away as if the act of turning on took precedence over listening. My youngest brother, Connie, would switch on, as he passed out of the room to change his clothes. When he returned and seated himself at the supper table, it would dawn on him half-way through that someone had turned off the wireless. He bounded up to switch it on again and then ignored it, but not before he had voiced his chagrin. 'Who turned off the wireless?'

Worst of all were those who simply lowered the sound. I would come in to see a lighted dial and would know that the battery had

323

been wasting for hours. In my quest for monitoring and control, I was volunteered to be the custodian of the energy supply. When the batteries ran down, it was my fault: I hadn't taken the spare to be charged, nor funded the acquisition of the dry. I was a wireless addict by then and it was up to me to fund the craving. In my father's words, he wouldn't lose any sleep if the dial never lit again, my mother had far too many demands on her limited finances to invest some on the radio. No one else had money.

Billy was good at funding but his requirements were of a different nature to mine. We hunted rabbits as a team and pooled our resources. In effect, that meant that I looked after the snares. He would be available on Saturday morning, when Horan, the egg-man, parked his van on the green triangle at Sluggaragh Cross. Horan was in an expansionary mode; he had first started in eggs but was now also trading in poultry and rabbits. Rabbits were worth half-a-crown each, in good condition, as ours always were because of the snares. A pheasant yielded the princely sum of one guinea. I had caught one in McAuliffe's stubble field. I saw it run into the hedge, and when I looked, it had covered its head in an ivy-tangled tree. I had simply to pull it out by the tail. Sometimes a hen or a couple of pullets would go missing; my mother would blame the fox because of the tell-tale trail of feathers I had discreetly laid down by the privet at the rear of the hay barn.

Billy haggled with the egg-man; the effort of the negotiation entitled him to 60 percent of the sale. Horan drew the line at everything else bar rabbits, eggs, and poultry. One cold November midday I heard him utter a phrase that would become well known to me in later years; a rustic forerunner of management speak. The brother asked him if he bought crabapples?

'No,' Horan shook his head. 'Crabs are not in my product range.'

Crabapples were in high demand then, as ingredients for jelly and jam. I learned about that possibility when a strange man came out from Rathkeale and asked my father's permission to take crabapples from the tree in the haggard. It was the way the man dressed and spoke that caused the wonder and that he should ask permission. He wore plus fours, argyle socks to the knee, a shiny waistcoat over a grandfather shirt, and brown brogues that glinted in the sunlight. His accent was posh, like the insurance man's, who some-times called to my mother's kitchen, vainly trying to sell policies for us children. Her refusal never deterred him. He would sit, take tea, and compliment my mother's delicious scones. It was the way he ate and drank that drew our silent interest and always created a half-circle of audience. His little finger stuck out like an extra digit when he raised the cup to his lips; he sliced each piece of scone before he transferred it to his mouth; after every bite he dabbed at his lips with a stark white handkerchief. But it was accent that held the semi-circle of audience. His voice was soft and fruity: every 'ing' received full exposure; expressions like, 'delightful', 'by Jove', 'my dear', speckled his conversation like the delicate dabs of his handkerchief.

The crabapple man had a voice like that insurance agent. We followed him, like the entourage of the pied piper, as he led us to the crab tree. He asked us if we would climb for him, throw the crabs down, and help him fill the sack. My mother was certain that he would fulfil his promise; to return and present her with a jar of what he called preservative. We never saw him again, but he led the brother and me to the discovery of the crabapple market. There were crab trees, in an abandoned state, all around Kilquane. They grew between the hawthorns, in several stands in the grove at Waterfield, out of ditches and earthen banks that had once been the surrounds of cabins and wattle huts.

Billy and I borrowed old Jim Kelly's ass cart and went to Newcastle West with a load that was neatly bagged and tied. That was strategy, because the man who bought the crabapples would open and check each bag and poke his hand down to the elbow. He would become exasperated, we hoped, winding off the loops of binding twine. Then he would make an act of faith in our honesty and fail to discover the middle layer of small stones below the elbow reach. It worked as we had planned. I don't recall now how much we earned, except that we had surplus to buy bottles of lemonade, ham and a loaf to make sandwiches with. I bought two dry batteries and stashed one in the drying press. Then I camped on the doorway of the BBC.

I could lie supine on the horsehair couch and, without rising, work the knobs above my head. I had an exclusive listening right during the milking period but I also had part of the evening, when the supper was over, until the news around eight o'clock. No one else bothered with the wireless before then. My mother lowered the lamp-pulley, read her books and rode rescue missions for French aristocrats with *The Scarlet Pimpernel*. My father smoked his cigarettes, basked in the aura of comfort to which his place by the fire entitled him and had someone find him the newspaper. Of the remainder, some came and went, scuttling back and forth to Barrett's house; the eldest brother was off planning dance hall excursions with the Clacker, the younger ones were struggling with home-work.

I found the mother lode of radio comedy that I would mine for the next ten years: Tommy Trinder, Tony Hancock, the madcap Goons, *Ray's a Laugh*, *Much Binding in the Marsh*, *Life with the Lyons* and Jimmy Clitheroe. It was wonderful. I kept the volume to the lowest pitch, so that I wouldn't focus attention on myself, distract the newspaper reader or alert the Bastille guards to the Scarlet Pimpernel. I could laugh only silently but perhaps that is the most pleasurable merriment of all. I remember that time as a kind of fun oasis that I alone inhabited. I think now that I was selfish about it for the others could have enjoyed it as much as me. But the enjoyment appeared to me as some kind of rare flower that could flourish only in a secret environment and, once taken out of there, would perish, like an orchid removed from a glasshouse. It was sensible, I thought, to keep the fun to myself; otherwise, and most likely, I would suffer the mockery of those who did not share my interest.

'What class of ould rubbish is that? Turn if off.'

I had a schedule of radio programmes in my head and it would lift my soul in the middle of the eternal turnip drills. Of the nations I can make comparison with, none to my mind, can write or present comedy as the British can. I used reach that conclusion in Jack Hayes' cinema in Rathkeale when I watched American films and could second-guess the contrivance of situation and dialogue.

We came very late to the wireless. In a similar way, other advances of technology would find it difficult to penetrate our bastion of tradition. It would be seven years, after that first broadcast in Kenneally's house, before electricity came into the parish. Matches had been broadcast on the radio as far back as 1931, Micheál O'Hehir had done his first commentary in 1938. When I went away to boarding school, in the autumn of 1947, no experience of mine raised an eyebrow of wonder. Most of my classmates, also from rural Ireland, had never known a time when there wasn't a wireless in their homes. The names I rattled off were commonplace, my passion with English comedy was mirrored a hundred times. But down in the depths of my unspoken exploration, lest it be smirked at, I felt that my experience was more profound than theirs. Even if one does come at the end of the wave, that joy of self-discovery, of finding new territory, though hordes of people may have been there before you, will always remain high on the wonder scale. I never found it so with television; in truth, the opposite was the case. Wireless ranged far, wide and limitless across our imaginations, forcing us to visualise and abstract and be amazed. Television sets limits like a 23-inch screen.

And it went on. Many years after Kenneally's, in the flush of unthinking manhood, I would spend Sundays with Mike Barrett, hunting game with guns and dog. It would be dark when we arrived home, sodden and famished. My father would be sitting in his armchair; everyone else was out at the milking. He was getting feeble then, feeling the early spasms from spine and hips that eventually and permanently would confine him to a wheelchair. I took the Sunday dinner from the range oven, put it on a tray and sat beneath the radio. There was a programme then called Ceol do Páistí, presented by Gearóid O Tighernaigh. It was an odd title because the music and song had no age limit;

it spanned decades of great music and wonderful voices. Here again were Tauber, Pinza and Caruso, operatic arias and famous overtures, music that I had first heard on the BBC, on *Grand Hotel*, more than a decade before.

My father puffed his cigarette. The music filled the kitchen. The sheepdog barked in the yard, as the new batch of cows was shuttled into stalls. No other noise filtered in from the world outside. A little mound of peat ashes overflowed from the grate, fell near my father's toes and he moved his stockinged feet away from the spiral of dust. We listened in silence; he would comment only if touched by some memory or association within his sphere of remembrance.

Then John McCormick sang *The Last Rose of Summer*. My father exhaled slowly, as if the song carried the wellspring and the droplets of passed time and its ancient tradition.

'Now that's what I call singing.'

13

When she was a child, my sister Nora, the fourth youngest of the family, had gone to live with the Macks, who farmed in a place called Rathfarra. My father's sister, Annie, who was married to Jack Mack, had three sons and yearned for the daughter she could not naturally have. Abetted by Jack, who was mere clay in Annie's hands, my parents were persuaded, as a temporary measure, to let Nora join the family in Rathfarra, in the twin roles of companion and surrogate daughter to my aunt. I vaguely remember the Sunday that they arrived with pony and trap to take her away with them. She was just a slip of a child, about six or seven, with blonde hair and a smiling face, unable to fathom the monumental change that was about to affect her young life. In a few years, like the white child captured in an Indian raid, she would become assimilated into the family in Rathfarra and would regard it as her natural home. In her later life, she would fall between the stools of both our houses, into a limbo world that dragged her thither and yon, in search for a centre of family affiliation.

When I was twelve, I spent almost one whole summer in Rathfarra. Annie had been promoting my visit every time she came to Kilquane; perhaps she saw it as a bridge between our homes that would keep Nora in filial contact. I never wanted to go. I was selected because my escapist habits had rendered me more expendable than the others. Summers had become idyllic in Kilquane; the routes of evasion had widened. I was indulging blissfully in the freedom I had created. I promised to go to Rathfarra but went missing with the dog pack on the appointed day. Then they hoodwinked me. The Mack's eldest son, Davy, arrived with horse and cart, late in the evening after I had returned home. I was packed, scrubbed and seated on the rider of the cart before I had time to draw breath.

I had been to Rathfarra previously, riding the carrier of my mother's high-nelly. They were seldom pleasant times. Nora would hide herself in the parlour and refuse to appear. She had to be dragged out; she would hang her head, avert her face and cling to Annie's ample frame. To make matters worse, Paddy, the youngest son, would hijack the high-nelly soon after we arrived. I could see him dashing past the window in a blur of movement and hear the yells of exultation as if he were semi-demented by the thrill of speed. When we were ready to brave the journey home in the dark night, we would often find the bicycle thrown against the front wall, suffering a front wheel buckle or a punctured tube. Paddy had absconded.

The return trip was a silent one. I could sense that the mood didn't spring from the damaged bike alone. It had to do more with my mother's feeling that Nora was slipping away and did not see us as family anymore. She was frightened of us; perhaps she believed, or was led to believe, that we were ranged against her and would spirit her away from Rathfarra. When Jack and Annie came to visit Kilquane, Nora stayed in Rathfarra. Annie delivered messages of endearment in her absence, but we suspected that Nora neither conceived nor uttered them.

Jack laid down the law as soon as the supper was over that first night. If I were to eat and drink, Jack told me, I must earn the right by working; there were no drones in Rathfarra. I shared a bed with Paddy, in a room that was twice as large as any we had in Kilquane. It had a wooden floor, the ceiling was boarded, there was plaster coving all round the top edge of the walls. Rathfarra was a gentleman's farmhouse, a rural expression of opulence.

The parlour in Rathfarra was a gem. One wall was panelled and from it hung portraits of ancestral Macks, a seascape, and prints of racing horses. The other wall was almost completely covered by an ornate rosewood bookcase, holding a leatherbound collection. There was a great marble fireplace, coursed through with veins of apple green and threads of crystal white, like the fossilised tracks of prehistoric snails. The fireside chairs were upholstered in leather; their arms and surrounding wooden frame were bound in brass. The mahogany hunting table, the matching chairs and carvers would have graced any drawing room. I would stand at the threshold of the doorway and admire it, inhale the smell of leather, marvel at the furnishings and decor, and feel the ambience of old money.

We said the rosary before we went to bed. We would say it every evening, immediately the supper was over and also during thunderstorms, downpours, windstorms — any occurrence that was at variance with the normal weather pattern. Jack led off. He had a deep bass voice that filled the kitchen and reverberated off the walls. Everything about Jack was big: he had a huge head, his ears stuck out like jug handles, there was a large mole with its aureole of spindly grey hair on his upper lip. When he picked his nose, his little finger disappeared up the tunnel of his nostril. Jack suffered from what he called an acid stomach and when he belched in relief, which he did continuously, it seemed to erupt from his toes, making a series of minor eruptions as it coursed upwards and then exploded in full-blown blast.

As we knelt for the rosary, I saw Annie nod to Nora, who went and fetched a blackthorn stick that was leaning against the dresser. When the rosary began and Jack's intonation was filling the room, I saw the reason for it. When they first knelt, the three sons were as sombre-faced as undertakers, but as Jack's voice boomed out, they were beset by an overwhelming fit of skittishness. Laughter welled up and out through constricted throats and escaped in bursts of hilarity. All it took to set it off was the slightest deviation from the norm: a fly buzzing in the room, a mispronounced word, a donkey braying in the distance.

That was the reason for Annie's blackthorn. Each offender was rapped on the heels, which triggered spasms of amusement from the other two brothers. As the days went by, the rosary gathered volume and content, as if demonstrating to me the fullness of Rathfarra devotion, compared to my semi-pagan legacy from Kilquane. When we had finished the five mysteries, Annie called for a repeat. Jack led off into a double set and sometimes a treble. If that wasn't enough, he then launched into the trappings. We prayed for everything under the sun: sunshine, rain, sick animals, Paddy's toothache, Mike's carbuncle, the conversion of Russia, and lapsed Catholics the world over. The rosary developed into rigmarole: it went round and round like a processionary caterpillar and then spun off into eternal orbit. Every time the hilarity welled up, or when concentration waned, Annie's stick rapped out in sharp retribution.

I had noticed that Jack said 'Mayee' instead of Mary: 'Hail Mayee, Holy Mayee'. I shared the observation with the sons and afterwards told them the irreverent version of the Ave Maria, which I had learned in school. 'Hail Mary, full of grace, the cat fell down and broke its face. Holy Mary, mother of God, pray for my mother, she's stuck in the bog.'

Next evening when Jack led off with Hail Mayee, his sons went into fits. Annie's stick rapped repeatedly, but it was futile. The rosary broke up in chaos and Jack stormed out, accusing his sons of wilful disrespect towards their Lord and Maker. 'Mark my words but ye'll die without priest or doctor and burn in hell till it freezes over. An' that won't be today or tomorrow.' Annie stared in disbelief at the blackthorn, as if its powers had dissolved. I suspected that they blamed me: the frivolity had never reached this level before my presence amongst them. Every time I looked at Annie, a frosty glare had replaced her smile. But from then on, the penny dropped for Jack, and he sped through the rosary like a whirlwind.

On my first night in Rathfarra, Jack introduced me, in bated tones of warning, to the fearful Moider Do. In time I would figure out the derivation of the name. Moider Do was a corruption of Madra Dhu, the black dog. Jack came into the bedroom and found Paddy and I still awake. If we didn't go to sleep, he told us, the Moider Do would have us for his supper. Paddy covered his head, turned to the wall, and every time I tried to say something, he whispered a muffled 'Sshh, Sshh' from beneath the bedclothes. According to Jack, the black dog was the devil incarnate: it roamed the countryside in the dead of night, searching out misbehaving youngsters, especially those who laughed during the rosary. I knew the story was nonsense but I woke suddenly in the blackness, certain that I could hear panting outside the window and the scrape of toenails against the glass.

I woke again when the first light was streaking in the window. It was a bellow that roused me and, even in my stupor, I knew it could not be canine. There was Jack in the half-light, clad only in his shirt, his lower limbs like roughly hewn columns of Carrara marble. He left and I heard him bellowing in the next room where his two other sons were sleeping. It continued intermittently for the next two hours and would be repeated every morning.

'Get up, ye lazy hangmen! There are no drones in Rathfarra.'

The roaring had no effect; the sons would arise when the humour took them and the sun was high. I could hear Jack in the kitchen, railing about his lazy cafflers of sons. He announced a litany of disasters that would befall them because of their slothful regard for God's day and the opportunities He had put in their way.

'The house will fall down. There won't be a cow in the fields, or a meadow of hay cut or saved. Ye'll die, roaring from the hunger, like Jack Doran's ass.'

It was mid-morning when we were ready for the fields. And what fields they were: great expanses of lush green whatever the season. You could almost see the grass growing in

Rathfarra; it was truly the land of milk and honey. It reminded me of Miss Abigail's description of the Ukraine when we stood around the tattered map of Europe. It was the breadbasket of Russia, she said. It grew wheat in vast abundance and if you threw a stick on the ground overnight, it would be covered by grass come morning.

But however fertile Rathfarra might be, it served not a whit to alter my view of eternal routine chores in fields of hay and root crops. Thinning turnips in Rathfarra drills were just as bad at it was in Kilquane. And the man who was lord in Rathfarra, acted in the same way as did the boss in my home place. Jack never did the menial back breaking chores: squatting to thin between turnips drills, pulling up noxious weeds by their roots or collecting from new meadows the stones that might break the mowing bar. But I would be expected to do those tasks. I had declared my independence in Kilquane; I would now need to do so in Rathfarra.

I found a reluctant conspirator in Paddy. He had the same feeling for land as my brothers had. But he liked diversion too and as long as the elder brother, Davy, was not about, he would follow me. We made rabbit hunters out of sheep dogs that were, as Jack put it, 'even lazier than his own sons. An' who could blame them an' the example they got'. We roped in a terrier from Bond's, incongruously called Shep, a bastard greyhound belonging to Mick Collins, a straying Jack Russell, and we were on our way.

But there is always a busybody to sneak on indolent youth. We crossed a hump-backed bridge near the south boundary and found Jack waiting for us, brandishing Annie's blackthorn. He made a drive at us, tripped over Bond's terrier and fell in the briars. If he hadn't fallen, we would have escaped and faced his wrath when he had simmered down. But the sight of a thorn embedded in Jack's cheekbone stirred the offspring loyalty in Paddy. He went to pluck it out and was repaid with a roar and a sharp blow across the buttocks. Paddy said nothing; he leaped over the wall, selected the strongest ragwort and brought it up from the root with a rending declaration of renewed duty. The prodigal son had returned to the fold.

I was a marked man, Jack told me that night. Annie favoured me now with naked hostility in her hooded eyes. I, who was supposed to build the bridge between our houses, had mined and scuppered it.

'Of all the brood in Kilquane,' Jack would say, 'and God knows but they're hangin' from the ceiling over there, how come we got you, the father of all drones?'

Jack, however, was the greatest drone of all. But like many a drone he was a master at delegation. Jack issued orders like a mandarin. By mid-morning we would be gathered, bleary-eyed, round the kitchen table. In most farms in our neighbourhood, when the sun was high, the flush and welter of early morning activity would by now have settled into regular routine. Here we were, four hours behind and not an ounce of shame amongst us. Jack had made numerous trips to the rooms, returning to his bed after each one. He re-appeared twenty minutes later in Carrara thighs, bellowing lectures on indolence. Now he was at the top of the table — the prophet of doom, a male Cassandra with an acid stomach, grimacing pain towards offspring and relative.

'The house will fall down, the bank will take over the land, there won't be a cow to be milked.'

Jack roared out the commands: Davy to the creamery, Mike to draw out dung, Paddy to the thistles. 'And, Nestor, I don't care if you don't do a dammed thing, as long as you don't keep the rest of 'em idle.'

Annie was like a Polynesian queen, who had, in Jack's chiding observation, fallen into too much flesh. She was the last to appear, coming out regally from the inner room, escorted by her pages, Nora and Paddy. She beamed at us all, sending out shafts of love and affability to all the spaces that bodies occupied, except mine. Nora did the vesting; Paddy guided his mother's steps in the grand procession to the kitchen, Annie heaved herself into the armchair beside the range and waited for service.

Jack and Annie were totally different personalities. He was loud and bluff, given to fits of anger that, like the bile in his stomach, exploded outwards without any hint of pretension or camouflage. Annie was devious. When she wanted something, she would never be deflected from her goal. Jack might have brusquely dismissed the idea, told her to have goddamn sense and asked if she thought that he was growing pound notes on the dunghill. She would smile throughout the dismissal, but later she would come scheming again, now presenting her case from a changed angle that sounded vastly different from the original. Annie picked off his objections, bit by bit, like a sculptor working on a slab of granite. Finally Jack saw where she was leading and realised how much had already been chipped from him. Then he bellowed his submission.

'I may as well be pissin' agin' the wind.'

343

Annie used Nora like a conduit to put out the first feelers of exploration, testing the responses against the circuits of route and strategy. Jack listened to Nora with a stoic tolerance. There was an extraordinary affection between them; it had been forged in the days when he was trying to wean away from a period of hell raising. Jack had been the archetypal hard man. I had heard about it in Kilquane before ever I went to Rathfarra. He would take the cart to the creamery in the morning and wouldn't return until it was time for the evening milking. The long interval was spent doing the rounds of the pubs in Shanagolden. Jack brought Nora with him; she was his minder, his magnet to Rathfarra, the influence that would finally steer him from the irresponsible company of his cronies. Nora would drive him home in the heel of the evening, a little blonde-haired waif hardly able to see over the rim of the trap cart, a child thrust into the twin role of warden and confidante. I never heard Jack utter a cross word to her, even when Annie's temptations, conducted through Nora, were sorely trying his patience and his pocket. If she had been his own daughter, he could not have loved her more. The role of guardian had an eventual effect, however. Nora was sitting in public houses, awash in a sea of ribaldry, in the company of men four times her age, when she should have been at school and at play.

The sons, especially Paddy and Mike, had inherited the war stories of the hard man days. They would repeat them to me like school learning put into the memory by rote. Not a word ever changed, an inflection, or a pause for breath. They told the stories with intense adulation and without the slightest hint of criticism. Some I believed, others I took with a grain of salt, especially the one about the filly Molly Dear. Jack had taken her by row-boat across the Shannon to compete in a point-to-point near Dromoland. On the return trip, the filly panicked when the wind came up and plunged over the side. Jack went in after her, and him, as Paddy would say, without a stroke for swimming. He grabbed the filly by the tail, clung behind, and guided her safely to the shore at Foynes. It didn't take a feather out of him, Mike said.

In Bunratty now, beside the Castle and the folk park, there is a famous pub called Durty Nellie's. Originally it was owned by a man called Ryan and run by his sister. I used go there sometimes after work and catch the midnight bus to Limerick at closing time. The old man offered me the parlour couch to sleep on when I missed the bus one arctic night, but I didn't use it much because he never stopped talking. He was a brilliant raconteur; his memory was honed to perfection. He remembered trivia, importance, time and place, as if, in his old age, he had dwelled long and lovingly on the events of his yesterday. Then he stopped suddenly. Perhaps he realised that his dominance was ungracious.

'What part of the country do you come from, a *mhic*?

'Coolcappa in West Limerick. It's about midway between Rathkeale and Shanagolden.'

'Ah. Shanagolden. I knew a man from near there once. Wild as the wind. An' mad about horses. Where's this he was from? Rath, Rath something or other.'

'Rathfarra,' I ventured.

'The very place. You have it. Jack Mack. That's your man. You know him?'

'He's my uncle. Was he really a wild man?'

'Wild, stop. We were in this boat, goin' across the Shannon after a meet in Dromoland. He had a little mare called Molly Dear on board. The wind blew up and . . . '

Now in his advancing years Jack wanted to bury the reputation of the hard man. He would never mention his past image in the presence of his family, as if the lore might contaminate further, the lack of industry of his sons. He pulled the veil over it and I heard snatches of it once only, when I eavesdropped on a conversation he was having with the Doctor Kelly in the quiet of the cowhouse. Kelly was no medical man; the title arose from his penchant for suggesting cures for every common ailment of man and beast. The remedies were mostly rubs and I'm sure he concocted them himself. The basic ingredients in the mixtures were always the same: mare's urine and the milk of a heifer immediately after giving birth. The Doctor came often to Rathfarra to help with the harvest, but he was even more disruptive than me. He would just stand there yapping, indulging himself in his two great interests — the prophecies of Saint Malachy and the conversion of the pagans in darkest Africa. He stopped talking to me when I told him that I had once given half-a-crown for a black baby and never got one. I had forgotten all about it because he had raised no objection at the time, but later that night, when we were saying the rosary, he halted halfway through his decade and addressed me with the paled countenance of sudden and intense anger.

'You 'haythen' little bastard.'

In the wild days the Doctor had been a disciple of Jack's. Perhaps that was the reason why he was still treated with deference, as if there was something in the history of the hard man which made Jack feel that he owed him. He was paid for his presence in Rathfarra, though he never did a stroke of work.

Jack had been fearless in his heyday. He had faced down a quartet of Black and Tans, who had arrived to search the house, on the pretext that Rathfarra was a safe place for rebels on the run. He went for them with a fourpronged pitchfork; Paddy told me that they scattered like goslings before a sheepdog. I could well believe it because I saw him in action myself, long after he was past his athletic best, and even then he was a sight to behold. The Fitzgibbons drove their cows to the milking along the road in front of Rathfarra. They ran a bull with the cows, a vicious ill-tempered shorthorn, which was given a wide berth by all but the working hand, who had no other option. Paddy, Nora and I were in the front garden, trimming the boxhedge, when the cows came by. There was a small iron gate midway in the front wall and the bull halted before it with ferocious intent, bellowing anger, salivating spume, and kicking up a shower of gravel with alternate forelegs. The bull drove at the gate, forcing the iron bars inward, as if they had been beaten by a blacksmith's hammer. Jack was in the kitchen, concocting a mug of tepid milk and bread soda to relieve his heartburn. He came rushing out, looked around him in vain for a stick, pulled open the buckled gate, and punched the bull between the eyes. The animal's eyes glazed over, the forelegs sagged and it walked docile and silent to the farmyard at the top of the hill.

'Anytime you like,' Jack shook his ham fist after the bull, 'anytime you like, boyo. There's more of this here for you, you bad-minded hoor.'

★ ★ ★

The eastern gable of the farmhouse backed on to a field of oats. Shortly before it fully ripened, there was a thunderstorm and a cloudburst. A patch of corn was flattened by the battering rain. As the days passed, the patch grew bigger because, in domino effect, the standing oats at the edge of the patch lost support, leaned over and was felled with the first puff of wind or summer shower. It became a Mecca for crows and pigeons.

Jack lost the run of himself. He would see a shadow flitting by the window and it jerked him erect with tension. A few moments after the shadow had passed, a boisterous cackle of crows would rise from the patch, as the newcomer squabbled with its brothers in residence. Jack almost upset the table in his mad anxiety to drive them away: cups fell to the ground, the dog yelped when Jack trod on its tail, spilled milk flowed onto the floor in a minor cascade. Jack grabbed Annie's stick and headed for the patch of corn.

'I'll give ye caw caw, ye black 'sans' of bitches.'

This went on for weeks and the house was in turmoil. I couldn't find a sheepdog for the hunting. They were cowering between the columns in the hay barn and not even the rattle of a feeding bowl would tempt them out. Jack was in a foul mood; he yelled at everyone who crossed his path, except his beloved Nora. Annie told us that she was breeding a heart attack; his sudden bellows and the mad drive from the table were causing a pounding in her chest. It was the only time that the three sons made early morning starts.

Jack and I wrapped coloured ribbons to the ends of hazel sticks and planted them in the middle of the patch. I wanted to tell Jack that I had read about crows being colour blind and, if crows were, most likely so were the pigeons. But I thought better of it. The coloured ribbons were the Doctor's recipe; he had been reminded of it when the crows were included in the trimmings of the rosary. The whirring ribbons were never known to fail, he declared; they would frighten the shite out of the birds. But they failed to have any effect, as did the special supplication in the rosary. The Doctor concluded that it was no wonder our prayers weren't heard.

'How could you expect God to listen an' the haythen little bastard under the wan roof with us?'

Annie nodded.

Then Jack and I constructed a scarecrow. Jack stood a little way off, suggesting changes here, redesign there. The scarecrow was an awesome sight. It had a set of spindly legs, cut from the branches of the nearby ash tree and driven into the ground through a pair of Davy's old wellington boots. The arms were fashioned from barrel staves nailed together: one side was aimed at the sky, the other leaned to the ground, as if the scarecrow was walking a tightrope. Its face was half of a teddy bear, wearing a Halloween mask with gorilla features. The scarecrow was finally draped in one of Annie's summer frocks, topped by a shapeless hat that Jack kept on a nail in the cowbyre. It was successful for half a day; by dinnertime the dark shadows were flitting by the window, Jack was bounding out, waving the stick and bellowing, 'I'll give ye caw caw, ye black hoorin' bastards'.

Jack sent me for Mick Collins and his shotgun. Mick was a most placid pleasant person. He was then about sixteen, chubby and smiling. He sat with me one whole Sunday under the ash tree, on the sheltered side of the dividing wall. This would be the ultimate solution: Collins would shoot a crow and it would be hung on the scarecrow as a terrible warning to its feathered fraternity. Strangely, not a bird landed on the patch that day. The following morning they returned in hundreds: they covered the ash tree like black monstrous locusts, formed a skewed line on the outstretched arms of the scarecrow, picked at the eyes of the gorilla, and left a profusion of calling cards on Jack's hat. Jack stood on the top of the wall, waving his great arms like a windmill. 'I'll fix ye yet, ye black hoorin' robbers.'

The birds trotted around the patch, lifted with a languorous defiant laziness and settled again.

After the rosary was recited that evening, Jack went into the parlour, and came out with half-a-crown nestling in his hand. He held it out to us.

'That much, to man, woman or child that will shift them hoors of crows.'

I had a restless night. The sheep dogs

kicked up a racket when I was drifting off to sleep and Paddy put his head under the blanket. The Moider Do was abroad. My mind flew for comfort to Kilquane and I suddenly remembered my father's strategy for ridding the birds from lodged corn.

I was up early and cut a dozen saplings from the ash tree. I planted them round the fallen patch and then ran lengths of black thread, from stake to stake, in several layers. As soon as I had left the patch, the crows returned, swooping down in nonchalant confidence. They became entangled in the thread, fluttered and squawked and took off in a bedraggled flight of terror. Two were held fast to the ash saplings.

When I told Jack, he was standing by the dresser, mixing his morning stomach remedy. He was a more awesome sight than the scarecrow as he raced to the patch of corn in his nightshift. It rucked upwards in the movement, showing a splash of Carrara white and displaying, in full splendour, the equipment of his manhood. Jack jigged in delight when he saw my handiwork, despatched the two crows with a deft twist of his wrist and hung them from the yardarm of the scarecrow. He shook his hand at the flock of crows that were heading towards Langfords' wood, never to return.

'Ye wouldn't listen to me when I told ye. Didn't I tell ye? I told ye I'd give ye caw caw.'

A few days later I mustered up the courage to ask him for the half-crown.

'Is it coddin' me you are? Haven't I been keepin' a roof over your head and givin' you plenty to ate? Ou'r that with you.'

But his mood towards me changed. He would sometimes creep up behind me and ruffle my hair. I would be invited to accompany him, with Nelson the sheepdog, to bring home the cows to the milking. One Sunday, he brought Nora and me to the pattern day in Barrigone. He asked Annie too but she had a headache coming on and suspected it was the start of a migraine attack.

Barrigone was a hamlet with one public house. Its fame lay in the holy well that rose out of the shingle on the fringe of the Shannon. It was black with people: crowds of women and youngsters did the rounds of the holy well, the mumble of prayers rose in the air like a swarm of bees in flight. Nora and I joined the throng at the well with instructions to pray for a special intention. I told Jack that I couldn't pray for any intention unless I knew what it was.

'Questions. Always bloody questions. You'll catch yourself coming back some day, you're so goddamn smart.'

By the time we had finished the rounds, Jack was in full swing in the public house. He had reverted, dropping the facade of the sensible adult with his wild days behind him. The war stories were pouring out: madcap escapades, coups at race meetings, nights of wild binges wherever his meandering had led him. The moment he saw Nora, his eyes lit up. Jack brought her into the group he was regaling, raised her to sit on the counter-top and broadcast her goodness and talents in the same booming voice that had vilified the crows and pounded through the rosary. He plied us with drinks — ginger beer and Nash's lemonade — and stuffed us with coarse biscuits as big as saucers. But I was just an insignificant appendage to my sister; he made one single reference to me.

'That's her brother. Great man for trappin' crows. But the devil will get him yet for he hasn't an ounce of religion.'

We would have been in the pub all night if Nora hadn't prevailed on him after much cajoling. I could tell it was a practised art. She was like a petitioner in the court of the king: judging the mood, coming forward with a whispered word, ghosting away when the blackened frown telegraphed irritation.

Finally he came away with us. He weaved away from the counter and declared that it was time for all Christian men to be in their beds. We led him arm-in-arm to the place where the pony was hitched. Nora propped him against the stone wall and tackled the pony to the trap. She did it with an innate skill. Once we had hoisted him up and settled him in the seat, he dropped his head and fell asleep. Nora drove home in the darkness, her tiny hands working the reins with sure-fingered confidence. A mile from home she shook Jack awake. He grumbled, belched and then grew seriously alert. He took the reins and shook the pony into a steady trot. We slowed to take the bend of the road near Tobin's house and then stopped.

'A man talks awful rubbish when he has a few drinks taken,' Jack said. 'An' 'twould be better for all of us to leave it where it happened'.

★　★　★

The two eldest sons went every evening to Tobin's house. Collins would call and they set off with evident excitement as if something special was afoot. When they were starting out, Paddy gave tongue to his litany of supplication. His opening line was always the

same — a primer for the ensuing beseech-
ment.

'I'll go too.'

The brothers looked at him as if he had
said something insane.

'D'ye you hear him? What's he talking
about?'

Jack and Annie ignored him at first. Then
Paddy opened up with the litany.

'Will I go, Da? Will I? Will I?'

'Once and for all,' Jack barked, 'you're not
going. That's it.'

Paddy turned to Annie.

'Will I go, Ma? Can I?'

'When you're a big boy.'

'I'm big now. Will I?'

'I'll give him will I, will I. If he doesn't shut
up, I'll sink my boot in his arse,' Jack said.

He extended his foot to emphasise the
threat and then quickly pulled it away when
he realised that he had cast off the boots
before sitting down for supper. Paddy sulked
at the window as he watched the others head
out the front gate. When they had gone, he
ran out the front and stood on the roadway.
Every now and then a strangled cry wafted in
through the porch.

'He badly wants a root up d'arse,' Jack
sighed.

I wondered what was happening in Tobin's

house. Jack went early to bed, as did Nora; Annie stayed nodding by the fire waiting until the sons came home. When the silence settled like a pall over the house, Paddy and I escaped through the window and headed for Tobin's. We heard the sudden gush of laughter and a few raucous yelps when we approached. It died, like a tap turned off, the moment we appeared at the doorway. Traces of the merriment were etched on frozen faces like fossil tracks on limestone strata. We had killed the mood stone dead. They sat around the table making limp conversation: the weather, the price of cattle, what a fierce bad year it was for thistles.

I was twelve that year; Paddy was a couple of years older. But in their perception, the four or five years that separated us from Davy and his cronies was a gulf. They were experienced and knowing; comfortable on the fringes of adult conversation and innuendo. The worldliest of all was Smokey Nolan. His skin was the colour of smoked bacon; with his dark crinkly hair and the sloe hue surround to the eyes he could have passed for a Spaniard. Smokey was the local Casanova: he went dancing, drank pints of stout, was missing until the small hours of Monday morning and was often reported in the company of young women.

When I got to know them better I realised how simple and innocent they really were. They were merely playing on the margins of adulthood; their real pursuit was to laugh, be happy and to defer to the rakish court jester amongst them, as Smokey was. They paid him in the coin of their adulation.

We had no way of knowing it then but that easy simple flow of life would be cut off in mid-stream. Old Father Time came with a swathing scythe to the heartland of Rathfarrra and cut them off in their prime: Davy, Mick Collins, Smokey, Chris Tobin. And Paddy, a few years later.

The morning after the escapade in Tobin's, I had gone out early in search of mushrooms. Nora sought me out in the quiet of the porch when I returned; the rest were still abed. I had done a bad thing, she told me, leading poor Paddy astray like that. I tried to tell her that Paddy was a willing partner, but her sympathies were not on my side; the Macks were her family. It might be better, she told me, if I packed my bag and went home, adding that Annie thought so too.

'I'm going home,' I told Jack, when he did his next bellowing circuit of the house.

'You are in your arse,' he roared. Then he ruffled my hair, pinched the lobe of my ear and winked. 'Out there with you to the road field. There's loads of *buachallawns* to be pulled.'

Jack's brother Charlie came to help with the corn stacking. The brothers were as different as chalk and cheese. Charlie was a truculent man who lived a life of order and was irritated by any disruption to it. You could even see it in the way he moved: short mincing steps that never varied in pace. The truculence was present in the way he spoke; every response was prefaced by a question, as if to accost the hidden traps that had been laid for him.

'Are you trying to tell me? Are you asking me to believe? What class a question is that?'

Charlie's singular indulgence, was the pony and trap. They were both resplendent; the woodwork smelled of yacht varnish, the harness of leather soap, the pony's coat was clipped and curried. He kept a chamois cloth in the pouch that held the whip; he would remove it and dab at the harness whenever a spot offended him. His arrival in Rathfarra, one sweltering day in mid-September, took Annie by surprise. Charlie had a palate as ordered as his lifestyle: he had an aversion to home-cured bacon, brown bread and eggs. His first act on arrival was to unharness the cob and let it loose in the shelter of the apple trees. Then he and Jack repaired to the parlour to make fraternal soundings and break open a few bottles of stout.

Word came out to Paddy in the haggard that he should to go immediately to the shop in Kilcolman and fetch sliced ham and a loaf of bread. Kilcolman was two miles away and there was no transport.

'Take Charlie's trap,' Davy suggested. 'You'll be back before he comes out of the parlour.'

I was inveigled to accompany Paddy. We stole the cob from under the trees, pulled the trap out on the road, went past the first bend and yoked up. I should have read the signs. There was an expression of unbridled anticipation, like an aura, on Paddy's face. It was the same expectancy that lit him up when he hijacked my mother's bicycle. He stood up in the well of the trap, took out the whip and flourished it at the cob. The animal shivered; a spasm shook the rippling muscles, the legs bunched like a sprinter at a starter block. Paddy and the pony were soul brothers, united in a passion for speed.

We raised a storm of dust on the road. Paddy was like a young Ben Hur: hair flying in the wind, a look of sinful pleasure lighting his features. We survived the outward journey and would probably have survived the inner,

if, before we rounded the bend at Dunmoy-
lan, Paddy hadn't flourished the whip and
made it crack like the lion tamer's in Duffy's
circus. The cob veered towards the stone wall,
the wheel hub smashed and the near shaft
splintered like a mast in a hurricane.

We pulled the trap onto the grass margin
and rode the pony home. It was Paddy's
intention to slip quietly into the haggard and
tell his mother what had happened. She, in
turn, would diplomatically tell Charlie, in a
way that would mollify the injury to his
beloved pony and trap. But they all had
returned to the haggard. We were in full view
as we appeared riding the cob and it was
obvious that some disaster had occurred.
Paddy mumbled a response to Charlie's fury,
all the time using the plural 'we'. I was a mere
passenger, scared, blameless and shaking, but
I was made to share the rap. After the rosary,
when the hullabaloo had died down and
Charlie had left, reiterating that he would
never darken the door of Rathfarra again,
Annie sent out a probing tendril of
accusation.

'You know,' she ventured, as if musing out
loud, 'nothing like this ever happened before.'

'You never said a truer word,' the Doctor
agreed. 'The curse of the haythen is upon us.
An' that's for sure.'

Jack hawked and aimed the spit at a beetle emerging from a crack in the flagstone. He glued it immobile in a pool of phlegm.

'Will ye whist,' he thundered. 'Ye know full well who was doin' the drivin', but the pair of ye, if ye thought ye'd get away with it, would blame the Virgin Mary and she spotless.'

Annie smiled; it spread across her face in a glowing testimony of tolerant acceptance. The boss had spoken, but his authority was flawed; she knew better. It worried me because she came frequently to our house in Kilquane. Annie had the ear of my father. She was adept at influencing him too, dropping innuendoes here and there, knowing that all would take root in his mind and germinate.

I tried to get on her side, scratching around the perimeter of her universe in servile homage. I would never replace Nora in her affection, but I might be allowed to play a secondary role. Without being bidden, I sought out the wayward pattern of the laying hens and collected the eggs, I brought her cabbages from the garden, washed potatoes, swept the flagged kitchen floor and drew water from the well. But she never smiled at me again unless Jack was present. The moment he was gone, I would feel her eyes on me and when I looked, I was fixed with the steady glare and the pursed lips of rebuke. So I switched my allegiance to Jack.

★ ★ ★

Sunday mornings were chaos. Every Saturday night Jack announced that we were going to ten o'clock mass in Kilcolman. If his family wasn't ready on time, he and Nora would go alone. Annie oversaw the ensuing flurry of activity, as if she was the driving force behind the declaration. The Sunday clothes were brought out from the airing-press and laid on the bars above the range. They were set out in three neat bundles: each with a shirt, pants, gansey and a pair of stockings. Nora polished the Sunday shoes and ranked them in order of status on the floor beside the dresser.

On Sunday morning Jack was dressed and ready by eight o'clock; the rest apart from Nora, were deep in slumber. Then the routine of the circuit began; the visits to the bedrooms to rouse the sleeping occupants. The bellowing was like thunderclaps in the silence as Jack pulled his sons into sitting positions. When he returned, they had reverted to the foetal position of deep slumber. In between, he harnessed the pony and pulled the trap around to the front gate. He would take his seat, do a U-turn with the trap, crack the whip and roar at the pony as if he were setting off. Jack had a watch in the fob pocket of his waistcoat; he would take that out, dangle it by the gold chain and sigh in desperation every time he looked at it. Eventually one of the sons straggled forth, blinking sleep from his eyes.

Last to come was Annie; she ambled out as if time was a gesture to idiots and their schedules, and if all the arrangements the night before were but empty homage to a duped and simple man. Jack never blamed her, nor raised his voice in anger when she appeared. He had castigated each of the sons: called them irreverent lazy lumps, arch enemies of God and their heritance. Annie wore her widest smile: the visage of saintly suffering, the stoic forbearance of a mother keeping her senses in the face of trial and tribulation. I used wonder why he behaved like that towards her; it was apparent that Annie was the prime culprit. She would not rise until her acolytes had come to dress her.

We never ever made it to Kilcolman. We would go instead to Shanagolden mass, which was an hour later and notorious for the length of its sermon. We were invariably late for that mass too. All the way home, Jack would deliver a tirade. It fell on desert air because the two elder sons had met up with their cronies and had gone off. Paddy pleaded to drive the pony, and eventually, through Annie's intervention, was permitted, provided he slowed to walking pace. He wore the face of a frustrated charioteer, lost concentration and was roared at when the pony strayed and tried to crop the grass margin. Annie alone listened to the monologue. She clasped her hands and laid her chin on them in a posture of long-suffering but radiant sainthood. She nodded and smiled all the way to Rathfarra.

★　★　★

I went home the last week of August. Jack helped me onto the cart and seated me on a sackful of hay. He shook hands with me and pressed a wad of paper into my palm. Annie stood in the front porch with Paddy at her side. She was beaming. There was no sign of Nora and it bothered me. I had come no closer to her; I had failed as my family's emissary. I had a glimpse of her then, peeping out from behind the net curtain in the kitchen, and in the fleeting moment, I thought her face looked sad. My spirits lifted a little but ebbed when I realised what would happen in the wake of my departure. Annie would repair any breach I had made to Nora's loyalties.

The image of Nora haunted me as we jolted towards Kilquane. It stayed until the landmarks of home eased it away. When we came by Tynies, I remembered the wad of paper in my hand, opened it and found two half-crowns.

14

I stood at the window that looked out on Mannix's Folly and watched them return to the fields. My brother John led the red mare, the hired hand was walking at my brother's side. Fifty yards behind them came my father; the other horse, without rein or direction, muzzled his shoulder as he followed his master. The sheepdog brought up the rear. Towser was getting old. A few years before he would be snapping at my father's heels, sniffing in circles at his scent trail, cavorting in joyful leaps against his lower body. I watched until they went through the iron gate and the hedgerow hid them from sight.

There was a book on the windowsill. It had been the first book I had tried to read, but it had gone missing by the time I had mastered the skill. *The Little Shepherd of Kingdom Come* had been brought to Kilquane by an uncle, as a memento of his visit. He emphasised that it wasn't a gift and that it should be returned to him in the same pristine condition as he had delivered it. It was a hardback, burgundy red, and the page edges were in the same colour. Over the years the book had suffered the same fate as *A Tale of Two Cities*: the cover had been torn off, perhaps to repair a school reader, the pencilled messages scrawled through the pages foretold the ego journeys of my siblings' maturing minds.

I had found the book in the press in the far corner of the kitchen; it also held polish tins and brushes, my mother's sewing box, her milking stool. When the door was opened, the innards usually tumbled out and when the right item had been found, everything was piled back again in disarray. I remembered the book in its unsullied state. I had tried to read it first before I passed out of Miss James' tutelage, but my feeble attempts were scorned. I had promised myself that a day would come when I would embarrass them all with my reading prowess.

A shadow fell across the back-door threshold and my mother came into the kitchen. I chided myself for dallying because she probably had some chore for me. But she came and stood beside me at the window, took up the book and idly turned the pages. Then she told me that she had got a letter from the school across the Shannon where, in early June, I had sat the entrance examination. I had been accepted. She must have read some misgivings in my face for she went on to tell me that I had no option but to accept; there was no place for me in Kilquane. It was obvious to everyone there that I had no interest, and even if I had, it would be the wrong decision. The day school closed for Easter holidays; Miss Abigail had given me a letter for my mother. It said that on no account should I be kept at home in Kilquane because I would be wasted on the land, I should have greater things to aim at. My father clucked in sarcastic merriment when he heard that and blew bursts of cynical amusement through his nostrils. Whatever about me being wasted on the land, he observed, the land would certainly be wasted on me.

My mother handed me the book. Books were my way out, she told me, and I should be thankful that I was getting the opportunity. It wouldn't be easy for them to find the money to educate me but they would find it somehow.

She went out of the kitchen in a blur of movement; a few moments later I heard the snatches of tuneless song that accompanied her circuit of work. I have never known anyone so consumed with work as my mother was. She galloped from chore to chore as if each one was a new landfall in the frenetic route of her labour. I would call her from the kitchen door, pass her in the cobbled yard and she would neither see nor hear me. In later years, we had a hired hand who was nicknamed Ruck. He had a way of describing my mother; when she came out of the bedroom at the crack of dawn, she hit the flagstones running.

My mother was right when she read the misgivings in my face. Up to the time I sat the entrance examination, I had never a second thought about making my way in the world outside Kilquane. I was filled with confidence then. I believed that I was clever and whenever it was called into question, I was able to cope with ease. I wanted to learn, to make new discoveries in the territory of knowledge. But that day in the examination hall, it all changed. It seemed that I had crash-landed in another universe, far removed from my humble planet. I wore clothes handed down from my brother John, who had grown out of them. The legs of the short pants hung unevenly below my knees, the jacket cuffs were frayed. I had writing equipment a whisper away from the quill: a nib in a chrome holder, black ink in a Baby Power bottle. All round me I heard the swish of fountain pens. The youngsters in the examination hall appeared to me like pupils in English public schools, in the fashion in which they dressed and spoke. I hoped none would talk to me and no one did. They would laugh politely at me. If they knew that I passed my days rabbit-hunting and was enthralled by goldfinch song, I would be classed as a yokel. As I wrote, I thought again of the analogy of the fastest gun in the west; there were a hundred young guns in that examination hall faster than me.

I took *The Little Shepherd of Kingdom Come* to my hideaway in the haybarn. I tried to feel sorry for young Chad and his dog Jack, making their orphan way from Lonesome in Kentucky down to the Bluegrass country and beyond it to the Cumberland Mountains. But the visions kept re-appearing and when I was forced to indulge them and face their reality, I was filled with a black maelstrom of fear. I was like young Chad, going out into the unknown. Kilquane was my lair, my home place, but there was no room for me there. Like the fox, whose den mad Danaher had closed on the eve of the hunt, I was forced into the open. It loomed awesome and fearful.

I looked out from the ventilation square, high up in the gable of the barn. The saucer-shaped plain fell away to the Shannon and rose to meet the low hills on the horizon. I sought the landmarks of my known world, this little hidden kingdom that I had roamed over and knew, as if it were an extension to my soul. I saw the grove of trees far away in Knockaderry; the outer extremity of my territory, a place left deliberately uncharted for some future exploration. It was the first thing I saw when I scanned the horizon in the morning: the sun had returned, the earth had moved in its eternal axis, God was in His heaven, all was right with the world. The grove would be the first of my landfalls to disappear beyond the rim of a changing horizon; when I came home for Christmas holidays it had been cut down.

Over Harold's wood, the mackerel sky formed and reformed, then drifted away in trailing wisps of vapour like the trails of a squadron of jet planes. Everywhere I looked there was columns of smoke, spiralling upwards in auger-shaped patterns. The rising chimney smoke was our semaphore system. When a chimney top was smokeless, the nearest neighbour sped to the house to check the condition of its occupants. In many of those houses the fire had never gone out, it was unlucky if it did. The fire was raked over at night; the embers blown into flame in the early dawn, to light the kindling of decayed wood. In later years, when my parents moved into their new home, my father brought the fire with him in an old bucket and set it in the grate. In his generation and that of his father, the fire in Kilquane had never gone out.

I stood there at the square-shaped window and let the truth form in my soul. I knew that I didn't want to leave, but the die had been cast and I was the one who had shaped and tempered its ejection. My own cleverness was coiling back on me, like the spirals of smoke rising out of the clusters of trees that sheltered the houses. It was over. I knew then that when I left this place, I would never find it again, as once it had been. There would only be remnants of the hidden kingdom in the saucer-shaped valley, but never the original marvel. All would have moved on.

I saw Madge come up the passageway carrying a feeding bucket. She bore our surname, the last in the line of the other founding brother who had settled in Kilquane. Apart from my Aunt Hannah, Madge was the only one outside my family with whom I ever shared my inner self. But there was a difference; the warmth of Hannah's affection was like an enveloping cocoon. Her concern was visible, in wordless sounds of understanding, in the soft eyes that filled with sympathy, the ruffle of her hand in my hair. Madge was utterly practical; she made unadorned judgements in a take it or leave it style.

But she loved to hear stories of our escapades and to be involved when some prank was being conceived. Her eyes would light up; her feet would beat time against the flagstones, as if merriment was a tune in her head. She would search me out in the aftermath of some mischief.

'Don't tell me now. Come in when they're all at the milking and we'll have the place to ourselves.'

I would find her then, sitting in the armchair, her feet on a small stool, the fire glowing brightly, the floor swept, avid expectation on her face.

'Sit now and tell me. An' don't leave out a single word.'

Madge hunched her thin shoulders and they shook with the enjoyment that was welling up inside her. She would hold out a staying hand and make me tell the story again. There were stories I had to repeat so many times that they had become rooted in my mind, like the incident when we duped Nonie Sheridan, with mock lozenges. Nonie had a craving for those sweets, and once, when my mother handed her the packet, expecting that Nonie would take the one that was hanging out, the old woman took five, crammed them into her mouth and returned a single lozenge in a collapsed packet. The next visit we were ready for her. The baking soda in my mother's baking tin had hardened into slabs. I had cut them exactly to the shape and size of real lozenges and offered a palmful to Nonie. She scooped them into her mouth; the next moment she was spluttering, declaring to God that she had been poisoned. Nonie spat them out in a cascade of rage, took up her basket of trinkets, and swore that she would never darken our door the longest day she lived.

When there were no escapades to recount, Madge would ask me to read her a story from my schoolbook. She could read with the best of us, but she preferred to be entertained by someone else. I waited as she arranged herself before the fire, a cushion against her back, her feet resting on the fender as if she were in a private box. She inclined her head, looked at me intently with the sharp bright eyes of a curious bird and let the words create pictures, music and laughter in the fertile seedbed of her brain.

I could go down the passageway now and find her feeding a calf beside the ash tree. I could tell her my tale of woe and, before I got into my stride, she would put out that restraining hand and bid me to have sense.

What was I worrying about? Wouldn't it be worse if they had asked me to stay at home?

'You can't have it both ways, boyo.'

Above the pall of haze that shrouded the hedgerows, I saw the keep-tower of Lisnacullia. Hannah would make petition for me, but this time she would lose and I would be faulted for involving her. I decided that my predicament could not be solved by discussion or mediation. I would be flying in the face of my mother's generosity by doubting her plans for me. My father would concur with that. Either way I would be wrong.

The fear was replaced with remorse. It wouldn't be easy, my mother said. She and my father would bear the burden of hardship for my education. I thought of all the mornings I had lain in bed when the others were toiling in the fields; the days I had wandered the kingdom, while they sweated under the sun, or froze in winter fields under leaden skies. I had slipped away when another hand would have lifted the hay before the weather broke. And when I was forced to pitch in, I did so with bad grace and with workmanship that my father said, had the very stamp of laziness about it.

I would go to the fields now, hide the book behind the stall in the cow byre and cover it with the accumulated hayseed. That puerile deception was the wisdom of experience. Books, my father had told me, were fine in their time and place but not in the middle of the day. A few years before, I had saved half-a-crown from the money I had accumulated selling rabbits, and sent away for a book about speedway racing, which I had seen advertised in one of Paddy Mangan's Westerns. I had it in my jacket pocket when my father had caught me mooching by the hedgerow, making for Lisnacullia. He marched me to the hayfield to drive the red mare. It was a bad morning; the mood was black in his face, the red mare was in a temper to match his. I made a wrong turn at the headland; the bars of the tumbling jack stuck in the long grass and one stave broke off. It was my fault — me and my bloody books and my wandering mind. He pulled the book from my pocket and threw it into the hedge.

I resolved not to talk to him again, but the only one who suffered was me. My father never held a grudge: he had neither the temperament, the will nor the endurance to maintain it. But I had. I built a portrait of him in my mind that sustained my resolve. Only someone devoid of a soul would behave so to his own flesh and blood. It was the act of a Philistine, of someone who could not appreciate the finer things in life and belittled those who did. On summer evenings my father and mother would walk the land arm-in-arm, their heads together in animated conversation. That walk was like a management meeting, a period for reflection and analysis and to lay the foundations for tomorrow's strategy. I came up the avenue late one Sunday evening, after promising that I would be home in time for the milking. I rounded a bend and there they were.

'Come here,' my mother said. 'Shake hands with your father and stop this foolish nonsense.'

My father looked at her in perplexed silence as if he had never had an inkling that there was a disagreement between us.

★ ★ ★

Year after year, as constant as the rising sun, the swallows built their nests against the rafter crossbeams in the cowhouse, shaping them anew from the foundations of the old. They had learned to cope with us and to practice a wary vigilance as they flew in and out through the door. Beyond the door was a dunghill; the midges rose in swarms from its apex, the swallows flew intricate acrobatics as they gorged on the bounty. One evening, when my father and I had come late from the fields with the horses, the young fledglings had fallen from the nest and were piping mournfully in the straw bedding. The adult swallows were skimming in agitated swirls around them; someone had poked a hole in the nest where the crossbeams met. For a few moments, my father stood in silent dismay, shaking his head at the wanton stupidity of the act. Then he had me fetch the wooden ladder while he rounded up the fledglings and placed them inside his hat. He mounted the ladder, patched up the broken nest with mud and cloth and restored the fledglings to their home. I thought of that incident the day he threw my book into the hedge and wondered at the perplexities of human behaviour.

In September the swallows would leave. They would gather on the wireless aerial and chitter a rhapsody of mounting excitement. I wondered if their sound was a language, transmitting the intricacies of a navigational acumen too complex for us to understand. Did the young ones speak of their fear — the fear of the unknown that lay beyond this hidden valley and that beat at their breasts in fluttering spasms? One morning, when the sun was high, and the shafting light was brightening the inner shadows of the hay barn, they would rise in unison. The chitter would be muted, the fluttering breasts at calm in the greatness of the moment. Then they would be gone. Winter would creep across the land and this hidden valley would draw in to itself. But I would not share in the aura of spreading comfort that would inhabit the kitchen. The blast would sweep down from Mannix's Folly and batter against the rear door; it would howl in the eaves, droplets of rain would come down the chimney and hiss in the fire. And those within would shiver in the pleasure of the spreading warmth and spare a passing thought for others who did not share in it. Would they spare a thought for me? I would be gone before the swallows, I would be missing too when Hannah announced that the first scouts of the summer migration had been seen above the keep-tower.

I went to the fields. For weeks that summer I sailed voyages round my father. I tried to make footholds to reach him, to find those fleeting tendrils that once we had touched, explored but lost because one of us had stunted the growth. I wanted to find a place in his soul that I could harbour in. When the feelers touched, perhaps he would tell me that he loved me and that he would be sad when I left. It would need only a whisper in my ear or a hand to ruffle my hair. I would take the symbol with me when I went; it would sustain me when the dark palls of loneliness filled me with despair, as I knew they would.

I worked side by side with my father: turned swarths of hay in his wake, edged the mowing blades, trimmed down and tied the trams of hay to his standard and ignored the brothers when they sniggered at my conversion to his fastidious ways. But I never reached the harbour. I sailed close a few times, I stood off outside the marker buoy, but the welcoming flag was never run up.

So I invented my father. I built him from the tendrils he had touched me with and grew them into a spreading chestnut. Its roots grew out of the nights when we had crossed the fields in the darkness to Andy Connor's house. He took me by the hand, opened wide his overcoat so that I could put my head inside and find shelter from the blast. It grew out of a time when we were driving cattle to the Rathkeale fair in the small hours of a November morning. As we went by Aggie Butler's house, my father talked to me about the stars. He pointed out Orion's Belt, the Great Bear, Venus, and showed me how to find the Pole Star. And then he had me fix my eye on a star above Aggie's chimney.

'See that star. That star could be burned

out by now, but it takes so long for the light to come here that we're still seeing it.'

Things like that, my father told me, he had learned and remembered from his school reader. Once upon a time, until Galileo, people thought that the world was flat; if you went far enough, you would fall off the edge. They believed too, he said, that strange creatures existed in the unexplored parts of the world. So the men who made maps, wrote on the outer margins, Beyond Here Be Dragons.

When we came to Benson's Cross, in that cold star-bright November morn, he turned to me with a sly grin and observed that he wasn't as stupid as some people might think.

I invented my father from a time when he and I were on the outward journey with the hay float. His face that day was like the lighted face of the moon: bright, full of laughter. He turned to me suddenly and made a remarkable request. 'Hey, young fella, why don't we sing?' I couldn't believe my ears. In the lore of that place, my father knew two tunes: one was *Faith of our Fathers*; the other was not. 'Tell you what,' he offered, 'I'll sing a song. You'll pick it up quick and then we'll sing it together.'

Johnny get your hair cut, Johnny get
   your hair cut,
Johnny get your hair cut short like
   mine.

It was outlandish. In the still of a summer's day — float wheels swishing in the aftergrass, air shimmering against the hedgerows — my father and I were singing. We sang the verse over and over and when we stopped to winch up the tram of hay, he said to me, 'Know what, son? We should sing more often.'

Yes, my father, we should have sung more often, again and again and again. You should have held my hand or I should have thrust mine in yours. I should have burrowed my way into your heart the way I put my head inside your jacket. Frostbright nights and mornings we should have stopped and talked and shared. And I wouldn't be building you up now, tendril by tendril, to take you with me; forming you into a spreading chestnut tree with its canopy of love and invented fatherhood.

I never made the landfall with my father. One Saturday morning, I was standing on a haycock, building for the pitcher, Pat the Dog, who was helping us that day. As we built higher, the vista over the hedgerows opened up; out there was freedom but in that meadow was an eternity of mown hay. I had given it my best shot; circled round him, knelt all day in the furrow between turnip drills, waited for a word of appreciation. When the haycock was completed, I slid down, trimmed the butt, fastened the ties, then stuck the two-pronged fork into its side.

'I'm going,' I told Pat the Dog. He sucked deep on his cigarette, searching my eyes, looking for some trickery.

'How do you 'mane' you're goin'?'

'I'm off. Anywhere. It doesn't matter.'

'Jaysus, take it aisy, Tomeen. You'll be kilt.'

★ ★ ★

I went by Lissocolagh, Cooltomin and Ardlaman; out to the very edge of the saucer-shaped land. The dog pack followed me, all except Towser, who stayed lolling in the shade. I fixed the landscape in my brain, etched and burned it in: every hedge and tree, the shape and twists of dry stone walls, the way the land lay, the journey of the glacier, the sculpture of weathering. I studied faces: my parents, brothers and sisters, neighbours, Hannah and Madge. I put them into the album of my memory. I would bring them with me for all time.

And one day that same summer, sitting on

385

a mound beside Absalom's fishpond, my bare feet salving in the ooze, it dawned on me. In all this saucer-shaped plain, in the country beyond the rising hills, there was hardly a youngster as fortunate as me. I had been granted freedom. I had been allowed to become a child of the landscape; to abstract the landscape to mindscape. It was a wonderful journey; piecing together the story of rock, land and water, the wild creatures that passed me on the way. I should be eternally grateful to those who had made it so, who had yielded their priorities to the frivolous consequence of mine.

That day by Absalom's pond, I built them all an amphitheatre. I scoured out the peaty soil, exposed the rock strata and raised it in tiers. I placed them sitting there: the faces of my hidden kingdom, kids from the Long Road and the road to Creeves, Rathreigh, Lisnacullia, Coolcappa and Kilbrathern. In the island in the pond I put specimens from the landscape and a patch of blacktop where the goldfinch might gather. Looming above them, I planted a spreading chestnut. I put my father sitting with his back to the bole and when the leaves stirred in the young wind, they formed the features of his face, like the image of God I had once seen in the clouds above Harold's Wood. The island I named for

Absalom and I chiselled its creation in my heart. It would come with me forever.

I walked home from Absalom's fishpond and thought about Wandering Aengus. Miss Abigail had given me Yeats' poem to read and a few days later asked me what I thought it meant. I had learned it then by rote and its music ran round and round in my mind. She shook her head when I told her how I had interpreted it and explained that I had missed the symbolism. The glimmering girl whom Aengus was pursuing was the poet's unceasing quest for the beautiful.

I could see the analogy starkly as I walked home. But, unlike the poet, I had found the beauty: it was all there in the mental amphitheatre in Absalom's pond. I would remember it, and all through my life, in good times and bad, in blackness of mood, in the pain of hurt, I would fly there, as still I do. And I would pluck from there, till time and times had done, the silver apples of the moon, the golden apples of the sun.

I went away in September. I left before the swallows. When I had gone, the mist rolled down from the low hills and closed off my hidden valley.

And I never found it again.

We do hope that you have enjoyed reading this large print book.

Did you know that all of our titles are available for purchase?

We publish a wide range of high quality large print books including:
Romances, Mysteries, Classics
General Fiction
Non Fiction and Westerns

Special interest titles available in large print are:
The Little Oxford Dictionary
Music Book
Song Book
Hymn Book
Service Book

Also available from us courtesy of Oxford University Press:
Young Readers' Dictionary
(large print edition)
Young Readers' Thesaurus
(large print edition)

For further information or a free brochure, please contact us at:
Ulverscroft Large Print Books Ltd.,
The Green, Bradgate Road, Anstey,
Leicester, LE7 7FU, England.
Tel: (00 44) 0116 236 4325
Fax: (00 44) 0116 234 0205

PLAIN DEALER

William Ardin

Antique dealing has its own equivalent to 'insider trading', as Charles Ramsay finds out to his cost. Offered the purchase of a lifetime, he sees all his ambitions realised in an antique jade cup, known as the 'Loot'. But as soon as the deal is irrevocably struck he finds himself stuck with it like an albatross around his neck — unable to export it without a licence, unable to sell it at home, and in a paralysing no man's land where nobody has sufficient capital to take it off his hands . . .

NO TIME LIKE THE PRESENT

June Barraclough

Daphne Berridge, who has never married, has retired to the small Yorkshire village of Heckcliff where she grew up, intending to write the biography of an eighteenth-century woman poet. Two younger women are interested in her project: Cressida, Daphne's niece, who lives in London, and is uncertain about the direction of her life; and Judith, who keeps a shop in Heckcliff, and is a divorcee. When an old friend of Daphne falls in love with Judith, the question — as for Cressida — is marriage or independence. Then Daphne also receives a surprise proposal.